P9-BYR-631

LIBRARY
AUSTIN PREPARATORY SCHOOL
101 Willow Street
Reading, Massachusetts 01867

BOOKS BY LEONARD MOSLEY

NONFICTION

THE DRUID   *1981*

BLOOD RELATIONS: *The Rise and Fall of the du Ponts of Delaware*
   1980

DULLES: *A Biography of Eleanor, Allen, and John Foster Dulles and
   Their Family Network*   *1978*

LINDBERGH: *A Biography*   *1976*

THE REICH MARSHAL: *A Biography of Hermann Goering*   *1974*

POWER PLAY: *Oil in the Middle East*   *1973*

BACKS TO THE WALL: *London in World War II*   *1971*

ON BORROWED TIME: *How World War II Began*   *1969*

HIROHITO: *Emperor of Japan*   *1966*

THE BATTLE OF BRITAIN   *1965*

HAILE SELASSIE: *The Conquering Lion*   *1964*

FACES FROM THE FIRE: *Biography of Sir Archibald McIndoe*
   1962

THE GLORIOUS FAULT: *The Life of Lord Curzon*   *1962*

THE LAST DAYS OF THE BRITISH RAJ   *1961*

THE CAT AND THE MICE: *A German Spy in Cairo*   *1960*

DUEL FOR KILIMANJARO   *1959*

CASTLEROSSE: *The Life of a Bon Vivant*   *1956*

GIDEON GOES TO WAR: *A Biography of Orde Wingate*   *1948*

REPORT FROM GERMANY, 1945   *1945*

DOWNSTREAM, 1939   *1939*

SO FAR SO GOOD: *A Fragment of Autobiography*   *1934*

FICTION

THE SEDUCTIVE MIRROR   *1952*

EACH HAD A SONG   *1951*

WAR LORD   *1950*

NO MORE REMAINS   *1938*

SO I KILLED HER   *1937*

THE DRUID

940.54
M 85

THE DRUID

Leonard Mosley

NEW YORK   *Atheneum*   1981

LIBRARY
AUSTIN PREPARATORY SCHOOL
101 Willow Street
Reading, Massachusetts 01867

14918

Library of Congress Cataloging in Publication Data

Mosley, Leonard, 1913–
    The Druid.

    1.   World War, 1939–1945—Secret service—
Germany.   I.   Title.
D810.S7M58   1981   940.54'87'43   80–69367
ISBN 0–689–11106–1

Copyright © 1981 by Leonard Mosley
All rights reserved
Published simultaneously in Canada by
McClelland and Stewart Ltd.
Manufactured by
American Book–Stratford Press,
Saddle Brook, New Jersey
Designed by Kathleen Carey
First Edition

CONTENTS

THE DRUID

Introduction

IT IS the proud boast of the British intelligence services that not a single spy sent to Britain by the Nazis during World War II remained uncaptured. Most people know by now that each and every one of them, whether dropped by parachute, landed by submarine, flown in by flying boat, infiltrated by merchant ship, hidden among troops retreating from the European continent, or sent over in the guise of a visiting businessman or diplomat, was eventually trapped by the security forces. There were some thirty-nine in all. Six, including two women, were tried and hanged. Three others were sentenced to jail.

The rest, however, became tools of a remarkable British intelligence machine called the Double Cross System. Under the control of their British captors, they fed a mixture of genuine and false news from Britain to their Nazi controls without ever revealing that they were under British supervision. They did their best work in the weeks leading up to D-Day 1944, when their combined (false) reports succeeded in convincing the

3

German High Command that the main thrust of the Allied invasion of Europe was going somewhere entirely different from where it actually made its impact.

The claims made for British intelligence are astonishing. Did no spies slip through the vigilant security net which the British spread for them? Did no Nazi agent remain at large in Britain during World War II? "Not a single one," insist former members of the Secret Intelligence Service. And one of them, Rodney Dennys, now Somerset Herald of Arms at the College of Heralds in London, adds: "It is ninety-nine and nine-tenths percent certain we caught them all."

It is a self-confident assertion by no means shared by the confraternity of intelligence experts in other countries, particularly among former members of the security services of the Nazi Reich. All national intelligence systems are, not unnaturally, reluctant to talk about their successful espionage operations (*force majeure,* they have no option about their failures), and they usually take special care to make sure no documents are available to outsiders which would betray the name, sex, or even the presence of an agent who has firmly established himself or herself in the enemy camp. It is true that the principal Nazi intelligence system, the Abwehr, which ran a very sloppy organization, left abundant evidence lying around at the end of the war about its espionage activities in Britain. Allied experts would have found it invaluable had they not known all about it already through the Double Cross System.

But the Abwehr was not the only German intelligence service. Working alongside it, often against it, was the SS. The Abwehr was the traditional service; the security service of the SS was rather more efficient. It made an effort to preserve at least some of its secrets in the last days of World War II, and put a considerable number of documents to the bonfire before the Allies moved in. All the same, there is a rumor, probably well founded in fact, that despite these efforts both the British and the Russians discovered some intriguing material about the espionage activities of the SD branch of the SS,[1] both at home and abroad. If so, they have so far released only selective portions of it. They have certainly said nothing to confirm the fact that one Nazi spy did land in Britain, did operate without detection by the authorities, and did evade capture at the end of the war. To admit this was so would be embarrassing to both of them—to the British because of what he got away with during the war, and to the Russians because of the manner in which he evaded detection afterward.

To find out who he was, where he came from, what he did in Britain, and to reconstruct the story of how he evaded capture, it has been necessary to go elsewhere.

It was in Egypt as long ago as 1942 that I was given the first hint of the existence of the man I came to know later as "the Druid." That was the year when the fate of the Suez Canal and the whole of the Middle East (or, rather, British control of it) trembled in the balance. The German Afrika Korps under the command of General Erwin Rommel had driven the British Army out of Libya, out of its port and stronghold of Tobruk, and back across the Western Desert to the gates of Alexandria and the Nile Delta. Both sides having run out of breath and matériel, an ominous pause had supervened while German and British armies alike began to build up for the decisive battle which was now looming. Upon its outcome depended the future course of the war.

Which army would be ready and strong enough to strike first? And strike where?

To discover British intentions, Rommel sent an Abwehr spy to Cairo charged with two main tasks: to find out the time and place of the attack, and to liaise with a group of dissident Egyptian Army officers (including the late President Nasser and the present President of Egypt, Anwar el-Sadat) and per-

---

[1] Sicherheitsdienst des RFSS, Security Service of the Reichsführer SS.

suade them to rise up in revolt once the battle began. But before the Abwehr spy could report, he was captured by a British field security squadron which stormed aboard a houseboat on the River Nile where he and his radio operator had established themselves.

The Abwehr spy went under the name of Hussein Gāafer and claimed to be an Egyptian subject, but in fact he had been born in Germany and his real name was John Eppler. He had been brought to Egypt as a boy by his mother after the death of her first husband. When she married again—to a well-known Cairo lawyer named Saleh Gāafer—her son was adopted by her new husband and brought up as a young Egyptian with good family connections. He learned Arabic, embraced the Moslem faith, went on a pilgrimage to Mecca, but also attended a fashionable English school in Alexandria.

Through his mother he kept up his German connections, and he was in Berlin shortly after the war began, having been recruited into the Abwehr. In 1941 he moved to Rommel's headquarters in Tripoli and, the following year, was smuggled into Egypt. It was mainly through a series of Abwehr blunders (they sent him to Egypt, for instance, with traceable money and forged five-pound notes) that he fell into British hands.

As a result of Eppler's capture, a conspiracy in the Egyptian Army was broken up and many officers arrested, including Anwar el-Sadat. To put pressure on their captured spy, the British played a trick on him. They rigged up a fake court-martial and solemnly sentenced Eppler to death for espionage, allowed him a few days to contemplate his forthcoming appearance before the firing squad, and then approached him with a proposition. He could "buy" his life by cooperating with them and becoming a double spy. Very sensibly, he agreed to do so at once.

This is no place to go into details of Eppler's work for the intelligence services in Egypt, except to say that it was considerably more effective than anything he ever did for the

Abwehr.[2] To deceive the Germans about his status, he was allowed to move freely about Cairo and to go on patronizing the nightclubs and the belly dancers who performed there of whom he was especially fond.

I first met him about this time and found him an easygoing and amiable young man with no particular political convictions, equally contemptuous of the Nazis he had met in Berlin and the officer types he encountered around British GHQ in Cairo. But most of all he resented the ordeal by fake court-martial to which the British had subjected him, an experience which had completely terrified him.

"Why did they have to put me through that torture?" he complained indignantly. "Why didn't they just say they wanted me to cooperate? All they had to do was ask!"

He talked at great length about his experiences in Berlin and the training as a spy which the Nazis had given him. He also let slip the fact that during his stay in Germany an attempt had been made by the SS to enlist him into the Sicherheitsdienst. He had acted as interpreter during a meeting between Adolf Hitler and the Mufti of Jerusalem, a notorious plotter against the British regime in Palestine. Among those present at the meeting was Ernst Kaltenbrunner of the SS, and he had been visibly impressed by Eppler's fluent handling not only of the Arabic-German exchanges but of the English-language documents which he had also been called upon to translate. At the end of the meeting, Kaltenbrunner took Eppler to the Adlon Hotel for a drink and asked him whether he would like to work for the SD.

They were planning a special mission, Kaltenbrunner said, and looking for an exceptional agent to carry it out. The SS, he went on, had become increasingly dissatisfied with the intelligence it was receiving from the principal Nazi espionage service, the Abwehr, and had decided to put its own agent in place, not only to send back information but also to check on

[2] See the author's book *The Cat and the Mice*.

7

the quality of the work being done by the rival organization. Would Eppler be interested? There was an Iron Cross in it once the mission was successfully accomplished. And not only that: a half-million Swiss francs would be deposited in a Zurich bank in Eppler's name the moment he began training.

Eppler was wary at once. The Iron Cross tempted him not at all but the half-million Swiss francs certainly did. On the other hand, he was aware that the SS would hardly pay that amount of money in precious foreign currency for anything but a highly dangerous mission. As casually as he could, he asked where the special agent would be expected to operate.

England, Kaltenbrunner replied.

Barely concealing his distaste—England, with its bombing raids, its rationing, and its weather was the last place he wanted to visit—Eppler quickly invented reasons why it would be impossible for him to accept. Kaltenbrunner accepted his excuses with ill grace and departed, leaving Eppler to pay for the drinks.

It was not until some time later, just before Eppler was leaving for North Africa on his Egyptian mission, that he ran into Kaltenbrunner again. He couldn't resist asking the SS leader if he had ever succeeded in recruiting his special agent. They were at a Berlin cocktail party, and, as usual, Kaltenbrunner was more than half drunk.

"Not only recruited but already in place!" he said triumphantly. He then added, with a menacing scowl: "And if you mention that to Canaris and his gang, I'll make sure you don't live long enough to tattle twice!"

Eppler never did tell the Abwehr that the SS had sent a rival spy to England. But later, when being debriefed in Cairo by the SIS, he mentioned it to his British interrogators. That was in 1942. Undoubtedly they passed on this fascinating item of information to London. Neither Eppler nor I knew anything about the Double Cross System at that time, but the SIS was well aware that all Abwehr agents in England had already been captured and "turned." Eppler's information must have

8

given them their first warning that an independent spy was still running loose in Britain, even though he could give them no information at that time as to who and where he was.

I lost touch with John Eppler for some time after the end of World War II, but some years later I found him again in Saar-brücken, and began a long series of conversations with him about his wartime experiences. It was in the course of them that the business of that spy from the SD cropped up again.

Eppler had by that time established himself as a successful operator of a do-it-yourself bookshop in the Saarland, but his return to civilian life had not been without its traumatic moments, and had it not been for the help given him by his erstwhile collaborators in British intelligence it is extremely doubtful if he would have made it. It was they who rescued him from a prison camp for "incorrigible" members of the SS into which he had been mistakenly consigned after his return from Egypt to Germany. He had then become a trader in black-market cigarettes in Hamburg and amassed a large amount of German occupation marks. Overnight, the German authorities decided to call them in and issue new currency, and Eppler would have lost everything had not his same British friends warned him in time and helped him convert his questionable gains into viable new money before the deadline.[3]

While he was in prison camp, threatened with prosecution by the German authorities for "war crimes," he received a visit from two British Army intelligence officers and a stenographer. They had evidently been through his dossier, for they quoted some of the remarks he had made during his debriefing in Cairo; but when he suggested that since they obviously knew who he was and what he had done during the war, they might explain to the German authorities that he was certainly no SS thug and get him released, they brushed this matter aside. That

[3] Other black-market operators, unable to account for their ill-gotten gains, and with no one around to vouch for them, lost everything.

wasn't what they were there for, they said.

What they wanted, in fact, was more information about his conversations with Ernst Kaltenbrunner, and, in particular, more details about the SD spy who had been sent to Britain by him. Who was he? Where did he come from? What was his background?

Eppler was so astonished that he burst out: "Do you mean to say you never caught him? Did one of us actually get away with it?"

Rather grudgingly, the interrogators let slip the fact that there were rumors an SS agent had somehow managed to infiltrate into Britain during the war and had succeeded in operating without being detected. Moreover, Eppler gained the impression that he had contrived to vanish in the confusion created by the end of the war, and the British had lost track of him. Captured senior SS officers were being stubborn and uncooperative, and the records had been burned. They made it plain they hoped Eppler would prove more sensible and accommodating than his senior colleagues.

In vain, Eppler insisted that he had never been a member of the SS and knew nothing of its intelligence operations. He was hectored and browbeaten for hours by his questioners, who ignored his repeated declarations that he had told all he knew. The security men finally departed, their questions unsatisfied, but still obviously convinced he had been holding out on them. As to his own predicament, they remained impervious to his pleas for help.

But John Eppler could be an extremely resourceful young man when his own skin was at stake, and the visit had given him an idea. For his mission to Cairo, the Abwehr had furnished him with a copy of Daphne du Maurier's novel *Rebecca* on which to base his code messages back to his controls at Rommel's headquarters and the Abwehr station in Athens. He had continued to use the book to send fake information from Egypt under British control, and by war's end he knew the book by heart and could recite whole paragraphs from it when simply given a page number.

His photographic memory of that "dreary and ridiculous book," as he called it, stood him in good stead now. He sat down and wrote an emotional love letter to a girl telling her how much he missed her and how he longed to be back with her soon. He wrote it in a mixture of simple German and very simple English, and then, between the lines, carefully copied out a message in the *Rebecca* code. The invisible ink he used was effective if temporary—his own diluted blood, which shows up well when heated. Decoded, the message read:

CONDOR[4] CALLING. GET ME OUT. IF I AM TRIED WILL BE

FORCED REVEAL MY ROLE IN CAIRO ALSO TELL ABOUT DRUID.

The letter he addressed to: Captain Rebecca N. Elliot, c/o Field Security, British GHQ, Hamburg. After telling the guard she was his secret girl friend, Eppler bribed him to deliver it by giving him a gold Egyptian sovereign he had smuggled out of Cairo. There was no such person as Rebecca Elliot, but there was an SIS officer with the same last name who had acted as one of Eppler's contacts during the war. One of the security officers who had grilled him had let slip the fact that Elliot was in Hamburg.

And luck, as usual, was with Eppler. The message got through. He was released from the SS camp a few days later, and, thanks to British help, allowed back into civilian life in Germany with a clean bill of health.

"I really owe my freedom to a man I never met," Eppler told me much later. "I wonder who the Druid was—and how he got away with it?"

In the intervening years, both John Eppler and I have found out much more about the operations of the Druid, he, curiously enough, through an attempt (unsuccessful) to recruit Eppler into the Soviet intelligence network, I through some burrowing

4 "Condor" was Eppler's Abwehr code sign.

into German archives and researches in Washington, London, Paris, and (by correspondence) Moscow and Buenos Aires. It was while going through reports of the postwar interrogations of SS Standartenführer Walter Huppenkothen and his colleague Kriminal Inspektor Hugo Hoffmann that I realized how early in World War II the SS began to suspect the activities of Admiral Canaris and his Abwehr intelligence organization. From a strictly Nazi point of view, they already had good reasons in 1940 for believing that the Abwehr was not just an inefficient intelligence-collecting agency but probably a treacherous one too. Both men had evidence persuading them that not only was the Abwehr conniving at the penetration of its operations by Britain's SIS but was perhaps even collaborating with the enemy to help Hitler lose the war.

In the circumstances, as Huppenkothen pointed out to his interrogators, it was vital for the RSHA (the overall security arm of the SS) to find out what the Abwehr was up to in England, for it was upon the Abwehr that the SS relied for its intelligence from enemy territory. Was it reliable? Could the Abwehr's agents be trusted? There was only one way to find out—by sending an independent SS agent to Britain to make his own inquiries and report back.

Neither Huppenkothen nor Hoffmann made any mention of the agent the SS eventually dispatched to Britain, possibly because they were never asked by their Anglo-American interrogators nor questioned about him by German lawyers during Huppenkothen's subsequent trials (at which Hoffmann gave evidence). In his reports to Martin Bormann in 1944, SS Obergruppenführer Ernst Kaltenbrunner makes three references to "our information from England" also without specifying the identity of his informant.[5] Since their agent had successfully

[5] See reports of the trials of Walter Huppenkothen at Munich (February, 1951) and Augsburg (October, 1955), copies to be found in records of Kammergericht Berlin; records of his depositions and testimony of witnesses, copies to be found in the Institut für Zeitgeschichte, Munich; and Reports of Ernst Kaltenbrunner in the German Federal Archives at Coblenz.

escaped detection, they were obviously determined to preserve his anonymity, possibly in the hope that by allowing him to stay in place he might one day be useful to Germany again. It seems that Huppenkothen, Hoffmann, and Kaltenbrunner took the most rigorous steps to see that all references to their agent were either destroyed or expunged from what SS records were left behind.

But they missed one source.

In the late summer of 1944, Huppenkothen had been given the go-ahead by his SS chiefs to complete his investigation of the Abwehr and, to use the words of one of his subordinates, to "unmask the nest of traitors around Canaris." He and his assistant, Kriminalkommissar Franz Sonderegger began "intensive questioning" of three Abwehr officials whom they suspected of making peace overtures or working out deals with the British. They were Josef Müller,[6] Hans von Dohnanyi, and Dietrich Bonhoeffer, all of whom had certainly been in touch with the British at one time or another during the war, and had, in fact, once tried to arrange a working meeting in neutral Spain between their own chief, Admiral Canaris, and General Stewart Menzies, "M" of the SIS. (The meeting was vetoed by the British Foreign Office, on the grounds that it might offend the Russians.) In the course of the interrogation, Huppenkothen attempted to frighten his prisoners into confessing their treachery by letting them know he had "a special source of information in England." Several times he remarked that "our observer in London has told us all about your treasonable activities," and on one occasion he even mentioned that "our Welsh comrade knows what you have been up to."

For some reason, the transcripts of these sessions escaped destruction by the SS, and they eventually found their way into the records of the Public Prosecutor's Department at Lüneburg and were used—though not the words "our observer in London" or "our Welsh comrade"—in a German prosecution of Franz Sonderegger.

[6] Not to be confused with "Gestapo" Müller, a notorious SS torturer.

What was the reason for this omission? It struck me as both odd and intriguing. As most students of wartime espionage in Britain are aware, a number of Welsh Nationalists worked as agents for the Nazis during the war, in the belief that Hitler would have given Wales its independence had he won. It had been my understanding that none of the Welsh spies escaped detection by SIS, and that they spent the war working as double agents. But in the light of the Lüneburg documents, there was good reason to have my suspicion confirmed that one spy had got away with it—and that he was a Welshman. The visit by two security men to John Eppler in his SS prison camp also took on a new significance. Was the missing spy they were seeking a Welshman too, and had he used the code name of *der Druide,* or the Druid?

It seemed a supposition worth pursuing.

By the 1960s I had made sufficient progress in my researches both in Germany and Britain to be certain that I was on the right track. This was the period when any details of British intelligence and counterintelligence work during World War II were still officially secret. Those who knew about the Double Cross System were debarred, under pain of prosecution, from writing about it, and officers of the Special Branch at Scotland Yard were soon on the doorstep waving summonses under the Official Secrets Act at anyone who dared to suggest in public or in print that all Nazi spies—with, whisper it, one exception had been caught and "turned" during the war.

About this time I was in Düsseldorf, Germany, having a series of conversations with Herr Erich Kordt for a book I was writing about the origins of World War II.[7] Kordt had been chief assistant during the war to Joachim von Ribbentrop, the Nazi Foreign Minister, but had also been a secret anti-Nazi and one of the chief plotters against Hitler. In the course of our talks, Kordt described in some detail his collaboration with

[7] *On Borrowed Time: How World War II Began.*

General Hans Oster and other members of the Abwehr in schemes to overthrow the German Führer, and revealed that the Abwehr had been quite well aware that its agents in England—about whose work Admiral Canaris boasted so frequently to Hitler—had in fact been caught and "turned." He added that I was correct in thinking that certain members of the SS had begun to suspect this and, to frustrate it, had sent their own agent to Britain. He confirmed that the SS man was of Welsh origins and thought his code name might well have been the Druid. Though some of the more vital SS documentation was missing, he thought he might be able to check on this and give me the agent's real name.

I went back to London, and weeks passed. Finally, I reminded Herr Kordt of his promise, and he said he would keep it but that there were unexpected difficulties. Shortly after this, I had a desperate message from Frau Kordt in Düsseldorf. Her husband had gone out for an evening walk, she said, and had not returned. The police had found his body floating in the Rhine. A subsequent inquest decided that he had committed suicide.

Shortly after this, I decided to try something which, I hoped, might flush out the truth. At the request of a well-known British film producer, I wrote a script about a German spy who had succeeded in escaping detection and stayed on in Britain after the war. I deliberately falsified the facts and made the spy a German national. I had him marry a female officer in the Royal Air Force and become, after the war, the domesticated father of a family. The only suggestion of the truth which I did allow myself was that the spy did collaborate, during some of his activities, with a Welsh Nationalist.

The film was never produced. British productions relied heavily, at that time, on government subsidy to get made, and scripts were submitted to an official department before the money was forthcoming. The script came back marked "Un-

LIBRARY
AUSTIN PREPARATORY SCHOOL
101 Willow Street
Reading, Massachusetts 01867

suitable. No subsidy." Perhaps the quality of the script or story was responsible for the refusal. But there were plenty of judges of film scripts who doubted this. . . .

Then came a series of revelations about Soviet penetration of the British intelligence services, catalyzed by the defections of Guy Burgess and Donald Maclean, followed by H. A. R. (Kim) Philby, and culminating in the arrest of George Blake, an SIS operator who betrayed scores of British agents in Eastern Europe to the Russians. There was a panic purge of intelligence personnel in consequence. Some of those who were thrown out of the service were completely innocent of any involvement and were therefore considerably aggrieved at the abrupt termination of their careers. Others found to have been involved, directly or peripherally, with the Soviet KGB were given the choice of being tried for treason or of continuing their lives as double agents—this time *against* rather than for the Russians. Indications of the identity of some of these individuals will be found in the narrative which follows.

It was from some of these elements, their lips loosened by the unexpected turn of events, that details began to emerge of the British side of the wartime espionage story, from which came clues to the background and activities of the Druid and those with whom he associated or operated. This enabled further researches to be made in Germany.

Among the characters who turned up were several of the agents originally sent to Britain by the Abwehr who then became, willingly or unwillingly, vital cogs in the Double Cross machine. Undoubtedly the most successful of the willing ones was Dusko Popov, an intrepid Yugoslav who risked his life with the Nazis several times during his remarkable career as a spy in furtherance of the Allied cause. When searching him out after the war, I was surprised to discover that he was living only a few miles across the hills from my South-of-France home.

Much more enigmatic was the part played by the Welshman Arthur Owens, known to the Abwehr as "Johnny" and to the

SIS as "Snow." The British intelligence authorities are anxious to emphasize that they were aware of Johnny's questionable activities almost from the start of the war, and that for safety's sake they put him in Pentonville prison and only allowed him out for the purposes of deceiving the Germans—as, for instance, when they allowed him to make two trips during wartime to Lisbon to contact his Nazi controls.

On the other hand, there was much about Johnny's byzantine career as a spy that they never did learn about. Nor did the Abwehr, for that matter. As this narrative shows, he was often deceiving both of his masters at the same time in order to help the Druid. After the war, he tried to write an account of his checkered career as not just a double but as a *triple* spy, but could never get permission to publish it. But extracts have been seen by some of his ex-colleagues, and they have found them more than surprising. They certainly add some startling new facets to the story of the Double Cross System.

So, over the years, the story of the Druid has been slowly constructed. I make no apology for recreating some of the incidents, reconstructing and rejigging others, and reproducing conversations to which I could hardly have been privy. I can say no more than that they are based on memories and recollections. A word of warning about that: as I write later on in this narrative about the motives of professional intelligence people, which of them are you to believe? Are some of them deliberately deceiving you for their own dark purposes? But all the code names (both Nazi and SIS) used in this narrative are the actual ones by which the agents involved were known during World War II. So are all the names of the characters—with four exceptions and I have concealed their identity for personal reasons.

PROLOGUE

The Woman in the Padded Cell

I

IN THE AUTUMN of 1940, Regierungsrat and SS Sturmbann-führer Walter Huppenkothen became convinced there were traitors working inside the Abwehr, the principal German intelligence service, and that they had already betrayed vital military secrets to the enemies of the Reich.

The only trouble was that, given the climate of the time, it was difficult for him to do much about it. How could he unmask the guilty men and turn them over to the tender mercies of his colleagues at Gestapo headquarters, when the Abwehr still had such influence with Hitler, and, by doing so, he could put his own career in jeopardy? That he was certainly not ready to do.

Walter Huppenkothen was thirty-three years old in 1940, and it is doubtful if there was a more dedicated Nazi working for the security services of the National Socialist regime. Among his colleagues, and particularly among his rivals for promotion, he was already known as the most determinedly ambitious operator in the RSHA.[1] They called him Ice Water, because, as one of them had once wryly remarked, "When Walter pisses, ice water comes out."

The Second World War had given Huppenkothen the chance to display the qualities that made a first-class Gestapo security official. Sent to Poland in November, 1939, after the Nazi blitzkrieg had shattered Polish resistance and rolled up the country in the space of a few weeks, he had been appointed chief of SS security police first in Cracow and then in Lublin. His instructions from his chief, SS Oberführer Reinhardt Heydrich, were to keep the inhabitants of these two great Polish cities docile and to discourage any tendency among them to thwart the plans of their Nazi conquerors, even when they learned that these plans included the eventual wiping out of the Polish people. He had more than succeeded in following orders. By simply cutting off all food, power, heat, and other amenities through the bitter winter of 1939–40, he had cleanly and efficiently starved a large proportion of the population to death, transforming Cracow and Lublin into ghost cities where, according to one German soldier's diary, "the dead are such bags of bones they don't even stink when you pass them in the street." Huppenkothen had also sent his minions into the nearby camps of Polish prisoners of war, the tattered, shell-shocked, rueful remnants of the defeated Polish armies which had been left behind when the victorious German war machine passed over them. Here too he had displayed his efficiency at "relieving the strain on limited Polish resources," as he had put it in his subsequent report, by instructing his men to go among the POWs and eliminate all those displaying overt "anti-German" tendencies. Since the miserable Polish soldiers could

[1] The Reichssicherheitshauptamt, or state security organization, which had been formed by Heinrich Himmler in 1939 by bringing together a combination of Gestapo officers, SS men, and trusted members of the civilian criminal police.

hardly be expected to display signs of affection toward their Nazi jailers, the SS squads found plenty of material for executions. At one camp alone they managed to reduce the POW population by 3,000, including 150 shot on Christmas Day, 1939, for refusing to interrupt a religious celebration.

It was shortly after this episode that Sturmbannführer Huppenkothen was summoned back to Gestapo headquarters on the Prinz Albrechtstrasse in Berlin. He returned not, as he had anticipated, to receive Heydrich's congratulations and perhaps the award of the Iron Cross, which his subordinates had insisted he had more than earned, but to learn that there had been complaints about the quality of his administration. What particularly angered him was the fact that the complaints came from, of all people, Abwehr officers operating in Poland, who claimed to have been outraged and disgusted by the behavior of SS troops toward Polish POWs and by the way civilized laws, particularly the Geneva Convention for the treatment of prisoners of war, had been flouted by the murderous actions of Huppenkothen's execution squads.

It is true that rivalry between the Abwehr and the Gestapo security services was such that Heydrich was not likely to be influenced by charges from that quarter. But the letter of complaint had been signed by no less than Admiral Wilhelm Canaris, chief of the Abwehr organization, and it had been sent to Heinrich Himmler in his official capacity as Reichsführer SS and Chef der Deutschen Polizei.[2] That meant official cognizance would have to be taken of it, and a note about it would go into Huppenkothen's record. He was somewhat mollified when both Heydrich and his assistant, Ernst Kaltenbrunner, told him to forget about the complaint.

"The Reichsführer has told Canaris to stick it up his ass," said Kaltenbrunner, with his arm around Huppenkothen's shoulders. But Heydrich had then taken him to one side and urged him to be more circumspect in the future when Abwehr men were around. They believed, rightly or wrongly, he said,

[2] Commander in Chief of the SS and Chief of the German Police.

that the Gestapo was scheming to take over their intelligence service, and their way of fighting back was to make mischief for the RSHA with the Führer, Adolf Hitler. In this case, Canaris had sent his letter to Himmler, but next time he might address his complaint to Hitler himself, and that could be embarrassing.

Huppenkothen spent several hours that night chasing schnapps with beer in the Prinz Albrechtstrasse mess. He did not get drunk but neither did the drink lighten his mood. Toward the end of the evening he found himself pouring out his story to a small, bespectacled, round-faced man named Hugo Hoffmann, whom he knew to be one of the criminal inspectors the RSHA had recruited from the Berlin police department. Hoffmann had a reputation around the organization for succeeding with interrogations where the SS musclemen broke the limbs but failed to break the spirits of the cases they were "investigating." He never raised his voice and he never failed to look and sound sympathetic, and time and again he made the toughest anti-Nazi crack and begin to talk.

Now his warm eyes were turned upon Huppenkothen as the Sturmbannführer drained his glass and suddenly said, "God damn those high and mighty Abwehr prigs! Who do they think is winning this war, anyway?"

At which Hoffmann leaned forward and said softly, "Perhaps they don't want us to win the war, my friend. Have you thought of that? Perhaps they would rather that we lost it—and are doing their best to help us do so."

There was something about the little man's tone of voice that drove some of the liquor fumes out of Huppenkothen's head and made him wish he was stone cold sober.

Before he could say anything, Hoffmann went on, "I realize I am taking a risk in what I have just said. I am just a humble civilian police inspector, and I don't have any influence around this department. But I do have reason to believe there are traitors in the Abwehr—and that the treachery goes very high up indeed in the organization. The only trouble is, I can't prove it—yet. And it could mean more than my job if I spoke out too soon."

Hoffmann abruptly reached out a pudgy hand and grasped Huppenkothen around the wrist with a grip that was as cold and firm as a handcuff.

"But you can do something, Sturmbannführer. They will listen to you. You are their bright-haired boy, and they will pay attention when you tell them."

"Tell them what?"

"That some of the high-ups in the Abwehr, maybe even Canaris himself, are selling us out—that they want us to lose the war—that they want to see our Führer, Adolf Hitler, dead!"

There was silence while the Sturmbannführer stared at the fat red face of the podgy man across the table. Then the tension went out of Hoffmann's expression, and he smiled, as if at some joke he had suddenly remembered.

"You see my predicament, Sturmbannführer?" he whispered. "You have every reason to hate the Abwehr—but you don't believe me either. It just doesn't seem possible. Can you imagine what Oberführer Heydrich would do to me if I told him Canaris was an anti-Nazi? His old naval buddy *a traitor?* He'd have my head for daring to suggest it. But if I can't prove that —yet—I can at least show you what some of the members of the Abwehr are up to."

Again there was silence. It was one of those times when Huppenkothen realized that a wrong gesture, a wrong remark, could spoil everything. It was as if Hoffmann was making a decision, and, to judge from the expression on his shining face, it was as painful as indigestion. Finally he seemed to make up his mind.

"There is an institution for the mentally disturbed at Bad Freienwalde," he said, "and there is a patient there I would like you to talk to."

It was such an unexpected statement that Huppenkothen burst into laughter.

"What the hell are you trying to get me into, Inspector?" he asked. "Are you now going to tell me that the person who's got the goods on the Abwehr is some"—he hesitated—"some maniac, some madman in a lunatic asylum?"

"Not a madman," said Hoffmann quietly, undisturbed by the outburst. "The patient is a woman—and she is not mad. She is a perfectly sane and rational female—at least she was when I last saw her. And what's more, you know her, Sturmbann-führer." He paused, and then went on: "I do not imagine you have forgotten the name of Katie Pruck, the young wife of Colonel Erich Pruck. If I remember my files correctly, you once spent two most enjoyable days—and, I hope, equally enjoyable nights—with Frau Pruck at the Wannsee last year, just after her husband was posted away to Norway."

"Katie Pruck!" Huppenkothen could not keep the astonishment out of his voice. "How the hell did you know about her? My God, you had us followed!"

"We like to keep in touch," said Hoffmann mildly.

"Katie Pruck!" the Sturmbannführer said again, allowing a little reminiscent pleasure into his tone this time. "But Katie's no madwoman. That minx has her head screwed on. What the hell is she doing in a lunatic asylum?"

Hoffmann sighed, and then said, more softly than ever, "Poor young woman, she tried to tell the truth about the traitors in the Abwehr—only she told the wrong people."

II

As Inspector Hoffmann had surmised, Walter Huppenkothen had not by any means forgotten Katie Pruck and the forty-eight hours they had spent in each other's company the previous spring. As his nickname Ice Water indicated, the Sturmbannführer was not exactly an emotional man, and all he demanded from the women with whom he formed tempo-rary liaisons was a bodily catharsis which could be quickly forgotten afterward along with the female who had helped provide it for him. He had expected no more from Katie Pruck when he had first met her and decided that he was going to sleep with her. It was true that in her case there were some extra ingredients involved which, he calculated, could add some sweetness to the sexual purging when it came, though he did not imagine these would change its fundamental nature.

For one thing, she was an old man's darling, and Huppenkothen always got a special kick, as well as a sense of justification, from cheating on an elderly husband with a wife at least twenty years too young for him. In the case of Major Erich Pruck—this was before his promotion to colonel—there was an additional incentive. The Major's age was compounded by a rumored physical disability. It seemed it had been brought about by a riding accident Pruck had suffered while on maneuvers with his regiment, a crack cavalry outfit. Invalided out as a result, he had been recruited into the Amtsgruppe Ausland (or foreign section) of the Abwehr by Admiral Canaris himself, who believed Pruck's fluency in foreign languages would be useful. Huppenkothen first encountered him and his wife at a reception at the Hungarian embassy in Berlin, and in the short conversation which followed their introduction the Major had made it plain what he thought of the Gestapo, especially the lower ranks among its officers. After a glance as curt as the flick of a whip at the insignia on Huppenkothen's epaulettes, there was a sneer almost visible on his thin lips as he inquired whether the young man was, by any chance, related to the Graf von Huppen from East Prussia; and when the Sturmbannführer replied that he came from the Rhineland, where his father was a carpenter, Pruck turned away as if to signify that the Sturmbannführer was dirt beneath his elegant riding boots and he had no time to waste on someone so obviously his mental, military, and social inferior.

On the other hand, the slow-burning fire in the eyes of the beautiful young woman hanging on the Major's arm told him she saw him in quite another way. He realized that she was mentally undressing him even while he took her cool and delicate hand in his, and to judge by the spasm which passed through her fingers just before she loosened them, by the time he moved away she was seeing him stark naked.

Huppenkothen had been acting as Ernst Kaltenbrunner's aide-de-camp on that particular evening, which must have made it simple for her to discover later how to get hold of him. Among the notes subsequently reaching him in Cracow after his posting to his new security job in Poland was a penciled message from Kaltenbrunner's office to tell him "Frau Pruck called." When he came back to Berlin on leave in the spring, he searched out the telephone number of the Pruck home in the suburbs and called during the morning hours, when the Major was most likely to be working in the Abwehr office on the Tirpitzufer. The sleepy voice of Frau Pruck came on the line at once, and it turned out that he could hardly have called at a more opportune moment. Major Pruck had left with an Abwehr unit for Norway the week before to set up intelligence lines in that newly occupied country. Would it amuse the Sturmbannführer to come out for a light lunch, and perhaps a little walk together afterward?

The Pruck home was a quietly luxurious villa on the shores of the Wannsee, with a well-manicured private beach and an indoor pool looking out on it through huge plate-glass windows. It was through these that Inspector Hoffmann's spies must have watched them as they emerged at intervals to disport themselves in the pool. Otherwise, from the moment Katie, in her bedroom, did physically to Huppenkothen what she had done in her imagination all those weeks before at the Hungarian embassy, they spent practically every waking moment of the next forty-eight hours making love. Katie Pruck knew it all, and she was hungry. Huppenkothen would never be satisfied with a simple catharsis again.

The light lunch consisted of Dom Pérignon and canapés of fresh pâté de foie gras which, she indicated, the Major had brought back from a recent visit to occupied France; and later on, when Huppenkothen's furious ardor showed signs of flag-

ging, she introduced him to the sustaining and reviving qualities of plovers' eggs, which the Major had had shipped to her
from Norway. Each time she talked of her husband, Huppenkothen did not miss the distaste and contempt which entered
her voice, and he soon discovered it was not just his physical
incompetence which aroused these emotions. She made it plain
he was not only a failure as a man but a disappointment as a
careerist as well. She had tried to dissuade him from joining
the Abwehr, since, with the exception of Admiral Canaris, she
considered that organization to be composed of effete types
totally lacking in fervor for National Socialism and devotion
to the Führer. As a good Party woman, she would have preferred him to offer his services to the SS, where, for certain,
the officers were loyal and inexhaustibly (she nuzzled him
fondly) dedicated men, and there would have been incentives
for her to help her husband in the furtherance of his career.
But, she pouted, he had refused to listen to her.

Ravished and fixated though he had now become, Huppenkothen still remembered to report in by telephone to the Prinz
Albrechtstrasse, and at the end of the second night with his
seductrix he heard the crisp instruction for him to report to
Tempelhof airport, where a plane for Warsaw would be leaving within the hour. They swore that they would see each
other again the moment it was feasible, and Katie vowed that
she would wait, faithful as Penelope, until he returned from
the wars, but then added, with a warning moue from her
bruised lips, that he must be discreet and "not cause us any
embarrassment" by writing to her while he was away.

So it was not until he had been summoned back to Berlin
that he telephoned Katie Pruck again, only to learn that the
house phone number had been disconnected. He drove past
the villa on the Wannsee and saw that the gate at the entrance
was padlocked. Major Pruck, he gathered from discreet inquiries, was back in the capital and in some trouble with the
Abwehr. As for Katie Pruck, she had simply "gone away."

III

It was a time when Adolf Hitler still had great faith in the efficacy of the Abwehr and in what he believed to be the loyalty as well as the uncanny acuity of its chief, Admiral Wilhelm Canaris. Later in the war, the Admiral's lukewarm feelings for National Socialism and his willingness to betray the Führer to the British would become plain even to Hitler. But for the moment, neither Canaris nor the Abwehr could do wrong in the Führer's eyes. And that was why their jealous rivals in the SS had to tread carefully.

"We knew the Abwehr could not be trusted, and we knew who the traitors were," said Inspector Hugo Hoffmann later.[3] "But the trouble was proving it to the Führer's satisfaction. He had to have overwhelming proof. And it was this proof that we were seeking before the Abwehr could destroy it."

He explained his feelings toward Canaris to Huppenkothen as they drove through the forests east of Berlin on their way to Bad Freienwalde and a rendezvous with Katie Pruck. As both men later recalled, it would have been hard to guess from the landscape that the war was nearly a year old. In the West the roads were jammed with army vehicles, and in Berlin itself soldiers in uniform were everywhere. Every night the Luftwaffe sent its bombers against England, and faithful Nazis waited eagerly for Hitler's announcement that the invasion and subjugation of Britain had begun at last. But here the fields between the forests were golden ripe with shocks of gathered wheat and barley, and old men and girls waved from laden horse-drawn carts as they sped along otherwise empty roads. It is doubtful if either man waved back. Huppenkothen recalled wondering when the Führer would get around to calling up women.

Hoffmann explained that it was Reichsmarschall Hermann Goering who had warned the SS that there was treachery brew-

[3] In statements to Allied interrogators.

ing in the Abwehr. Goering's Luftwaffe ran the Forschungsamt, the Luftwaffe research organization. One of their main tasks was tapping embassy telephone lines and reading diplomatic telegrams. For ten days the previous May, just before the Wehrmacht invaded Holland and began the blitzkrieg in the West, they tapped the calls made by the Dutch military attaché Major Gijsberthus Sas to his superiors in The Hague. Each day, Sas warned them that Germany was about to invade Holland, and indicated almost exactly when and where the thrust was coming.

It hadn't done them much good, Huppenkothen commented, laughing. Four days to capture Holland. A month to roll up Belgium and France.

Hoffmann acknowledged the truth of the remark, but pointed out this was only because the Dutch were afraid of acting on Sas's information. They thought the Führer would be angry with them if they declared a general mobilization and rushed to defend their frontiers. But, he went on, the fact remained that Sas knew the Germans' plans. *And* he kept telling The Hague to pass on his warnings to the British and French—which, luckily for Germany, the Dutch were also afraid to do. But think of what might have happened, and what might happen again, if the traitors stayed active. Someone had told the Dutchman and it was someone high up who knew the details of the German High Command's military plan. Someone who hated his country so much that he was prepared to commit *Landsverrat* (high treason).

Huppenkothen asked him if he knew who it was.

"I suspect," said Hoffmann, "but have no proof." And then he added: "But Frau Pruck. She knows, and I think she can prove it."

Katie Pruck had not been entirely sincere when she told Huppenkothen she would stay faithful to him until he came back from Poland. As Hoffmann could have told him, there were quite a few handsome young Luftwaffe and Wehrmacht officers—and even another Gestapo man—who had become acquainted with her talents during the weeks following his abrupt departure for the East. Nor had she been quite truthful in letting the Sturmbannführer believe that her husband, Erich, was entirely impotent as a result of his riding accident. She had methods of giving him satisfaction in her own special way, and she resumed her ministrations when he came back from Norway in June, 1940, when by this time he had been promoted to the rank of colonel. It was during one of their sessions that he revealed to her that some of his Abwehr colleagues were far from being loyal to the Führer and National Socialism. He named an officer who had warned the Danes just before the Nazi occupation of Scandinavia, another who had informed the Vatican of the coming attack on Holland and Belgium, and the senior Abwehr official who had tried to tip off the Allies about the imminent blitzkrieg in the West. What secretly infuriated Katie Pruck was that her husband, far from being shocked at such treasonable behavior, was much more worked up about the brutal conduct of the SS toward the people of occupied Norway. As his Abwehr colleagues in Poland had likewise done in the case of Huppenkothen's activities in Cracow and Lublin, Colonel Pruck had officially complained about SS behavior in Norway. Hence his return to Berlin to write his report.

Katie Pruck brooded over what a loyal Nazi should do in such a situation. Finally, she sat down and wrote a letter. She recounted what her husband had told her about the SS, but insisted it was far less worthy of investigation and punishment than the disloyalty and treachery which was going on in the Abwehr. She then proceeded to name names and describe incidents in which certain high Abwehr officials had been implicated.

Unfortunately for her, she chose to send the letter not to the SS—who, she feared, might make trouble for her husband—but to Admiral Canaris himself, at the Abwehr. The Admiral reacted at once. He dispatched a note to Reichsführer SS Heinrich Himmler telling him that a certain Frau Pruck, wife of an Abwehr officer, had made some outrageous accusations against SS behavior in Norway. He made no mention at all of her charges against his own officers, but suggested to Himmler that Frau Pruck was a severely disturbed young woman and that she ought to be arrested and sent to a mental asylum without delay, before her wild and hysterical statements became public.

That was when Hoffmann came into the story. As Kriminal Inspektor of Special Cases in Amstgruppe IVE, he was instructed to pick up Frau Pruck and take her to the police prison in the Alexanderplatz, where she would be detained pending her removal to a mental institution. It was while she was in the women's section of the prison that he decided to interrogate her. He was not surprised to discover that Frau Pruck was young and attractive, but he was startled to find that, in spite of what he had been told, she was no more insane or even mentally disturbed than her captors. In fact, the only mad thing she had done was send the letter to Canaris. And how was she to know the Admiral was determined to protect his staff, whether they were traitors or not? Poor Frau Pruck, she had acted in the belief that Canaris was as loyal to the Führer as she was!

Hoffmann did not have a copy of Frau Pruck's letter, but only of the summary he had been given by Himmler's office. But after an hour or two of interrogation, it became apparent that what the Colonel's wife had written and what Canaris had reported about it to the SS were two very different things. She had been arrested for making "scandalous" charges against the conduct of the SS, but the burden of her message had been much more serious: treachery against the state from within the Abwehr.

Hoffmann had waved the copy he had been given in the Prinz Albrechtstrasse and challenged her to prove that it told only half the story. Frau Pruck told him all he had to do was go to her home on the Wannsee and look in her boudoir. There he would find the typewriter on which she had written the letter. What's more, in the drawer of her desk he would find a carbon copy. And in that carbon copy would be found all the charges she had made—including the names of the traitors.

Colonel Pruck had taken up residence again, and it was he who let Hoffmann into the villa; he was plainly angry at the sight of the Inspector, making it obvious he loathed the SS. From the start, he treated Hoffmann like dirt, like a peasant. He certainly wouldn't have let the Inspector inside the house if he hadn't brought the right papers with him. Even so, he actually made him take his boots off when they went into his wife's bedroom—said he'd ruin the carpet! Hoffmann pretended to make a general search of the whole room and bathroom, but the Colonel obviously guessed that what he was looking for was the portable typewriter and the desk where Frau Pruck had written the letter. Hoffmann finally got around to opening the desk drawer where she said the carbon copy would be. It wasn't there. All the drawers were empty. Someone had obviously been there before him. He couldn't tell from the Colonel's face whether it had been he or not. All he could see was the sneer pasted all over it.

Huppenkothen asked whether he had questioned Pruck, and Hoffmann's expression was pained at the memory. Oh, he had tried to question him, all right. But the moment he mentioned Frau Pruck the Colonel said he didn't want to talk about her, didn't want to hear her name ever again. When he insisted, Pruck got into a temper and started shouting that not only was she a madwoman but she was also a slut—the kind of slut who mixed with Gestapo scum and brought shame on him. Hoffmann must have glanced sideways at Huppenkothen as he said that, for he added that someone must have told the Colonel about his wife's affair with the SS man, because he said she had not only disgraced his family name but had also ruined his army career.

Tears had come into the Colonel's eyes. He was going away,

he said. Closing up the house for good. Taking steps to divorce his wife as quickly as possible. And then he said again that he didn't want to talk any more about her. He didn't want to know where she was, what was happening to her. She was a slut and deserved everything she was getting. Then he went to the door, picked up Hoffmann's boots "as if they had shit on them," and flung them at him. "And now get out!" he said.

So Hoffmann came away without a copy of the vital letter. Nor did he have the chance to question Katie Pruck further about it.

When he got back to the Alexanderplatz lockup, Frau Pruck was no longer there. She had been signed out. The reception office showed him the authorization, signed by Canaris himself. Two men had come for her and booked her out. They hadn't said where they were taking her, either. And it was not until a week later that he got a tip from friends inside the Abwehr that the place where they had hidden her was out here in East Prussia, at Bad Freienwalde.

IV

The Kaiser Friedrich Sanatorium in Bad Freienwalde had formerly been one of the most fashionable private nursing homes in East Prussia, if not in all Germany. For the first thirty years of the century, it had been the favored retreat of wellborn German ladies who wished to rectify the results of their sexual indiscretions. Since the advent of National Socialism and the state's campaign to bolster the birthrate ("Make a son for the Führer!"), its highly profitable trade in clinical abortions had had to be abandoned, as had its sideline specialty of psychoanalysis for ladies with hysterical rather than physical problems. Gradually it had changed the nature of its activities, and by 1940 had become a private clinic for the treatment of the mentally disturbed. It was also known in Nazi security circles that the Abwehr had lately taken to using its

33

facilities for experiments of its own into schizophrenia and paranoia.

Not that there was any sign of Abwehr, or military, presence anywhere around. The woman who passed them through the lodge gate might have been a hausfrau or a nurse. The drive to the big house lay through opulent, well-kept parkland with a lake, woods, deer grazing on a slope, and odd figures wandering along the paths or sitting gazing over the water.

"If I ever go loony, this is where I would like to end up," said Huppenkothen.

"Don't be too sure," Hoffmann said.

They showed their papers to a severe young woman in the reception office at the big house, and were led down a brilliantly lighted corridor to a doctor's office where a middle-aged man in white smock was awaiting them. He did not seem to be surprised to see them, but at the mention of Frau Pruck's name he immediately shook his head.

"A sad case," he said. "Such a beautiful young woman she was, too."

"*Was?*" Hoffmann asked softly.

The doctor smiled, a sad smile. "These hysterical cases, they often damage themselves so badly, you know. It's not just the suicide attempts. They actually get pleasure out of—well—er—disfiguring themselves." He shook his head again. "But you would like to see her, I take it?"

"We would like to *talk* to her," Hoffmann said.

"Ah."

The doctor seemed to hesitate and then suddenly reached out across his desk and pushed a button. Presently, a burly young man who *could* have been a soldier came into the room and was introduced as Hermann, a male nurse. With Hermann and the doctor in the lead, they went down a succession of corridors, out across a paved courtyard, and into what seemed to be an annex of the big house. Inside was a large room, its floor covered with a green linoleum of patterned tiles, its walls whitewashed, and its only furniture a table and a chair in which sat another burly man, who could have been Hermann's twin. Behind him was a door with what both Hoffmann and Huppenkothen instantly recognized as a peephole in it.

As the second attendant rose to his feet and took out some keys, the doctor said, "This is Frau Pruck's room."

"Cell," whispered Hoffmann. And then, looking at the doctor: "Padded cell?"

He made a deprecatory gesture. "We don't use those terms nowadays. Sometimes our patients need—well, protection from themselves. So we call it the protective room." He hesitated as the locks were turned and the attendant's hand was on the handle of the door. "I don't know what you two officers expect to find, but—"

Huppenkothen had stepped forward, and while the doctor was still talking, he thrust the attendant away from the door and opened it.

V

To begin with, neither of them was certain that it actually was Katie Pruck. There was a cowering heap of flesh in the corner of the padded cell, the limbs curled into a fetal position, barely covered by a green shift. The head was entirely swathed in bandages. There were more bandages, bulkier this time, as if covering a cast, bound around the jaws.

No one said anything until, at last, the doctor cleared his throat nervously and broke the silence: "You see, there were two suicide attempts," he said.

He pointed at adhesive tapes around the wrists.

"She tried to cut her veins and bleed to death in the bath. They often do that. Then she managed to get to the roof and was very hysterical. I don't think she meant to jump, but she slipped and fell and hurt her head. Only superficial cuts, but she was very disturbed and we gave her electrotherapy." He coughed again. "The spasm broke her jaw. That also happens sometimes."

Hoffmann drew closer to Huppenkothen and muttered, "Do you recognize her as Frau Pruck? Looking like that, really, I can't be sure. It could be any—"

The Sturmbannführer turned to the doctor, who was pretending not to be listening to them. "Is she violent?" he asked.

The doctor shook his head reassuringly. "Oh, no, not now we've given her sedatives—against the pain, you know. But she's still conscious. If you want to try to talk to her—"

He gestured to the attendants and they went to the corner, took the quivering bundle by the arms, and held on, waiting for them to approach. It was Huppenkothen who came forward. He dropped to his knees in front of them, and it was as if she sensed his presence. The bound head turned so that the eyes faced him, but they were rolling so wildly they could not focus, and the only expression in them was fear.

The Sturmbannführer switched his glance to the body. In the last hours of their time together on the Wannsee, Katie Pruck had laughingly secured a pledge from Huppenkothen. He carried with him one of the indelible markers with which the SS categorized the Jews in Poland. They marked them with a "J," for *Jude,* on their arms, chests, or bellies until such time as they reached a camp and could be tattooed with a number. She took it and wrote a "K" on his foreskin, making him swear not to wash it off until they came together again. He knew it would last several months at least, anyway. In turn, he had taken the marker and drawn the shape of a heart on her flesh and then written "W," for Walter, inside it. Had she kept her pledge too? He reached out and raised the shift covering the human wreck on the floor, gently turned her, and then put his hands on the buttocks and pulled them apart. It was very faint now, as if she had scrubbed at it, but it was still visible on her skin.

He rose to his feet and nodded to Hoffmann. "It's Katie Pruck."

The Inspector let the breath out of his lungs in a defeated sigh.

"In that case," he said, "there isn't much we can do. Let's go, shall we?"

V I

It was almost an hour later, and they were approaching the outskirts of Berlin in the gathering dusk. In all the time they had been driving, neither man had said a word. But now Inspector Hoffmann spoke.

"You know you have a nickname in the service?"

"So I have heard," said Huppenkothen dryly.

"Ice Water." Hoffmann whispered it, half under his breath. "Now I understand why they gave it to you. You have steady nerves and admirable self-control, Sturmbannführer. In your circumstances, I do not think I would have behaved so well when I saw what they had done to Frau Pruck."

Huppenkothen's voice was flat. "I was sorry for her. A waste of a beautiful woman." He shrugged. "But there are others. . . . It's what they've done to Germany and the Party that worries me. What are they planning next? And what can I do about it? The Reichsführer would laugh his head off if I went to him with this story. 'That will teach you to play around other men's wives, Huppenkothen!' I can hear him saying it. And Heydrich would say his pal Canaris did exactly the right thing—that wives have to be taught not to fuck around while their husbands are away at war."

By contrast, Hoffmann seemed suddenly almost cheerful, and indicated to his companion that he did not despair. He was far from being finished with the Abwehr. True, for the moment the war was going well and Canaris was getting all the credit. But he knew the truth about that, and he would get them yet. It might take a little longer, that was all.

He had put on the blackout headlights of the car now. Here in the suburbs the air-raid precautions were punctilious, and the streets were black and deserted. Driving was difficult, and the Inspector concentrated until his eyes adjusted. Then he relaxed, fumbled for a cigarette, and offered one to Huppen-kothen, who brusquely refused. Hoffmann drew in a lungful of smoke, and then remarked that there was one thing Frau Pruck had mentioned during his interrogation of her that was not included in her letter to Canaris, and he had found it intriguing. He had been going to ask her about it today, if . . . He trailed off, and then went on to remind Huppenkothen that Reichsführer Himmler had always opposed the monopoly which the Abwehr had established in the control of intelligence from enemy countries. It was Canaris who picked the agents Germany sent to England to provide them with information about conditions there. The Reichsführer SS had several times asked the Führer to be allowed to organize his own intelligence agents for service in England, but Canaris had always intervened and persuaded the Führer that competing services would clash and impair the effectiveness of his system. At the same time, he had assured Herr Himmler that every scrap of information he received from his agents would be channeled through to the SD[4] section of the Gestapo. But, Hoffmann went on, it was not working out that way, and Frau Pruck went part of the way to explaining why.

Katie Pruck had mentioned to the Inspector that her husband, after being brought back from Norway, and while his report on SS misbehavior was being read, had been posted to the agency's office in Hamburg. Abwehrstelle Hamburg was one of the principal operational headquarters of Amtsgruppe Ausland, and from it control was exercised over a number of German spies who had already been parachuted, landed by submarine, or infiltrated from the Continent and Ireland into

[4] SD, Sicherheitsdienst (Security Service).

England. To Hamburg they communicated regularly by radio. From Hamburg they received radioed questionnaires, and were supplied—usually by parachute drop—with sabotage equipment and other materials, including money. To begin with, Colonel Pruck had been much impressed by the devotion of the control officers to the welfare of their distant and endangered charges, and even more so by the high quality of the information which the spies were obtaining in England and relaying back. It was true that some agents had been caught, tried, and, according to reports which had filtered back, executed. But most of the agents had evaded capture, established themselves, and were bravely performing tasks of great value to the Fatherland.

It so happened that while Pruck was in Hamburg, some new volunteers for espionage service arrived at headquarters for final briefings. The Colonel sat in on some of them, and became at first perplexed and then astounded. As he later explained to his wife, it was not that any of the agents lacked dedication or determination to serve the Führer and serve him well. It was the nature of their qualifications which worried him. A fluent English, French, and Polish speaker himself, he was greatly disappointed with the linguistic abilities of the potential spies. One young German girl, a former BDM (Bund Deutscher Mädel [Nazi Girls Movement]) member from the Rhineland, who had lived in Scotland with her German father and Scottish mother, spoke English with such a distinct German accent that she made him wince. She had not been to Britain since the age of eleven, had no particular technical knowledge, and would be expected to gather information about the RAF (an Abwehr priority at that moment). The Colonel could not imagine her mixing with any middle-class English with any ease, let alone flirting in bars and pubs with RAF pilots and airmen. How many days would she last before security pulled her in?

The remainder of the agents were no more reassuring. There were some Spaniards who had worked as waiters in

London and Brighton, and a very pro-German Pole who had once served in the Polish consulate in Southampton. After what he had heard of SS depredations in Poland, the Colonel did not believe there were any pro-German Poles left. And finally, he was introduced to one agent who, it was claimed, was a genuine Englishman who had been on holiday in France during the campaign there, had been captured by the Wehrmacht, and had immediately volunteered to work against his country, out of hatred for Churchill "and his drunken gang." He spoke English perfectly but with an exaggeratedly affected accent and an extremely pedantic mode of speech. He said he was a graduate of Cambridge. A few questions from the Colonel, who had, by chance, been to Trinity College, Cambridge, himself, quickly revealed that the agent had never been inside a British university in his life. Moreover, his accent changed wildly during the course of a wide-ranging conversation, and at least twice he was trapped into German mannerisms.

Finally, the Colonel turned to the ABT1[5] controllers who were doing the briefings and said: "This man is no more English than I am! If he continues to speak in that atrocious drawling way, and insists he has been to Cambridge, he'll end up in front of a firing squad."

Everyone burst into laughter, including the "Englishman," and it was explained that "James," as he was called, was, in fact, a German who had worked in London for several years in the branch of a German bank, and had become, according to the controller, "a master of English accents." He had simply been showing off his skills. They expected big things of him.

Colonel Pruck was not placated. As he confided to his wife later, "If that lot are typical of the types of spies we are sending to England, then the British must be more stupid than I thought they were. I cannot understand how they have all done so well, both in escaping detection and in providing us

[5] Abwehr's Hamburg division.

with intelligence. They do not seem to be of the right caliber for the job."

Huppenkothen had listened to the Inspector's account in silence, but now he broke in. "I have understood that the information our agents are sending from England is exceptionally good," he said.

"It's certainly what we have been wanting to hear," the Inspector said. "And Admiral Canaris is continually boasting to the Führer that never have his agents done so well on enemy territory. But if the Colonel is right, there is something fishy about the whole operation."

"Those shithounds!" exclaimed Huppenkothen suddenly. "Could they be deliberately faking—the Abwehr, I mean. Making things up just to keep us happy?"

Hoffmann said, "There is only one way to find out. We need a trustworthy agent of our own—in England. Sent over there unknown to the Abwehr, to discover the truth for us."

"And what," asked Huppenkothen, "if the truth turned out to be that the Abwehr is doing the magnificent job they say they are? What if the spies are indeed in place, doing brave and magnificent work for the Reich? Wouldn't we look like fools—or worse?"

"Not necessarily," the Inspector said, adding virtuously: "Why, we would be the first to bring to the notice of our superiors what we had discovered, and recommend that each and every one of our heroic agents be decorated with the Iron Cross. First Class, of course."

The Sturmbannführer brooded.

"Reichsführer Himmler would never authorize it," he said at last. "It would be like pissing in the Admiral's face."

"But why should the Reichsführer need to know?" asked Hoffmann innocently. "And why would we need to inform Oberführer Heydrich and put such an unfair strain on his friendship with Canaris? On the other hand, there is *your* friend and patron, Kaltenbrunner. If I remember my facts, he is not exactly a friend either of the Abwehr or the Admiral."

"He hates the whole shithouse," said Huppenkothen. "They patronize him, the bastards. Yes," thoughtfully, "he might be willing to give us his backing! He listens to me. I believe I could talk him round. But only if—"

His voice had risen with excitement, but now it fell again.

"There is one problem. Where do we find this agent? Could there be someone good enough? Haven't all the potential volunteers been recruited already by the Abwehr?"

"Not all of them," said the Inspector softly. "There is someone I have had my eye on for a long time, ever since I was in the criminal police. I think he could be trained to do the job."

"My God!" breathed Huppenkothen, worked up again. "If we could bring it off and show up those ass-licking traitors, why—why, for us, Inspector, it could mean everything. Promotion. The Iron Cross—"

"With oak leaves," said Hoffmann, and added gently, "And perhaps even a decoration from the Führer for poor Frau Pruck."

Huppenkothen shrugged his shoulders. It was evident that for him, at least, Katie Pruck no longer mattered. No wonder they called him Ice Water, thought Inspector Hoffmann, and sighed. He would have been quite distressed if he had known what was going through the Sturmbannführer's mind at that moment. He was thinking that one of the first things he was going to do when he got back to Berlin was get under the shower and do a thorough scrubbing job on the place where Katie Pruck had written her name.

CHAPTER 1

Two Down, One to Go

I

ON THE NIGHT OF May 10, 1941, a heavy force of Luftwaffe planes crossed the English Channel on what was to prove one of the last major night-bombing offensives against Britain during World War II. The Nazi invasion of the Soviet Union was about to begin, and this was a last exhibition of Hitlerian spite against British lives and property before the Führer turned his armies and air forces eastward. More than five hundred planes picked out targets over London, the Midlands, and the cities of Bristol, Swansea, and Cardiff, and wreaked heavy damage on people, their homes, and their historic buildings.

There would be no point in picking out this raid from the ones which had preceded it were it not for the fact that, on this occasion, two other Nazi planes used the cover of the raid to infiltrate British air space. They were dropping spies instead of bombs. The first spy, a seasoned Abwehr veteran named Captain Heinz Richter, landed in the flat marshlands of Lincolnshire, in eastern England, and was immediately taken into custody by British security police. He had £4,000 in British sterling in his money belt and a supply of explosives and dried secret ink. They were meant for a German spy already in England who had sent repeated messages desperately asking for them. Richter, who was his control working out of ABT1 in Hamburg, spoke English fluently and knew Britain well, and had impulsively decided to deliver the badly needed supplies himself. What he did not know was that his trusted and (he believed) brilliantly successful agent was, in fact, already in British custody and had long since been "turned." He had enticed Richter into the trap, and the British hoped to get another double agent out of him. Unfortunately for them (and for him), Richter happened to be one member of the Abwehr who was genuinely pro-Nazi and completely loyal to the Führer and the Fatherland. He adamantly refused all efforts to turn him around and induce him to work for the British. In consequence, he ended up on trial for espionage at the Old Bailey, and in December, 1941, he was executed.

The second spy who parachuted into Britain that night was more fortunate. That was almost certainly because he arrived under Gestapo rather than Abwehr auspices. The Junkers courier plane which the RSHA had commandeered from an airfield near Cherbourg slipped around the wall of anti-aircraft fire which the defenders of Swansea put up in a vain attempt to keep the Nazi bombers away from their port installations and the dwelling places around them. Swooping low through a valley in the Cambrian mountains, the pilot throttled down to a hundred knots, and it was the agent himself, staring down hard through the misty moonlight, who pressed the button which illuminated the amber warning light both in the cockpit and the open door of the plane. Hitching the parachute to the static line, he leaned forward for one last look at the ground. The plane was yawing badly and the agent yelled into the ear of his dispatcher that he was going down "before this old crate stalls itself into the ground."

He pressed the button first for red and then, as it set up a howl, changed it to the green. *"Heil Hitler!"* he shouted, and was away. The pilot did not stay to watch him descend but gunned the engine and swung round, making back for the Cotentin Peninsula before any night fighters caught him.

The agent could not have asked a better night for parachuting. The clouded moon gave just enough suffused light to illuminate the Welsh hills but not enough to define a figure or a canopy against the sky. There was a slight breeze which did not blow him off his course, but gave him the extra seconds to pick out his landing. With expert fingers, he tugged at the shrouds to guide himself first across a craggy summit from which it might have been difficult to climb down, and then out of the way of a mountain stream, which could have given him a soaking. He touched down on a gently sloping hillside covered with burgeoning herbs and heather, and filled his lungs with the scent of thyme as he rolled a short way down the incline. Then, with no sense of shock or bruises, he scrambled to his feet and gathered in the canopy of his parachute.

Half an hour later, in a small cave just above the mountain stream, he put a match to the chute and watched it burn, aware that the flames were screened from view by the bank of the stream and that no one would see the smoke against the night. He was very cool and confident. Strapped around his stomach, he carried a leather tool bag from which he now drew, first, a bar of chocolate, which he nibbled appreciatively, and then what appeared to be a rubberized battery, four valves wrapped in rubber, and coils, keys, and strips of metal. By the light of a pencil torch, he worked swiftly and efficiently, and by the time dawn was beginning to lighten the sky, he had set up his radio on a crag facing Cardigan Bay. Holding the telescope aerial high with one hand, he pressed the Morse key, and four times, with a pause of four minutes between each, tapped out the same message.

"Eisteddfod!"
"Eisteddfod!"
"Eisteddfod!"
"Eisteddfod!"

He had no great hope that it would be picked up, except by some British ham or listening station. And what could they make of it other than that some Welshman was signaling the name of his country's annual festival of poetry and minstrelsy? But if an RSHA station in Ireland or France or the Channel Islands did bring it in, and passed it on to Gestapo headquarters in Berlin, then that would be different. For "Eisteddfod" to them had a much more important meaning. It meant:

"The Druid has arrived!"
"The Druid has arrived!"
"The Druid has arrived!"
"The Druid has arrived!"

By the time the sun was over the mountaintop, the agent had dismantled his radio again and strapped it back in its case. He began walking southward, just under the brow of the hill, making for a road he remembered seeing from the air which would take him to a village, and, eventually, to Swansea. After about an hour, he struck a footpath leading down toward the valley, and presently he came across a flock of sheep grazing contentedly beside it, paying him only momentary attention as he passed by.

The old shepherd who now came in view was equally incurious. He would surely not have spoken had not the agent stopped, smiled, and called out a greeting to him.

"Dai bach! It's a beautiful morning. But that was a queer sort of night we passed, my friend! Did you see all the lights? It was as if all the stars and the moon as well had gone suddenly crazy!"

He spoke in Welsh, easily, melodiously, the lilt of the words like the sound of music. At the sound of him, the surly expression on the old shepherd's face changed, and it was as if he had run into a friend. In a torrent of Welsh, he described the raid on Swansea and Cardiff as he had seen it, piling on the drama as he told of swarms of enemy planes roaring over his head before they turned toward the Bristol Channel to drop their bombs.

"There'll be hundreds of dead and dying down there," he declaimed solemnly. "Let's hope some of them are those devilish Germans."

"Indeed, let us so hope," the agent said. "I pray for my people down there. I have relatives in Swansea. I'm going down to see them before the army gets me, and may they still be around to wish me luck."

They exchanged mutual good wishes and then the agent strode on, following the shortcut the shepherd had suggested to a bend in the main road where the morning bus would come by. He felt such a sense of relief that he began to whistle. His first encounter in Britain had gone by without a hitch. He had not even needed to hesitate when the shepherd had asked him his name.

"Gwyn Evans," he had said. "From up north, near Llanfyllin."

It was true. That was where his relatives had haled from. His real name was Gwyn Evans, and in that name he carried in his pocket a membership card in the Welsh Nationalist Party, which was genuine. He also had a British identity card in another name, food and clothing coupons, a picture of himself as a member of a Welsh choir (also genuine), as well as his radio and material for communicating with his controls both in France and in Lisbon.

Gwyn Evans was twenty-five years old in 1941. He spoke Welsh, English, Spanish, and German equally well. And how that had come about, how he had been recruited into the SS, how he had acquired the name of the Druid, and why he hated the English should be explained before this narrative goes any further.

II

In 1865 the Cardiff brig *Mimosa,* three months out of its home port in Wales, made landfall 8,500 miles away, on the southern shores of South America. The brig had brought a hundred and fifty-three Welsh colonists to the inhospitable shores of Patagonia, where the Argentine government had given them a grant of land along the Chubut River. The Welshmen were refugees from English arrogance and intolerance. Forbidden by the government at Westminster to teach their children to speak and read Welsh in their village schools, they had rallied under the leadership of a fiery nationalist named Caradog Evans and made an abortive, not to say pathetic, attempt to form a movement that would give them independence from their English neighbors. Evans had gone to jail for his part in the agitation, and when he emerged from Liverpool prison and was transported by his triumphant followers back over the border into his native North Wales, he addressed a mass meeting and declared that true Welshmen should not stay in a land which banned them from speaking the language of their fathers.

But of the thousands who cheered his fervent words, only a hundred and fifty-three made the journey with him across the stormy south Atlantic to the little harbor of Puerto Madryn, where the *Mimosa* finally tied up, to be greeted by two surly native Indians and a flock of stolid penguins. None of them budged or made a sound until Caradog Evans let down the gangplank and drove a herd of sheep among them.

Evans had brought his family with him to South America: his wife, Gwyneth, and his two sons, Alun and Dai, aged ten and five. Together they started a sheep farm on the bleak windswept hills above the small town of Gaiman, in Patagonia, and there, or roundabout, the rest of the Welsh decided to settle. But soon they were expanding across the valleys, unde-terred by the hostile climate and the thin, sour soil. They were much tougher than the Indians and the local Spanish-speaking Patagonians, and seemed to relish hardship. Settlements sprang up with names that rang of home: Bethesda, Bangor, Bethel, and Bryn Crwn. In their village schools, as well as in their homes, Welsh was taught and they sang it with resonance and fervor when they gathered in their Wesleyan chapels on Sunday to hail the Lord with their time-honored Welsh hymns.

To begin with, the Welsh kept themselves to themselves, and marriage with anyone else was frowned on. If Caradog Evans, now sporting a long white beard, had had his way, even the speaking of any language but Welsh would have been taboo. But the new generation coming along soon saw that that was impractical. The Argentinian government, which ruled Patagonia, was Spanish-speaking, and official communications had to be kept up in that language. Moreover, the railways and many of the principal shipping firms in Bahía Blanca and Buenos Aires were still controlled by the British, and they insisted on dealing and corresponding in English. So gradually the colonists became trilingual, and many of them soon began to speak Welsh only when they were singing or reciting poetry. This they did annually at the Eisteddfod they held in Gaiman, a small expatriate version of the great yearly festival that had always been the highlight of the national year in their native Wales.

At the Gaiman Eisteddfod of 1880, Caradog Evans was crowned archdruid and sent the following year as druidical envoy to the 1881 Eisteddfod in Wales. He was drowned at sea on the journey home, and Gwyneth Evans wasted away from grief and died the following year. But both sons had married girls in the colony and there were families on the way. A few years later, first Alun and then Dai were made druids, and it thereafter became a tradition of the Evans family that at least one of each succeeding generation should become a druid. There was keen competition among different branches of the family to win the druid's robes or the bardic crown, which was awarded each year for a song or a poem or an epic story in Welsh and about Wales. Alun's son Caradog, named for his dead grandfather, won it on his twenty-first birthday with a resounding narrative poem about the men of Harlech and their fight for freedom against the hated English. The family tradition meant that no matter how slack and lazy the rest of Patagonia's Welsh became about their native tongue, the language stayed alive in the Evans family. They used it always among themselves, and when they spoke English or Spanish, there was a beguiling Welsh tone to their voices that fascinated all who came in contact with them.

It may have been the lilt in his voice that first attracted Hedwig von Forbath to Caradog Evans II, but there were other things going for him too. He was tall, with a tousle of fair hair and a tiny beard tipped with ginger, but what made people look twice at his pleasantly ordinary face were his intense, burning, cerulean-blue eyes. As he stood before the assembled Welshmen in the autumn of 1913 and sang the saga of the men of Harlech, Hedwig von Forbath was caught up in the passionate music of his voice and the blazing glory of his eyes and became as excited as if she understood every word. When it was over, and he had solemnly been awarded the crown at the bardic coronation, her only thought was to discover exactly what story the young man had told. She asked for a translation into Spanish or English, but there was none. To find out what he had said, it seemed that she would have to talk to Caradog Evans himself. With her heart in her mouth, she presently did so—and from then on there was no turning back for either of them.

Hedwig von Forbath was eighteen years old in 1913, the only daughter of a German shipper who specialized in running supplies to the whaling fleets. He had already made a fortune in Scandinavia, and had now opened operations in the Argentine, and had set up headquarters for his stores and ships in Bahía Blanca, which was convenient for the British, American, Russian, and Scandinavian fleets hunting the great herds of whales in the South Atlantic and Antarctica. Hedwig was on vacation from school in Germany, and had brought some of her school friends with her to Gaiman to watch the Eisteddfod ceremonials, which had now become a tourist attraction in Patagonia, as had the Welsh themselves in their quaint native costumes and druidic robes. Her companions had been highly entertained, but Hedwig had been enthralled.

After only an hour together, Caradog Evans and Hedwig were convinced they were soul mates. As he translated his epic poem to her word for word into English, for he had no German, she realized that, in addition to unspoken urges, they had in common a mutual antipathy for the English, he because they held his people in bondage, she because, like all good Germans, she believed the English were the bullies of the world. It took her six months to convince her doting father that the young Welshman was the only man she would ever marry, and in his family Caradog was never really forgiven for seeking a wife outside his own nationality. He vowed to his mother that any children of the marriage would be brought up in the true family tradition, speaking Welsh and staunchly anti-English, but she was not really mollified. As for his brothers and sisters, they looked with a mixture of suspicion and contempt at this highborn German outsider who didn't know a mountain sheep from a Patagonian goat, got a rash from ticks at shearing time, and flinched and looked squeamishly away when the men bit the balls off the yearling lambs.

To add to their disdain, she miscarried with the first child of the marriage. But Hedwig was in love and passionately wanted a child, and within months she was pregnant again. A boy was born in 1915, and they christened him Gwyn in memory of his great-grandmother. By this time, World War I had begun, and to Hedwig's amazement and dismay this Welsh family, which had been taught through the generations to loathe the English and wish ill upon all their enterprises, turned out to have mixed feelings about the war. She automatically assumed that, like her, they would pray for Germany's victory and do everything in their power to help the Kaiser triumph over his hated enemy. To her distress, they were all smiles when the Germans were pushed back from the gates of Paris, and downcast when the Allies were beaten back at Passchendaele and heavily defeated at Gallipoli. They would talk among themselves in Welsh about the war, confident that she would not understand; but she had a good ear for languages, had picked up the Welsh tongue in the best of ways, by listening to her husband pouring out his passion to her in Welsh as he made love to her, and she knew enough to understand generally much of what they were saying. It was not complimentary to her or her people. She held her tongue, but sometimes she found it hard to bear.

One day she came into her dressing room to find that someone had disfigured the picture of Kaiser Wilhelm which she had hung on the wall. There was a smile of triumph on the face of Mifanwy, the Welsh nurse, as she watched Hedwig's expression change from astonishment to outrage, but she angrily denied her own guilt or knowing who had done the desecrating deed. That night Hedwig and Caradog had their first quarrel when he refused to bar the house to his brothers and sisters in future.

Gwyn was, of course, too young to be aware of his mother's distress, and by the time he was sitting up and taking notice the war was over. But Hedwig never forgot the way her in-laws had behaved toward her and her native country, and she never got over the humiliation of Germany's defeat. She did not interfere in any way with her son's Welsh education, and became proficient in the language herself in order to converse with him. But she also saw to it that he learned German, and, when he was sufficiently fluent, read him German books extolling the heroic deeds of her fellow-countrymen in the war. Carefully and subtly she bred in him a contempt for England and the English which, aware as he quickly became of the reason for his family's exile to Patagonia, he was never to lose. He was entered in a British prep school in Buenos Aires and there had the temerity to tell some English fellow-pupils that it was they who had cheated the Welsh people out of their country. He got a bloody nose out of it, but he inflicted a few black eyes on the English boys in the course of the melee, and, for their different reasons, both his mother and father were proud of him.

Each Sunday when he was home, Gwyn Evans sang in the choir of the Wesleyan chapel at Bryn Crwn, and in the Gaiman Eisteddfod in 1928, when he was thirteen, the choir won the prize. The result was an invitation to sing in the international Welsh choir competition at the Eisteddfod in Wales the following summer. They gathered in the courtyard of Caernarvon Castle, overlooking the Menai Straits and the Isle of Anglesey, and for the first time in his life Gwyn Evans felt the tug of nationality and realized what being a Welshman meant. In the course of his visit he and his companions also met their first Welsh Nationalists, and found confirmation of what his father had repeatedly told him, that the urge for an independent Wales was still present in the hearts of the Welsh people. Now here were men and women who were ready to fight for their freedom. He took no persuading when they asked him to become an overseas member of their movement.

He went back to the English school in Buenos Aires, and did well in his studies. His love of music made it easy for him to learn the piano and the violin, and his facility with languages enabled him to speak Spanish and English without thought, though, like his father, he never lost the Welsh lilt when he used either of them. Gwyn's German lacked, as his mother repeatedly pointed out, modern usage and colloquialisms, and those she felt he could only pick up in Germany. Over the years Caradog Evans had become weak and sickly, racked with a constant cough ever since he had caught pneumonia while rescuing newborn lambs in a sleeting Patagonian spring, and he did less and less around the family farm. He tried not to be too conscious of the fact that only subventions from Hedwig's family fortune kept them going. And when she wanted something badly, he no longer opposed her, but let her have her way, even though he had begun to suspect that her way would one day take his son away from him.

As the years passed, Hedwig saw *her* son as a German rather than a Welshman. In 1932, a week after his seventeenth birthday, a training ship of the German Navy called in at Bahía Blanca after a rough journey across the South Atlantic, and Hedwig's father gave a party for the captain, the officers, and the cadets. His daughter brought her son, who had already proved himself an adept yachtsman with small boats in and around the Chubut River. The German ship was sailing on its next stage around Cape Horn on its way to Valparaiso, and Hedwig, still a blazingly handsome blonde at thirty-seven, was at her charming best as she cornered the captain, presented her son, and asked if he could sign on for the voyage as a member of the crew.

With a face pickled a deep bronze from sun and salt water, his hair bleached golden, a grown-up young man instead of a callow boy, he was back on the farm a month later bearing a letter from the captain which brought tears of pride to Hedwig's eyes.

"It is a pity," the captain wrote, "that this young man is not a German citizen. He would have made a good commander in the German Navy."

It was this, perhaps, which decided her that Gwyn must be taken to Germany to complete his education. By this time they had all been reading in *La Prensa* of Buenos Aires how, at long last, the turmoil in Germany had come to an end, and Adolf Hitler and the National Socialists were in power. *La Prensa* was a great liberal newspaper and it did not conceal its distaste as its correspondents described the Jew-baiting and bullying which accompanied the rise of the Brownshirt revolution. Some of the Patagonian Welsh were disturbed when they read the reports, and so were many of the more thoughtful members of Argentina's German community. But Hedwig insisted—and half convinced Caradog, if not the rest of the

Evans family—that these were the simple growing pains of a reborn Germany. When branches of the Nazi Party began springing up in South America and a unit appeared in Bahía Blanca, Hedwig signed up for herself and for her son. She hung up a picture of Adolf Hitler in her dressing room, but this time she kept the door locked.

Gwyn Evans was now a paid-up member of two militant parties, for he still kept up his membership in the Welsh Nationalists. Each month he received a bulletin from the Nationalist headquarters in Cardiff, written in hortatory Welsh, and he did not fail to notice that nowadays the more inflammatory polemicists in that party often singled out Hitler and the Nazis for praise, even proclaiming in one issue that someday Wales would have a Führer of its own. He showed them to his mother, who then saw that they were passed on to other members of the family.

Nowadays there were two big events in the year for Gwyn and his mother. One was the annual congress of the Nazi Party (overseas division, South American section), which was usually held in Buenos Aires, and in 1935, when they arrived in the Argentine capital, Hedwig revealed that she had obtained Brownshirt uniforms for the two of them, and they wore them in a parade before a visiting bigwig from the Party in Germany, Baldur von Schirach. It was a thrill for Gwyn Evans, and he liked the snapshots which Hedwig took of him in his uniform (though he understood and accepted her suggestion that he should not show them to his father or "the others" back home).

In truth, however, he got a bigger lift from the annual Eisteddfod in Gaiman, for there was more of a challenge to it; the whole of the year every member of the family—every keen Welshman in Patagonia, in fact—was dipping deep into his Celtic soul for the inspiration that would win him a bardic crown. And he had to beat them.

In 1936, Gwyn Evans won the crown for a long epic poem about the mythical Welsh hero Owen Glendower. Hedwig, who had only vaguely heard of him before, listened to the impassioned passages with growing excitement, and at one point burst out: "He sounds just like the Führer!"

Those other members of the family who heard her remark snickered in derision, but they too were impressed by Gwyn's skill with words, the resonant delivery of his deepening voice, and the handsome spectacle he made as he declaimed from the platform.

Caradog, who was now very feeble, had insisted on attending the ceremonials, and when it was over he clasped his son to him and said, "Next year, maybe, or the year after, they will certainly make you a druid, my son. It is the only thing I am waiting for."

But the next year, 1937, when the Gaiman Eisteddfod came around, Gwyn Evans was no longer in Patagonia. He was in Germany with his mother. The year before, Hedwig's father, Ferdinand von Forbath, had left a manager in charge of his Bahía Blanca office and gone back to his old home in Bremerhaven. He wrote back enthusiastic letters about the "wonderful new atmosphere" in the Reich now that the Nazis were in power, and beseeched his daughter to come home—at least for a visit. She sailed with Gwyn early in 1937, and though she did not tell her son, she had no intention of coming back. Her once virile young husband was now a feeble wraith, and she was still eager and full of life. What was there left for her in Patagonia? The Evans family would never allow her to marry again.

As for her son, he had been enrolled at once in the University of Berlin, where he studied languages and literature. He played the violin in one of the college orchestras, sang in the glee club, and, like most of his fellow-students, was an active member of the Nazi Party. He wrote long dutiful letters to his father each week—in Welsh, of course—but otherwise did not miss Patagonia. Berlin was exciting. There was always something going on. The nation was on the march. Austria had been taken over by the Nazis without a fight.

Now there was the Czech question to be settled. What would the English, the French, and the Russians do when the Führer finally decided that the German Herrenvolk of the Czech Sudetenland must be freed from the foreign yoke and brought back to the Reich? Would there be war?

Gwyn Evans could hardly wait for the next drama to begin. He liked what was going on in Germany. He was excited by it all, and proud to be a National Socialist.

But what was he going to do when he finished college? Go back to herding sheep in Patagonia? No! He would stay here and fight the English!

III

The bus was almost empty when the Druid flagged it down and boarded it at the foot of the mountain, and long before it reached the outskirts of Swansea all but three passengers had disembarked. He realized why, once they were into the streets of the city and the driver was forced to pick his way through the smoke and around the piles of rubble. Swansea had taken a pasting in the night, and both ambulance men and bomb disposal squads were still hard at work. It took the bus half an hour to reach the depot—or, rather, what remained of it, for the shock wave from a bomb-hit in the next street had sheered away half the building and toppled three of the buses onto their sides. While the driver and the conductor were gaping at the damage and repeating "Glory be to God" the Druid picked his way over the broken glass and went into the railway station, which was still intact, even if there were no trains running. He spotted a canteen and hesitated as he looked at the girl behind the counter dispensing tea from an urn, watching whether coupons were now being demanded. The girl looked up, caught his eye, and grinned at him.

"You look as if you could do with a cuppa," she said. "Brought any sugar with you?"

He came forward, shaking his head. She poured a pale brown liquid, steaming hot, into a mug and dipped a hand into the pocket of her slacks. "Here you are, dear. You can have the lump I was saving for my dog. He's getting too fat anyway. That'll be fourpence."

He puckered his lips over the comforting warmth and gave a grunt of satisfaction.

"Thanks," he said. "You are right. I needed that. Come a long way, I have," he went on, slightly exaggerating his Welsh accent. "Up from North Wales to visit my relatives. God only knows what's happened to them. You wouldn't know Kidwelly Street, by any chance?"

"Not me," the girl said. "I'm a stranger in these parts. From London. Came to Swansea to get away from the bombing!" She shrieked with laughter, then gestured to the door. "There's a copper out there somewhere. He'll know."

The last communication he had had from the Welsh Nationalists was a copy of the party newspaper, *Y Cimru,* which had been forwarded to him from Patagonia in 1939. On its masthead had been the name of the Swansea branch secretary, Cledwyn Jones, and the address 16 Kidwelly Street. He was well aware of what had happened to the Nationalist Party now that there was a war on, for, like Mosley's BUP (the British Union Party, a Fascist organization), it had been proscribed and many of its members rounded up and put in jail under the British government's wartime Regulation 18B. On the other hand, he had heard from the RSHA's spies in the Abwehr that several Welsh Nationalist members had succeeded in going underground and were working closely with Germany both as spies and saboteurs.

Well, that remained to be seen. But he was certainly not going to ask a Welsh policeman to direct him to an address which might immediately arouse his suspicions. Instead, he gave a polite greeting to the steel-helmeted officer standing by the station entrance, and walked on toward what, he hoped, was dockland and some more raffish, less suspicious folk from whom he might make inquiries. Instead, the closer he got to the water—he had caught a glimpse of the sea as he walked downhill—the more uniforms he saw. There were policemen, ambulance men, soldiers, and air-raid wardens everywhere, and from one vantage point, through a bombed gap in a row of small shops and houses, he saw the reason for it. A couple of ships in the harbor had been hit and one was completely overturned, its keel and screws sticking into the air, the other half evidently on the bottom and still ablaze, black smoke pouring from its hold. He could not see any firemen but he could see jets of water making a spectacular fountain display. A warden came round the corner, caught sight of him, and bustled up.

"You'd better skedaddle, man, if you know what's good for you," he said. "That crate's liable to go up at any moment. There's grain aboard, and that means gas. If the fire gets close, they'll be scraping us off the walls. So be a good chappie, will you now, and bugger off quick!"

"Where's Kidwelly Street?" the Druid asked.

"Right down there." The warden pointed vaguely toward the docks. "You don't want to go that way. In any case, we've evacuated everyone. If you're looking for relatives, go back up to Bethel Hall and ask someone."

"I'll do that," the Druid said, and then added, in Welsh: "And good luck to you."

"Leave it to the Welsh!" the warden said, in the same language, grinning broadly.

The Druid turned around, went back up the main road, then crossed over and doubled back through the maze of streets, toward dockland again. Ten minutes of reconnoitering (there was no one around to ask) and he had found Kidwelly Street. There was a row of mean two up-and-downers on either side, leading down to the water, and No. 16 looked even shabbier than the rest. The windows had long since lost their glass and were boarded up, half with wood and half with cardboard. Pinned to one of them was the tattered remnant of a Welsh Nationalist poster, with a cock crowing defiance at a bloated John Bull and Y CIMRU! in red letters underneath it. In fading letters across the sheet had been overprinted the words UP THE WELSH! and below them was a penciled addition: UP YOU!

He looked cautiously along the street, but it was hushed and deserted; even the cats and dogs seemed to have been taken away. He tried the front door, and, as he had expected, found it locked. So he counted the doors to the nearest alleyway, and went down it, through a nauseating smell of urine, until he came round to the back. Counting the back gates carefully, he slipped into the yard of what he calculated was No. 16. There was no lock on the scullery door, and he carefully depressed the latch and went inside. In the kitchen, too, the windows were boarded up and only small cracks of light from outside gave dim illumination to the room. There was no one in it, and no sound from anywhere. But when the Druid sniffed, he could smell something—tea. He went across to the gas stove against the wall and gingerly put a finger on the old kettle on one of the rings. It was still hot.

"Who the bloody hell are you?" said a voice suddenly. There was a Welsh lilt to it.

"I'm looking for Cledwyn Jones," said the Druid, in Welsh, carefully not turning around. "I was told I would find him here."

"Then whoever told you," the voice said, in Welsh this time, "is a bit out of date. Cledwyn has been out in North Africa for nearly a year now, fighting for his King and country!" There was a derisive snort. "Can you imagine that? Cledwyn Jones a bloody patriot! The party will never get over the shame of it!" There was a pause, and then the Druid heard the sound of slippered feet coming into the room. From close behind him, he felt a breath on his neck, and then the smell in his nostrils of tea—and alcohol. "And who," breathed the voice, very close now, "would you be, my friend?"

"Up north in my village," he replied slowly, "they have

60

been known to refer to me as the Gwynnedd minstrel. That's because I'm always hoping my modest poems will someday compete for the bardic crown. My kindlier friends call me Eisteddfod, because that's where I'm always going."

"My God!" There was a quick sucking in of breath and then he felt arms on his shoulders, twisting him round. He found himself looking into the pale blue eyes of a middle-aged man with flowing hair who might have been a brother or a cousin of his father, and the family resemblance gave him quite a pang.

"My God," said the man again, "then I know who you are. You're the Druid! I've been waiting for you, my friend. I've got quite a tale to tell you."

He had a mug in his hand, and now he went across to a cupboard and took out another mug and a half-empty bottle of whisky. With a trembling hand, he slopped some into the empty mug and handed it across to the younger man, then filled up his own with a mixture of whisky and tea. He took a draft, and held out his hand.

"You must know my code name," he said. "I'm Johnny! Did they tell you in Berlin about me?"

"They also told me your real name," the Druid said. He took the sweaty hand of the Welshman in his.

"Arthur Owens," he said. "Hallo, Mr. Owens. I can't tell you how happy I am to meet you at last. I have brought some money for you. And I have a special message for you from the Oberführer himself."

CHAPTER 2

Snow Job

I

ADMIRAL CANARIS and the Abwehr played the espionage game very close to the chest, and neither Hitler nor the Sicherheitsdienst had any exact idea of how many agents they had operating in Britain in the summer of 1941. From their own spies in the Abwehr, the RSHA estimated that between nineteen and twenty-four agents had been infiltrated into Britain by one means or another, and the British had allowed it to be known that they had caught, tried, and executed four of them. But who were the rest? The RSHA, in spite of all their efforts, had succeeded in discovering the identities of very few of them and the code names of not many more.

But about one of them they were confident they knew everything, and even more certain that he was completely under their control. This was "Johnny," otherwise Arthur Owens. The reason they were sure of Johnny was because they had in their possession the only thing in life he really loved—more, even, than money and booze—and that was his girl.

"If you have any trouble with Johnny," Inspector Hugo Hoffmann had told the Druid, "tell him you wouldn't like anything unpleasant to happen to Trudy. He'll toe the line."

On his good days, Arthur Owens was a brisk, bustling little man with a light step, twinkling eyes, and the kind of mischievous charm that would have made you think of a leprechaun if he had been Irish rather than Welsh. On his bad days, he was a moody wreck. Born in the Rhondda Valley, trained as an electrician while serving an apprenticeship in the RAF, he had become a traveler in electrical goods for a British firm in the 1930s, and thereafter made frequent trips to Germany and other Continental countries. What he had never told the Abwehr—but the RSHA had subsequently learned from Trudy—was that during those years he had begun working for British intelligence snooping around the dockyards in Hamburg, Kiel, Wilhelmshaven, and Bremen, and selling what naval information he picked up when he got back to London.

He did it, he emphasized to Trudy, only for the money, because, like every good Welshman, he despised the English. The thing that irritated him with the SIS characters he met when he handed over his information was that they not only paid him very little money for it but they patronized him for being so obviously a member of the Welsh working class and lacking that *sine qua non* of their circle, a public school education. What's more, they called him "Taffy," and that, as he told Trudy, "really got my goat."[1]

As a way of getting his own back on these "English snobs," he secretly joined two organizations of which they would certainly not have approved. One was the Welsh Nationalists. He actually put on a false mustache and dark glasses and joined a parade through Hyde Park demanding independence

[1] There is an English nursery rhyme which goes: "Taffy was a Welshman,/Taffy was a thief,/Taffy came to my house/And stole a piece of beef."

for Wales, and that made him feel much better. And he signed up as a member of the Anglo-German Fellowship, which supported Nazi causes, in the hope that it would put him in touch with German intelligence, for whom he decided he would like to do some work on the side.

It was through the Fellowship that he discovered a social club which the Nazi embassy ran for German and other foreign *au pair* girls working in London, and Owens was invited to their evening dances. It proved to be a happy hunting ground for one of his favorite hobbies: girls. He was a great sucess with the *au pair* girls. He was tiny, far from handsome, and much older than they were, but they liked his irrepressible good humor and sense of fun, and his willingness to listen to their problems.

It so happened that the social manager of the *au pair* club was a talent spotter for the Abwehr, and he was told to sound out Arthur and discover whether he would be willing to work for the Germans. The Abwehr figured that if and when war came (this was 1938), they would need to have some spies on the ground. The approach was exactly what Arthur Owens had been waiting for. Almost immediately, he produced a plan of a new RAF airfield near London and the layout of the electrical equipment of the Hurricane fighter. ABT1 in Hamburg, to whom they were sent, was delighted and Arthur Owens was handsomely paid and highly praised for his work.

He was given a code name—Johnny—and assigned a number —3504—and Arthur Owens was now on the official roster of Abwehr's foreign agents. Though neither side knew it, he was, in fact, a double spy, for he went on working for the British whenever he was in Germany. The British had a code name for him too. They called him "Snow."

At which point, to complicate matters, the SS stepped in in the elegant shape of an RSHA operative in London named Trudy Körner.

I I

Gertrude Körner was ostensibly a member of the secretarial
pool at the German embassy in Grosvenor Square, but had
been a member of the SS since she was seventeen years old.
That was the year she came back from finishing school in
Switzerland and her brother, a captain in the SS, introduced
her to the organization. She was just what they were looking
for. A tall, Nordic, leggy blonde with an angelic face and a
sympathetic voice, she had, in fact, a heart of stone. Her job
in London was to spy on the German *au pair* girls and report
back to Berlin what they were doing and saying, which is how
she first encountered Arthur Owens at the *au pair* club the
Germans ran in Cleveland Terrace, Bayswater. She would
never have allowed her devastating bedroom eyes to give
him a second glance had she not had it whispered to her by
the social manager, Peter Ferdinand Brunner, who trusted
her, that the Welshman had been recruited into the Ahwehr.[2]
She informed the RSHA in Berlin about this, and was then
instructed to find out what made the Welshman tick.

It did not take Trudy Körner long to have Arthur Owens
hopelessly in love with her. She quickly divined that he was
oversensitive about his height and background, and she fed his
vanity by making it obvious that though she herself was tall
and aristocratic, she still thought him a most dynamic and
wonderful fellow. It was the fulfillment of his most cherished
secret dreams, and soon he was keeping nothing back from
her. She triumphantly reported back to Berlin that the prize
agent the Abwehr had recruited was, in fact, a double spy
who was also working for the British. She was ordered to say
nothing about it to anyone else, but from that moment the
SS decided to move in on Arthur Owens.

In the summer of 1939, at the moment when war clouds

[2] Brunner himself worked for Captain Hans Dierks, an Abwehr control
officer in Hamburg later killed in a car accident.

were gathering thick over Europe, the Abwehr urgently summoned the Welshman to Hamburg for training in espionage techniques. To the surprise of his control officer, Nikolaus Ritter of ABT1, he turned up with Trudy Körner. They were wined and dined well by the Abwehr, and sometimes late at night, when they were touring the sleazy nightclubs along the Reeperbahn and Arthur was getting sodden on too much wine and beer, Ritter would look for a sign of disgust on Trudy's face. Not a hint of distaste, but only concern, darkened those admirable features.

When the crisis began in late August, and it was inevitable that war would soon begin, the Abwehr wanted its agent back in Britain as soon as possible. But what about Trudy? The little Welshman made it clear that he was not going to be parted from his beloved. But Trudy was a German citizen. How could he take her with him?

Trudy answered that one (after surreptitiously consulting with the SS). They would travel back to England together, and as soon as they reached London they would get a special license and marry. Arthur Owens, hardly able to believe his luck, joyfully booked them a passage on the Hamburg boat to England. But when they came to the police desk at the dockside, an official motioned them aside and politely told them there were "some questions" to be answered. Trudy was taken one way, Arthur the other. He was kept waiting for an hour, after which the official, full of apologies, returned with his passport and told him he could go on board. Fräulein Körner, he was informed, was already there and waiting for him. He rushed up the gangplank, which was raised immediately he set foot on the deck. Trudy was not there, but a steward indicated he should go below and look in the saloon. She was not there, either.

By the time he got back on deck, in a panic by now, the boat was on its way, heading out of harbor. Rushing to the rail, he leaned over, staring toward the receding shoreline, looking so desperate it seemed likely he would fling himself

66

overboard and start swimming back to Germany and his beloved Trudy. What did it matter if he drowned? Life was not
worth living without her.

It was then that he felt strong arms pinioning him, and
when he struggled round, he saw two burly types holding on
to him. Quickly and efficiently, they swung him off his feet
and carried him below, where an SS official was waiting for
him.

Which was how Arthur Owens learned that henceforth he
would be not a double spy but a triple one. He would continue to serve the British and the Abwehr, but he would
report on both of them to the RSHA. It was made very clear
to him that if he valued Fräulein Körner and wished to see
her again, it was the RSHA whose orders would always have
priority. And heaven help both him and the girl if he ever
whispered a word to anyone about the arrangement.

III

"How much do you know about me, laddie?" the little Welshman asked, slopping some more whisky into his tea.

"I know about Fräulein Körner," the Druid said.

In fact, he knew more about Trudy Körner than Johnny
did. Johnny probably thought that it was love and desperation
which had enabled Trudy—once she had been left behind in
Hamburg—to get her old job back with the German diplomatic
service, and then arrange a posting to Lisbon. She had contrived to get news of her presence in Portugal to him through
a Portuguese newspaperman on a mission to London, and
begged him to try to visit her. The Welshman had then managed to organize a visit to Lisbon in connection with his
electrical business, and once there he had immediately made
contact with the Abwehr control officer in the Portuguese
capital and delivered information to him about British airfields and aircraft production. But he had also managed to

have what, for him, were some blissful hours with Trudy Körner in Estoril, during which she had demonstrated that her devotion to him was as passionate as ever. But when he pleaded with her to be allowed to remain in Portugal, she had tearfully refused, because, she said, she dreaded the horrible revenge the Gestapo would exact from both of them if he stayed on.

The Druid looked into Johnny's bloodshot eyes, noted his stubbled chin and trembling hands, and wondered cynically how such a pathetic little man could be taken in by such a charade. He knew that Trudy was already the willing mistress of her boss in Lisbon, Paul von Fidrmuc, and that when she talked about Johnny she called him "the dwarf" or "my little Welsh worm," or even more uncomplimentary names. During the forty-eight hours together with Johnny in Lisbon, she had thoroughly and systematically debriefed him between each simulated orgasm. Trudy's subsequent report to the RSHA made it abundantly clear that the information Johnny had handed over to the Abwehr about the RAF was false, and that he had deliberately cheated them. That meant the British must know about his Abwehr connections.

What the Druid needed to find out was this: except when he was pouring out his heart to Trudy Körner, was Johnny cheating the RSHA too? Had he also confessed to the British his SS connections?

Of course the Druid revealed nothing of this to the man facing him across the oilcloth-covered table. Instead, he said, "Our information from Lisbon is that Fräulein Körner is well but very lonely. She hopes you will perhaps be able to arrange another visit there soon, when you have business to do."

Johnny sighed and shook his head. "That won't be so easy to arrange. Why should I go personally when I can send the Abwehr all it wants by radio or secret ink? If I go too frequently, someone's bound to get suspicious. Besides, the authorities here are getting really sticky. Exit permits are as hard to get as booze." He stared ruefully at the nearby empty bottle, then banged his fist on the table. "This bloody war! Why should I be mixed up in it? Why don't those English donkeys admit that they're beaten?"

The Druid said, "The British don't suspect you? What reason did you give for being in Swansea?"

The Welshman grinned at him. "Oh, come on now, my boy. The SS knows I work for English intelligence. Trudy told me someone split on me. And you must know I'm an agent for the Abwehr too. I just try to see that my left hand never knows what my right hand's doing, and vice versa. One of the jobs I do for the English is snooping around among the Nationalists in Wales, finding out what the lads are up to. I come down here regularly and keep my ears open. They trust me, see? They know I'm one of them—and they let me in on their plans."

"And then you tell the English?"

"Only when it's too late—or when some daft bugger's trying to be too much of a hero, like the laddie who tried to blow up the Birmingham water-pipe line all on his own—and I arranged to have him ambushed and shot by the army before he could spill the beans about everybody." He added, emotion in his voice: "I'm a true Welshman, sonny, and I'd never let down my own side!"

The Druid looked at him coldly. He was tempted to reply: *You're a Welsh bag of wind and you'd let down your own side like a shot if the British offered you enough money or booze. You'd sell me out too if it weren't for our control over Trudy Körner.*

Instead, he rapped out briskly, "There are now twenty-four Abwehr agents operating in Britain. How many of them do you know?"

Johnny looked startled. "We're not supposed to make contact with each other," he said, and added: "Except in an emergency, of course."

"What emergency?"

"Well." He hesitated and licked his lips. "If they are in

trouble—ill—on the run—need money. Then we may be called in to help."

"And have *you* helped any of them?"

Again the hesitation. Then: "Last September, I got a radio message from Hamburg. 'Cassio' had dropped by parachute on the heath near Buckingham, sprained his ankle on landing, and had been sleeping out in bad weather until he could walk. He needed help. I was instructed to find him a safe hiding place until he'd recovered."

"What happened?"

"I picked him up on High Wycombe Station," Johnny said. "He was in a bad way, poor soul. Very bedraggled. I whisked him on the train double quick and fixed him up in rooms behind King's Cross Station. Kept by a little Welsh woman I know. She looked after Cassio and fed him like a fighting cock, while I made sure his papers were in order. Then I sent him off to Birmingham—he was going to report on armament production there and in Coventry—and that's the last I saw of him."

"Where is he now?" asked the Druid.

The little Welshman shrugged. "How should I know? He's vanished. I got a message from ABT1 on New Year's Day saying Cassio thought he'd been rumbled by the English narks and was going to make a run for it. He said he was dumping his radio set at Cambridge Station and I was ordered to check that he'd done that." He nodded. "It was there all right, and nobody picked me up when I retrieved his ticket from behind the number two toilet—where he said he'd left it—and checked out the suitcase with the set. But as for Cassio"—he shrugged again—"he's disappeared off the map. Killed himself, I wouldn't be surprised. He was a moody sort of chap."

Johnny was watching the Druid carefully while he spoke, wondering whether this cool young man was accepting his story. How could he tell him the truth about Cassio? It could blow the whole business wide open. How could he explain that on High Wycombe Station last September 17, Cassio—a young Dane named Goesta Caroli—had been taken into custody by security officers from MI5 and three weeks later had tried to hang himself at Camp 020, the interrogation center at St. Albans? But the English had broken and turned him in the end—or so they thought. Cassio was a double spy feeding false armament figures to Hamburg all through October, November, and December, 1940, convincing the Germans that Britain was becoming too strong to be invaded, when, in reality, she was still as weak and defenseless as in the earlier weeks of the summer. The English had a code name of their own for Cassio. They called him "Summer," and they were confident that they had won him over completely to their side; so completely, in fact, that they had allowed him to leave Camp 020 and live with his MI5 control officer at Hinxton, in Northamptonshire, close to the area where he was supposed to be spying for the Abwehr. From there he made his supposedly secret radio contacts with the Abwehr, and usually there were a guard and a radio operator on duty to oversee his operations.

But on New Year's Day, 1940, the British relaxed their watch over their charge, and allowed guard and operator to go home on leave. Cassio was sharing a celebratory drink with his control, and they were rather bibulously singing together the words of a German *Lied* when the German spy snapped. Leaping upon the Englishman, he wrestled him to the ground, strangled him until his tongue popped out, and then escaped on the control's motorbike, parked in the back garden. His intention was to reach Norfolk, steal a small boat, and try to make it back across the North Sea to the Continent. Unfortunately for him, the motorbike broke down, and he was picked up in the early hours of the following morning not far from Lowestoft; but not before police, army, and security forces had been alerted and a nationwide hunt for the fugitive begun.

How could Johnny reveal to the Druid that Cassio had not

just disappeared? He was indeed dead, but not by suicide. After his capture, the English had put him on trial for espionage and at Birmingham prison, in the first week of February, 1941, he had been hanged. Every old lag in the jail was talking about it. It was one of the executions the British had carefully not made public, in case someone in Germany wondered exactly what had happened to Cassio between his landing in Britain and his death four months later. But you couldn't stop warders and released prisoners from talking.

"Yes," Johnny said, "he's vanished right off the bloody map, has Cassio. Probably killed himself, poor fellow, when he realized he couldn't get away.

The Druid was watching him with no expression in his eyes, and it made Johnny feel uneasy. So far, he had always found it simple to deceive the Nazis, but that was chiefly because they were Germans, and Germans were never suspicious when you told them what they wanted to hear. But this young man was not simply a Nazi; he was Welsh too. He knew the way the Celtic mind worked. He must already have guessed there was something wrong with Johnny's story. Did he think he couldn't be trusted? Then he had to convince him otherwise, because he needed to persuade this strange young Welshman that he not only could be trusted, but that he would never betray him to the English. But at the same time, there was one secret he had to keep from him, because, if the Druid learned it, the whole intelligence network in England would collapse—and bring disaster on all of them, including Trudy and himself.

IV

The Druid did not mention it to Johnny, but there was a woman he had been told to find when he got to London. Her name was Polly Wright and she was married to a musician who worked in one of the orchestras run by the state radio system, the BBC. Polly Wright was what Inspector Hoffmann had called "friendly," especially with young men. In the last months of peace in 1939, she had accompanied her husband when a BBC orchestra had visited the Rhineland for a series of concerts, and while there, the Inspector went on, she had become "very friendly" with a young engineer working on the Westwall, the fortifications the Nazis were building along the French frontier.

Unfortunately for her, when the time came for the orchestra to return to London, Polly had become so infatuated with her young German that she had decided to stay on. Even when war began, her engineer lover assured her he could protect her and had prevailed upon her to stay with him. Of course, she had eventually ended up in an internment camp, but the following spring she had been among those exchanged through Holland for Germans interned in England, and was now back home in London. Hoffmann warned the Druid that the young woman was completely non-political, and to beware of letting her know of his Party or German connections. On the other hand, she could be useful to him, because she knew everybody in the London musical world, including quite a few Welshmen who worked for the BBC.[3]

Johnny spent some time going through the Druid's papers, checking his identity card, his ration book and clothing coupons, pointing out that the Abwehr could be careless over their documentation. But when he passed them back he grudgingly admitted that the RSHA were smarter in their handiwork. The documents looked genuine.

"They should," said the Druid. "They are genuine."

But though Johnny waited, he gave no further explanation.

As one of the perks of his work for the English, the little Welshman had a car and a liberal petrol allowance, and later

[3] Musical life in Britain tended to center around the BBC, and its Music Department was—and still is—a major part of the British radio system.

that morning he went back up the hill to the garage where he kept it and brought it down to Kidwelly Street. As soon as darkness fell, the Druid slipped out the front door of No. 16, and spent an uncomfortable night lying on the floor of the old Austin pickup. There was only a tarpaulin sheet to cover him, and he was cold. But just before first light, he heard the car door open and a hand came over the back seat.

"Get this inside you," Johnny's voice said.

He must have found replenishments, because the mug of hot tea was well laced with whisky. The Druid drank it gratefully. He was still gulping down the last drops when the car started and they were off.

No one stopped them. It was about three hours later that the car began crossing a wide river—he was sitting up by then—and he realized this must be the Clifton suspension bridge. Presently, Johnny pulled into the side of the road.

"This is where I turn off," he said. "You can pick up a bus at the next corner. Bristol's twenty minutes away."

They had already made their rendezvous arrangements, and there was nothing more to be said. Johnny grinned as the car pulled away; there was an air almost of smug satisfaction on his puckish face. It was hardly surprising. He was having it all ways. He was being paid by the Abwehr for working for them. He was double-crossing them with the British, and getting paid for that too. And in his pocket was £500 which the Druid had brought him over from the RSHA.

The only thing he had to worry about, in fact, was Trudy—and what the Gestapo might do to her if he didn't keep his mouth shut about the Druid.

V

The train from Bristol delivered him at Paddington Station in the early evening, and the first thing the Druid did was find a small café on Praed Street, where he bought a cup of watery tea and a plate of beans on toast. Then he smiled at the blousy waitress and asked where he could find a room. She jerked her thumb toward the back of the café.

"Ask 'im, why don'tcher?" she said. "'E runs the place next door."

CHAPTER 3

Vera Gives a Clue

I

ON THE EVENING of October 20, 1941, an officer of the Secret Intelligence Service named Denzil Roberts drove back to his office in Pimlico, London, after a frustrating session at the interrogation center of the counterintelligence section at St. Albans. He had been to see Captain Heinz Richter, the Abwehr officer who had parachuted into Britain on the same night as the Druid, but, unlike that SS agent, had fallen straight into the hands of waiting British security police.

Everyone in the SIS had been hoping for great things from Richter. He was one of the professionals in ABT1 in Hamburg, and it was quite a feather in the cap of MI5 (the internal wing of SIS) that they had succeeded in enticing him into their net. As one of the control officers of the Abwehr's Amtsgruppe Ausland, his principal activity, until he foolishly left Hamburg, was feeding instructions to and directing the welfare of one of the most successful spies the Nazis had infiltrated into the United Kingdom. This was a young Austrian (supposedly a refugee) who operated under the code name of "Alto" and had, thanks to great personal charm and good family connections, done extremely well for the Nazi spy machine. He had built up a network of subagents in all parts of Britain, and provided a steady flow of most vital information.

But recently Alto had signaled that he had run into difficulties, mainly financial. He desperately needed money to keep up appearances and to pay his subagents. Getting money to their spies in Britain had always been one of the most vexing problems the Abwehr had to deal with, and in Alto's case it was particularly complicated. For one thing, he needed so much. Some pro-Nazi embassies, mainly Spanish and South American, had their attachés make cash-drops for him, and once a Spanish newsman smuggled in over £1,000; but Alto used it up quickly and was soon asking for more. He needed a really large sum, and since both Richter and his Abwehr superiors thought he was worth it, they pondered emergency measures, especially when Alto hinted he would have to close down if help was not soon forthcoming.

Finally, rather than lose his favorite spy, Richter decided to take the risk, and persuaded Admiral Canaris to let him go personally to Alto's rescue. Carrying a money belt with him containing £4,000, he parachuted into Britain—and into the trap the SIS had set for him.

Only now, more than three weeks after his capture, was Richter beginning to realize what had happened to him. Relays of interrogators, some brutal and threatening, some gentle and persuasive, set out for him the situation that faced him. Either he would tell all he knew about the Abwehr, and henceforward work for the British as a double spy, or he would be put on trial as an enemy agent—which would mean his almost certain execution. When he proved first obdurate and then defiant, the British confronted him in his cell with none other than Alto himself, who confessed to him that he had been working for the "enemy" ever since he arrived in

Britain.[1] But even the bitter knowledge that his favorite agent had betrayed him did not persuade Richter to change his allegiance, a fact which surprised neither Alto nor Roberts, both of whom knew Richter as a fanatic Nazi and a devoted admirer of Hitler. But before he was taken off to a normal prison and held pending his trial, Denzil Roberts had hoped to mine one small gem of information out of the Abwehr agent. On that fatal night in September when Richter parachuted into England, had he been aware that the Abwehr had also sent in another spy? If so, who was he and where was he? Why had the unsuspecting Abwehr not alerted Alto or any of the other German double agents in England, enabling this second spy too to be trapped by waiting security men?

But no matter how circuitously Roberts had tried for the information, he had soon realized that Richter was not going to be of any help. And Roberts was convinced that it was not because he was being stubborn or holding back; he simply did not seem to understand what the SIS man was getting at.

Yet Roberts was sure that Richter had not come alone. On the night in question, during the Luftwaffe attack on South Wales, three different air-raid wardens had reported a plane coming in behind the main bomber force and making in the direction of the Cambrian Mountains. One eyewitness swore that the plane had cruised at a surprisingly low altitude through one of the valleys, as if it were about to machine-gun the road, as some of them sometimes did. But he had heard no sound of gunfire; instead he had seen the plane bank and turn sharply, and shortly afterward he caught a glimpse, from far off, of what looked like the canopy of a parachute. A search of the neighborhood had revealed no trace of any German crewman who might have baled out, but some charred rope, which might have been the shrouds of a parachute, had been found amid a pile of ashes in a mountain cave; and a shepherd spoke of meeting a young man on the morning after the raid.

[1] The British had a code name for him too: "Tate."

He was on his way down the mountain and he had stopped to exchange greetings.

"Man, what a strange but beautiful Welsh he spoke," the shepherd had said. "But he said he was from the North, you know. Sounded just like a poet."

The words had intrigued Denzil Roberts, for he had heard something like them before.

I I

Denzil Roberts was a veteran of the counterespionage business, with scars to show for his service. Recruited into the SIS in the late thirties because of his fluency in German and his deep interest in archaeology—which implied a capacity for digging deep into national background—he had been an SIS courier and paymaster during the so-called "phony war" period of 1939–40, and he narrowly missed capture by the Nazis as a result. Passport Control was the embassy section the British used for their counterespionage services, and one of the principal centers was in Holland, still neutral at this time. The chief of station at The Hague was Major Richard Stevens. Shortly after the start of the war, Stevens fell into a Gestapo trap of uncanny similarity to the one the SIS used two years later to capture Heinz Richter. Enticed to the Dutch-German frontier town of Venlo for a rendezvous with one of his agents, Stevens and a fellow-agent, Captain Payne Best, were seized by a squad of SS men from the RHSA and wrestled into Germany amid a blaze of gunfire. A young Dutchman, Lieutenant Klop, accompanying the British spy chief, was shot in the back and killed when he started to run. But what no one (including the Germans) noticed was that Roberts, who had been delivering dispatches and had gone along for the ride, was in the British party; he managed to slip into the Dutch customshouse and hide in the toilet until the SS men had disappeared with their captives. He returned to The Hague to tell the tale and rise in the service of an organization whose secrets were now being extracted, by torture and drugs, from the unfortunate Stevens.

It taught him a lesson about the nature of the business he was in, and of the ruthlessness of the Sicherheitsdienst, particularly as compared with the rather more gentlemanly activities of the Abwehr, against whom he had sharpened his wits so far.

Roberts spent some time at the St. Albans interrogation center while waiting for an assignment overseas. It was there that he encountered the first German spies to be captured by British security since the outbreak of war. He was not impressed by their caliber, but they did give him ideas.

There were three of them. One was a Swiss-German named Werner Heinrich Walti, who had once worked as chauffeur for the French consulate in Hamburg and spied on the office for the Abwehr. Another was a confidence trickster, on the run from the German police, who had operated in the black market in Brussels and used the name Theodore Drücke. And the third was his mistress, a fair-haired Danish-German cabaret girl from Schleswig-Holstein called Vera de Schallberg (though she used other names too). They had been landed from a seaplane on a remote stretch of coast in northern Scotland with the task of reporting on British preparations to resist a Nazi invasion. (This was at the time of the Battle of Britain, when German troops were expected to cross the Channel at any moment.)

Right from the start, things had gone wrong for them. The bicycles which the trio had brought with them in the seaplane fell into the water and went to the bottom, which meant they would have to travel by bus or train, and no one had briefed them about public transportation in wartime Britain. They got well soaked when their rubber dinghy collapsed close to shore, and they were forced to wade up the beach.

There they split into two parties. Drücke and Vera de Schallberg found a local railway station, asked its name and

the time of the next train, and were arrested a few minutes
later by a policeman who arrived breathless on his bike. The
stationmaster had been suspicious about Vera's accent and
their soaked clothes. Walti went as far as Edinburgh, but was
picked up there as he got off the train from Aberdeen. They
were taken to St. Albans for interrogation.

It was quickly obvious that neither of the two men was of
any interest. They had little information. They had come
along with Vera de Schallberg principally because she was a
beautiful girl who was generous in her favors to both of them,
and they thought the venture would be (a) exciting, and (b)
of short duration because the Nazi invasion forces would be
arriving soon. Both men subsequently regretted that assumption. The Germans never came, but their trial for espionage
did. They were found guilty and hanged; and news of their
execution was shortly afterward allowed to filter back to Germany *pour décourager les autres.*

Thanks to Roberts, the British authorities were not quite
as quick or as callous with Vera de Schallberg. The SIS had
discovered from their own sources that the girl, alone of the
three, had been put through a course of training for her task
at a parachute-*cum*-sabotage school run by the Luftwaffe in
East Prussia. Roberts was anxious to learn more about it and
whom she had met there. To his surprise, he found her completely uncooperative. Dressed in a rough smock, because her
soaked dress had shrunk badly and no longer fitted, she
hunched in a corner of the interrogation room with her hair
lank over her drawn face, her lips downturned, her expression
surly. He wondered how on earth she had ever made a living
as an entertainer, or persuaded a lover she was worth sleeping with.

She refused to talk to him, and he thought: If she goes on
like this, she'll hang too, poor lamb.

Talking about her later to his girl friend and colleague, Ann
Kirby, he had an inspiration. Perhaps she was disgusted with
men—and, having seen her two companions, he couldn't blame

81

her—and would be more forthcoming with a woman. Would Ann go and talk with her?

The matron who accompanied Ann to the interrogation room was smirking.

"She's got the curse," she said, "and keeps asking me for sanitary towels. But I've told her repeatedly they're in short supply. Anyway, why shouldn't she be uncomfortable for a bit? It'll unsettle her and loosen her up."

Ann turned on her heel and went back at once to the main building to rustle up some tampons from one of the girls. When she came back, she also had with her soap, talcum powder, a lipstick and eye shadow, a set of underwear, and a dress of her own. Roberts had told her the girl was tall, and she was a tall girl herself. The dress might fit, in place of the shabby smock.

The first thing she said when she entered the interrogation room was, "I've brought you these. Maybe you'd like a shower first, and then see what you can do with them. Oh, yes, and here are some cigarettes."

Vera de Schallberg burst into tears. An hour later, glowing fresh, smelling clean, elegant in Ann's dress ("It fitted perfectly; she looked really quite distinguished once she got cleaned up; she's got breeding"), and puffing happily on a cigarette, she began talking.

It was a long and shabby story of a girl who runs away from a comfortable home after her father marries again ("I had a fixation on him"), has her first abortion a year later at the age of fifteen, works in a Copenhagen cabaret, and is eventually picked up by a German who takes her to Paris. His name is Hans Dierks and he turns out to be an Abwehr agent; she falls deeply in love with him and is devastated one night when he is killed in a motor accident. She goes to pieces for a time, then ties up with another pickup, Drücke, a phony salesman and trickster, and helps him con gullible businessman out of their money. Just as the police begin moving in on them, along comes another Abwehr man who offers to get her off the hook if she will go on a mission for the agency. In return for similar immunity for Drücke, and as a sentimental gesture to her dead lover, Dierks, she accepts and is sent to Camp 4 in East Prussia for training.

There were twelve or thirteen others being trained at the same airfield, of all ages and nationalities.

"All of them were men except me," Vera said. "It was strictly forbidden for us to mix or even to talk to each other beyond the usual *Heil Hitler* or *Guten Morgen*. But"—she smiled—"that's never seemed to stop boys getting to know me —not even when I was at school. Somehow, they all managed to make contact with me. Even our instructors. I don't think I got their real names, but I knew the code names they had adopted. There was the big dark Yugoslav named 'Ivan.' He was quite a boy!" She chuckled. "There was an Englishman they called 'Fritz,' and a Russian called 'Max'—"

She rattled them off, wryly filling in their psychological and physical characteristics, while Ann scribbled the details down.

Finally she said, "There was only one boy at the camp I never got to know. We caught glimpses of him at the other side of the airfield. Rücki, one of the instructors, told me he was being trained for a very special mission, and they were certainly giving him the treatment. He even had a plane all to himself when he did his training jumps, and he lived in quarters cut off from the rest of us by electrified fences and guard-dog patrols."

"Did you ever get his code name?" Ann asked.

Vera shook her head.

"Rücki used to call him 'the Monk'—but that was a joke, because he might just as well have been in a monastery, the way they walled him off."

But one day toward the end of her training, Vera got an attack of the blues and, desperately anxious to be on her own for a bit, managed to slip out of the camp and make her way to the seashore. (The training camp was on the island of Rügen, in the Baltic.) She had kicked off her shoes and was making her way through the dunes down to the sea when she caught a glimpse of a man standing with his feet in the light surf.

"He was very young and very beautiful," Vera said, a warm glow lighting her face at the memory of him. "He was wearing a training suit, so I knew he was from the camp, and he was up to his ankles in the water. From the way he was flinging up his arms and gesturing, I realized he was making some sort of a speech, though of course I couldn't hear what he was saying. I felt like an intruder, though, and I thought of turning back and going away, especially when it dawned on me that this must be our mystery man, the Monk himself."

She giggled. "But then I decided I just couldn't! He was so good-looking, such a *Torte* [a pastry] I wanted to eat him! And"—mischievously—"think of what they'd say back at the camp when I told them I'd met and talked to the Monk! So I went back around the dunes and came onto the beach at a spot where his back was to me, and then I walked up to him."

It was when she came within earshot that she realized he was speaking—declaiming, rather—in a language she had never heard before. Vera spoke English, Spanish, French, Italian, and Polish, as well as German and Danish, but she had never heard the tongue in which this young man was speaking.

"I didn't understand a word he was saying, but it was beautiful!" Vera said. "It was musical and it had rhythm, and I knew it was poetry. I knew he had to be a poet—but what on earth was he doing in this place?"

She never had a chance to ask him. Sensing that someone was approaching, the young man swung round. Vera put on her most seductive smile and kept advancing toward him.

"*Grüss Gott!*" she said, in a gentle voice.

"*Heil Hitler!*" he replied, and without another word, barely glancing at her, brushed past her and raced up to the dunes and back toward the camp. Vera never saw him again, not even as a distant figure on the other side of the airfield. But from then on, she always thought of him as the Poet and no longer as the Monk. And when Ann asked her whether she could remember how he had looked, the girl nodded vigorously.

"So would you," she said. "He wasn't someone *any* woman would ever forget."

I I I

"Now what language could he possibly have been speaking?" Denzil Roberts asked, after Ann had reported back to him. "She's a cosmopolitan girl. She'd recognize Hebrew or Arabic or Portuguese."

"Urdu?" said Ann. "Tamil? Gujerati? Japanese? Swahili?"

He shook his head. "Would any European call those languages musical? Or the man who declaimed them a poet?"

There was something about Vera de Schallberg's story which had nagged at him, even at the time. Now he was even more worried. The only thing he was thankful about was that he had scotched the public prosecutor's plan to have Vera tried, found guilty, and hanged for espionage.

"What are you going to do about Vera?" Ann had asked. "I admit she's told us all she knows, and she did come over here to spy. On the other hand, I feel sorry for her. She's had a raw deal. I hope there are no plans"—she hesitated—"for treating her the way they did her companions."

Roberts said, "She's safe for the moment. I've recommended keeping her in storage. She may come in useful one of these days."

But who was her mysterious poet? And what plans did the Nazis have for him?

Vera de Schallberg stayed in jail, but soon, under her code name of "Viola," the British began feeding back miscellaneous information to her control in Hamburg—simply to indicate she had escaped capture.

Roberts might not have believed Vera de Schallberg's story had he not, by one of those coincidences that sometimes occur in intelligence work, been able to prove the truth of what she had told Ann. It so happened that one of the most effective double spies now working for the SIS from London was a fellow-trainee of Vera's from the camp in East Prussia. He was "the big dark Yugoslav" known to the Germans as Ivan, and he had arrived in Britain at the end of 1940. Ostensibly he was an exporter of British goods to the Balkans, but his real mission was to spy for the Abwehr. What the Germans did not know, however, was that Ivan had all along kept the SIS informed of his activities, and from the moment he arrived in Britain all messages he had sent back to his "control" in Lisbon had first been vetted by his British friends.

Ivan's real name was Dusko Popov (his British code name was "Tricycle"), and Roberts could see why Vera's eyes had grown warm when she mentioned him, and why she had called him "quite a boy!" The SIS had already found that Dusko could not resist a pretty woman, and that women found him equally attractive. On his first night out in London, after his debriefing by the SIS, Roberts and another intelligence agent had taken him out to dinner at a fashionable Mayfair restaurant, the Mirabelle. There was a beautiful girl in WAAF uniform dining at a nearby table with an older army colonel. Halfway through their meal, Dusko got up and excused himself. Shortly afterward, so did the girl. Neither of them came back. Dusko did not put in an appearance again until the following morning.

When Roberts informed him that one of his former fellow-trainees had been captured, Dusko had shrugged his shoulders. But then Roberts had mentioned it was a woman.

"The Blue Angel!" he cried. "It's got to be the Blue Angel—

she was the only girl in the camp."

He explained that he had called her the Blue Angel "because when she took her clothes off and showed off those long legs, she looked just like Marlene Dietrich, only more so!" But he was appalled to think that the Nazis had ever sent her off on a mission ("She was just a dumb blonde cabaret girl"), and that she'd been caught.

"You aren't going to do anything nasty to her, are you?" he asked in alarm. He added, to show off his growing mastery of wartime argot: "All the Blue Angel's interested in is a nice bit of crumpet."

He was assured that nothing very terrible was going to happen to her, even if crumpets were going to be denied her for the time being. What Roberts wanted to know from him was whether, in their intimate moments, she had ever spoken to him of a trainee in the camp she called the Monk, or the Poet? It was then that he got his confirmation.

"She was the only one who ever saw him close up," Dusko said, "but we all had distant glimpses of him, and we all wondered why the Abwehr was keeping him under wraps. Except," he added, "that after a time, one or two of us began to wonder if he *was* Abwehr—or whether someone else was training him."

"Why don't we ask your control in Lisbon whether he knows anything about him?" Roberts suggested quietly.

CHAPTER 4

The Gluepot

I

IN THE COURSE OF her conversations while in internment camp in Germany (all of which had been carefully monitored), Polly Wright had mentioned the fact that her favorite "local" in London was a pub called the Gluepot, which was, apparently, not far away from Broadcasting House and other offices of the BBC. This made it a convenient meeting place for members of the BBC Music Department and for those—such as composers, instrumentalists, orchestral players, concert promoters, and critics—who had dealings with them. It was also (Polly had mentioned) a regular watering hole for the Welsh poet and tosspot Dylan Thomas, who worked off and on for the BBC.

It was not until several weeks after his arrival in London that the Druid decided it was time for him to go and have a drink at the Gluepot.

Exactly how he had spent his time in the intervening period is now difficult to track down. He confided to Johnny that he had spent one ten-day period lodging in Soho, though where and with whom he did not say. "Probably some tart," Johnny said, adding, with an enigmatic grin: "Though what sex we'll never know, will we?" The Druid said he had moved away because of "too many police," and, instead, had found himself rooms off the King's Road, in Chelsea, where he had registered for air-raid warden duties at Chelsea Town Hall. He produced a bona-fide certificate from a doctor, showing he was a chronic asthmatic, to explain his civilian status. But even health-exempted individuals in wartime London, especially if they were young, had to find work, and the Druid needed a job before the authorities "directed" him to one. He hoped Polly Wright might have some suggestions.

So far as his espionage work was concerned, he was in no hurry. A few nights before he had parachuted into Britain, Ernst Kaltenbrunner had hosted a farewell dinner for him at Horcher's in Berlin, at which the other guests had been Walter Huppenkothen and Hugo Hoffmann. The two SS men got very drunk and sentimental, and Kaltenbrunner kept embracing him and calling him *"ein echter Heldendeutscher"* and promising him the Führer's personal thanks if he succeeded in exposing the Abwehr. But it was the professional policeman Inspector Hoffmann, sober and paternal, who walked him back to his barracks and gave him his final piece of advice.

He counseled him, above all, to take his time. They wanted proof that Canaris and his crew were betraying Germany, and that would not be easy. Hoffmann repeated a saying they had in the Berlin police department: "A weapon in the culprit's hand is better than a signed confession, but produce both if possible." In this case, the Führer was not going to be satisfied with less. Canaris had his ear and his respect, and he had already talked his way out of one accusation. The SS would need solid facts and convincing ones, and that would take time. Turning to the young man at his side, he warned him not to let Kaltenbrunner badger him. He had a feeling, he said, that this was going to be a long war, and what the Druid reported from England could easily decide how long it would take Germany to win it.

The main task, he repeated, was for the Druid to get himself accepted as part of English life. The Inspector had implied that it would not be easy. But already the Druid had found it simpler than he had ever imagined, thanks to his Welshness. The English, he was discovering, were apt to forgive a Welshman any kind of gaffe, so long as he apologized in extravagant enough language and exaggerated his accent. Celtic theatrics had been frowned on in Patagonia, as, he suspected, they were in Wales, except on bardic platforms, and he was startled to discover that extravagances of voice and gesture were almost expected of him in London when it was noticed that he was Welsh. (Unlike Johnny, he was quietly triumphant when beery types thereupon came up to him and called him Taffy.)

He realized he had committed one of his gaffes on the day he wandered around the streets near Broadcasting House looking for the Gluepot. It had not occurred to him that this was not the true name of the pub, and he was surprised when the man he asked for directions cackled with laughter. But then he pointed across the street.

Its real name was the George, and it was a very ordinary pub indeed, with an underground toilet right next to the main door and a strong smell of stale beer and urine permeating the entrance. On the other hand, it was jammed with customers, and he had a great deal of difficulty easing himself through the pack to the bar and no success whatsoever in attracting the attention of the barmaid. She looked round him, over him, and through him, but never at him, ignoring his most placatory smile and his pleas for half a mild and bitter. It was not until a voice behind him said, "For God's sake give the poor sod a drink, May, before he dies of thirst!" that she slapped a jug in front of him and demanded his money. He turned and gestured by way of thanks that the owner of the voice should have one too, but the man held up his glass, shook his head, and edged to the back of the bar. It was evidently a very cliquey pub, because everyone seemed to know everyone else, and May the barmaid seemed to know them all by name. No one else spoke for or to the Druid, and when his glass was empty he did not try to buy another but slipped away instead. But next day he was back, and the next, and the next. By the end of the week, May had begun to recognize him as he came through the door and had his mild and bitter already drawn by the time he made it to the bar. He had also begun to be accepted as a regular by various little groups into which, he realized, the Gluepot's clientele was divided. The camaraderie of the ordinary English pub prevailed here too, he discovered, except that whereas in the others you were expected to talk about sex and girls, and tell dirty stories or good bomb tales, here the lingua franca was gossip about the BBC or some knowledge of music and musicians. He found himself one lunchtime sharing a loathing for Debussy and Brahms with a thin, dynamic woman whose facial features were so sharply etched that an Indian brave could have used her head as a tomahawk. She turned out to be a disciple of Alban Berg and Arnold Schön-berg, and had just been commissioned by the War Office to write a march for the WAAFs (the women's branch of the RAF). She explained at some length the complications of fitting a brisk, regular beat into the theme she had chosen. Her name was Lucille Long, and he proceeded cautiously after he had learned it, for her name rang bells in his head. He knew whom he was meeting, too, when he was shortly introduced to another composer called Constant Lambert, for one of the records in the music library at Berlin University was Lambert's "Rio Grande" Suite, and a version of William Walton's *Façade*, with Dame Edith Sitwell reciting and Constant Lambert conducting, was regularly played by his professors as an example of musical decadence in the democracies. They were presently joined by a tall, bearded music critic named Ralph Hill, whose attitude was as lofty as his build until, in a discussion of operatic themes, the Druid suggested Vaughan Williams ought to do one on the subject of Owen Glendower. He thereupon softly sang possible opening lines to the tune of "The Shepherds of the Delectable Mountains," and, moreover, sang them in Welsh. Hill was impressed. They were all impressed. They could hardly know that the singer had once written his epic poem on Owen Glendower, and were probably unaware that Vaughan Williams was a favored English composer in Nazi Germany.

Toward the end of their session, the Druid decided to take a chance, and asked about Polly Wright. Had they seen her around? At once he realized he had made one of his gaffes, maybe a serious one this time. All the members of the group stopped talking and stared at him.

"Haven't you heard?" asked Hill.

"She's in Holloway [women's prison]," said Lambert.

"They took her in under Regulation 18B," explained Lucille Long. "Suspected of being friendly with an enemy alien—just because she slept with a German." Her eyes flashed as she added: "That's the way a woman gets treated in this country. Now if it had been a man! Look at Ralph here. He went on that BBC tour and if I know him, he fucked every *Fräulein* in sight from Frankfurt to Freiburg. But no 18B for him!"

"Ah, but I didn't stay on in Germany to give them aid and comfort," Hill said mildly. "Polly ought to have had more sense —and more taste. After all, he was a Nazi." He turned a pair of shrewd eyes on the Druid. "What's your connection with her, my friend—if I might put it that way?"

"She probably wouldn't even remember me," he said.

He had a rigmarole ready which it would be practically impossible for them to check. He knew that before the BBC orchestra had gone to Germany they had given a performance in the Queen's Hall, just around the corner, of Delius's *Sea Drift*, and he explained how he had been on holiday from North Wales and had queued to hear it. He sang in a choir himself, and . . . Then after the performance he was leaving the hall, still very emotional ("It was a very moving performance by Boult"), when he had seen this very pretty redhead looking at him and smiling.

92

"I suppose I must have looked very flushed and excited," he said. "Anyway, I couldn't help it. I told her how wonderful it had been, wonderful conductor, wonderful choir, wonderful orchestra. She then said her husband played in the orchestra, and I said she must thank him for having given so much pleasure. And she told me her name, and her husband's name, and said anytime I was in London I must come and see them. And then"—he hesitated—"I was so, well, happy that I put my arms around her and hugged her."

"And she hugged you right back," said Long crisply. "Polly always did like them young."

He protested that nothing else had happened. He had gone back home to North Wales. But now he had come to London, unable to join the forces and in need of a job; he thought maybe she could help him, put him in touch with some organization.

"In music?" Hill snorted. "That'd be the kiss of death! On Polly's recommendation they wouldn't touch you with a barge pole."

They were joined by a BBC type and his young secretary and the conversation changed. But when the groups began drifting off for lunch, Hill took the Druid to one side.

"Have you tried CEMA?" he asked. "They're looking for people who know something about music."

The Druid looked at him in genuine astonishment, and decided he could safely display ignorance.

Hill laughed. "It's the initials for the Council for the Encouragement of Music and the Arts," he said. "It's a highfalutin organization that coordinates with the BBC and the music world and puts on concerts and shows for the troops. Their trouble is, they're short of organizers. You might just be what they're looking for. Very short of men, CEMA is."

He grinned, then reached in his pocket and pulled out a scrap of paper on which he scribbled a name and signed his own below it.

"Why don't you go and see her? Tell her I sent you."

Long had come up and heard the last part of the conversation. "She likes them young too," she said. "And she's Welsh."

II

The official job of H. A. R. (Kim) Philby at the headquarters of the Secret Intelligence Service in London was to act as liaison officer between MI5, which looked after counterespionage in Britain, and MI6, which conducted both espionage and counterespionage outside the United Kingdom. He also had control of the SIS Iberian sector and was responsible for keeping track of Abwehr's operations in Spain and Portugal, two neutral countries from which Nazi spy chiefs controlled the activities of their agents in Britain.

By the very nature of his job, and through the inevitable indiscretions of his friends in the service, he began to figure out why MI5 was acting with such surprising complacency over the possibility that the Nazis might have an active spy network in the U.K. It was supposed to be one of the most cherished secrets of the British intelligence system, and not even Prime Minister Winston Churchill knew everything about it, but it did not take Kim Philby too long to guess that the Abwehr—at least so far as Britain was concerned—had been penetrated. He made it his business to ferret out the facts, and soon was aware that all Abwehr spies sent to Britain had either been captured by MI5 or had given themselves up, and that of this mixed bag of enemy agents at least ninety-five percent had been "turned" and persuaded to double-cross their Nazi masters. The rest had either been jailed or executed.

Since all these double spies had perforce turned over their codes and code names to the British, and, as the price for their lives, agreed to continue communicating with Germany by radio, secret ink, or (later) microdot messages, it followed that they had effectively placed the Abwehr's operations under

British control. It was the British who wrote the answers to the questionnaires which their Abwehr spymasters sent them. When a new spy was being sent in from Germany, it was the British who, through one or another of the controlled agents on the spot, suggested the dropping zone or landing zone most convenient for British security patrols waiting to arrest them. And it was the British who stage-managed the "sabotage" of armament factories for which, subsequently, the Nazis awarded decorations to their agents for "heroic" acts of intrepidity and resource. One of the double agents who reaped a rich reward in medals and money, for instance, from British ingenuity and Abwehr gullibility was a bold and resourceful Scottish ex-safebreaker named Eddie Chapman. He was serving a sentence in Jersey, in the Channel Islands, for robbing a bank when the German Army captured the islands in 1940. He volunteered for espionage service against the English, whom he professed to hate, and was sent to Germany for training, then parachuted into Britain with the mission of sabotaging the De Havilland aircraft factory at Hatfield, near London, where Spitfire planes were being made. Chapman went to a telephone box immediately upon parachuting into Britain and called up Scotland Yard, who turned him over to MI5. Henceforward he became a double spy, known to the Germans as "Fritz" and to the British as "Zigzag." To help him deceive his German paymasters, a mock-up section of the De Havilland works was built, then blown up and set on fire, sufficiently spectacularly for Nazi reconnaissance planes to photograph the damage. When Chapman returned to Germany for new instructions from the Abwehr, he was decorated, lavishly praised, and richly rewarded—and sent back to England to continue his "heroic" activities. But he was under British control from start to finish.

So MI5 had reason to be proud of themselves. Gaining control of the Abwehr's network was undoubtedly the greatest coup ever brought off by British intelligence. (Or any other counterintelligence service, for that matter.) But it was obviously proof against detection only so long as two conditions prevailed. The Germans must never suspect that their agents—all of their agents—had been "turned." And no new Nazi spy arriving in Britain could be allowed to survive outside the Double Cross System, for he would blow the pretense wide open. By the very nature of his espionage reports, which would contradict the carefully controlled messages of the "turned" agents, he would lay bare the nature of the whole gigantic confidence trick.

Kim Philby was inclined to believe that MI5 was altogether too smug in facing up to the perils implicit in their success. It is true that, as one MI5 official later put it, "innumerable precautions" were taken "with every agent and with every message on the assumption . . . that the Germans had several and perhaps many independent agents of whom we had no knowledge, and that these agents' reports could be used to check the reports of our own controlled agents." But the same official added: "Only long experience taught us the extent to which the Germans depended upon our controlled agents and taught us too the gullibility and the inefficiency of some branches of the Abwehr."[1]

This was all very well. But Philby, from his frequent trips to Lisbon, was only too acutely aware that there were other Nazi intelligence systems in operation in addition to the Abwehr, and that they were altogether tougher and more efficient. Certainly they were more loyal to National Socialism. He knew that the Russian intelligence system, through its agents planted in Germany, suspected that some senior members of the Abwehr were probably quite aware that their espionage network in Britain had been penetrated, and were conniving at it because they hoped it would help the West defeat Hitler (whom they hated and despised) before the Russians became too important on the battlefield. They wanted Britain and America to win the war so that, between them,

[1] J. C. Masterman, *The Double Cross System* (New Haven: Yale University Press, 1972).

they could save Germany from both Adolf Hitler *and* Joseph Stalin.

Philby, of course, was a double agent himself, working for the Russians as well as for the SIS, and there were moments, he later admitted to friends and relatives who talked to him in Moscow, when he was tempted to blow the whistle on the Double Cross business, if only to sabotage the Abwehr's eagerness to split the Allies. But at his monthly meetings with "Ernst," his KGB control in London, he was dissuaded. Ernst (otherwise known as Nicky Rostov) was a German Jewish refugee whom Philby had met in Vienna in the fratricidal political riots of the 1930s, and it was he who had recruited Philby into the Communist Party. Ernst by then was already a veteran Communist, trusted by Moscow first as a talent spotter and recruiter and later as a control; he had been Philby's friend, adviser, inspiration, and conduit to the KGB since 1937, when he had first arrived in Britain. A chirpy, minuscule fellow with shortsighted eyes covered by thick glass spectacles, his cover in London was a job as a free-lance subtitler for foreign film distributors (he spoke French, Spanish, German, and Italian with a heavy accent), and he lived in the attic of a rooming house in Maida Vale. In appearance he looked like one of life's rejects, but Philby once revealed to a close friend that he admired him more than any other man alive. Underneath the shabby exterior and timid approach was a cool, calculating brain and an unswerving belief in Communism and its methods that never failed to steady Philby in his moments of panic over the double life he was leading.

In no way should he interfere with the Double Cross System, Ernst insisted. Thanks to Philby's reports (and those of certain other friends[2]), the USSR was being kept well informed of what the Abwehr was asking its agents and what answers the British were sending back on their behalf. He would not want

[2] As became known later, at least two and probably four MI5 officers working inside the Double Cross System and manipulating captured Abwehr agents were also working for the KGB.

that altered so long as the system worked. But of course, he assured Philby, the day of reckoning was coming for the Abwehr. The KGB already knew from information inside the Reich that the SS suspected Canaris and his gang, and he had heard that the RSHA had already taken steps to entrap Canaris. One day there would be an upheaval. Meanwhile—

"Meanwhile," said Philby, "they may already have sent someone over here to find out what is going on."

"In that case," said Ernst, "let us hope that we find him first, before MI5 does."

III

"We don't pay much, I'm afraid," the tall, dark woman said. "Ten pounds a week is all we can manage. But there isn't much you can spend money on these days, is there?" Then a sly hint of a smile crossed her face. "But we do get the occasional clothing coupon and food voucher. There are perks going, once you have settled in. You'll get to know about them. Now I'll take you along and introduce you to our secretaries. They'll type any letters you might want to send. But don't expect much from dictation. All the good professionals have either joined the Wrens or been snapped up by the BBC. We get the leftovers. Nice girls, but—" She shrugged.

As they walked along the corridor, the Druid said, "Have you anything in mind for my first job?"

"Yes, I have." She stopped and faced him. "We have this string quartet, German refugees from Holland. They're very good but a bit recherché about what they play. You know—Hindemith—that sort of thing. Well, we're sending them to Bristol for a concert, and we'd like you to go along and—well, persuade them to sort of popularize their program."

"Who will they be playing for?" the Druid asked.

"The Canadians," she said. "As a matter of fact, their entertainments officer called me up and told me he hoped we'd be giving them something cheerful. It's what the boys badly needed, he said. I expect they're just about to go on an exercise or an operation or something like that. So it's up to you to persuade our quartet to rise to the occasion."

She opened a door at the end of a corridor. Four comely young women were gossiping together by the window looking out over Baker Street.

They barely broke the flow of their chatter as their boss pushed the Druid into the room and said, "Elaine, Daphne, Gale, and Jane, I'd like to introduce our newest recruit to CEMA!"

I V

The Druid's control in Lisbon was Paul von Fidrmuc (also known as von Karmap), a tall, handsome, aristocratic-looking type whose tanned good looks were enhanced by a sprinkling of gray in his well-brushed brown hair. His background by no means belied his appearance, for he was a Sudeten-German of impeccably aristocratic stock, and his dashing reputation was confirmed by his war record in the Austro-Hungarian Army in World War I, when, as a subaltern of eighteen, he had personally captured an Italian general and a whole battalion of troops in the campaign in the Tyrol. He had been an early recruit of the National Socialist Party, and, in the 1930s, when he went to Portugal as representative of a subsidiary of the Krupp organization, he had joined the Auslandsorganisation of the NSDAP (the Nazi Party). On one of his trips to Lisbon, Admiral Canaris had met him and proposed that, as a sideline, he might like to work for the Abwehr. He moved in fashionable circles in both Lisbon and Estoril, where a classy, well-informed society of aristocratic exiles from old Europe had come to roost, and he found it simple enough to pick up useful gossip. The Abwehr paid him well for it.

Once World War II had gone into its blitzkrieg phase, and

the German Army had occupied Scandinavia, France, and the Low Countries, Sweden, Spain, and Portugal had become the only neutral countries through which the Nazis could keep open information lines to Britain. Portugal was by far the most convenient communication center, and the Abwehr had stationed at least three of its most important agents there for controlling messages from and sending out questionnaires to its spies in Britain. But when Canaris had asked Paul von Fidrmuc to become one of the controls, he had accepted on one condition only: that he be allowed to recruit his own spies, be solely responsible for communicating with them, and be personally in charge of sending on their information to the Abwehr in Berlin. Canaris had reluctantly accepted this condition, and never regretted it. The smooth-talking Sudeten quickly built up his own network of agents in both Britain and the United States, and it was so effective that the Abwehr gave it a code name of its own: the "Ostro Network."

What Canaris and the Abwehr did not know was that—at least until 1941—the Ostro Network operated with completely fictitious spies. Fidrmuc had invented them. He relied entirely for his information on British and American newspapers, gossip from travelers and diplomats, and a shrewd calculated manipulation of data in railway timetables and telephone and reference books for Britain, which he kept in his Lisbon office. That, plus a fertile imagination, enabled him to invent extremely plausible (and sometimes amazingly accurate) accounts of troop movements, Cabinet meetings, bomb disasters, military exercises, which not only earned him the personal congratulations of Admiral Canaris but also extremely generous monetary rewards from the Abwehr coffers. Much of it he spent on the tables at Estoril, for he was, not surprisingly, a heavy gambler.

The Ostro Network continued to flourish—as did von Fidrmuc —until the beginning of 1941, when disaster threatened the enterprise. The Sudeten had a German-speaking Portuguese secretary, Dulcinella, with whom, since she was young and attractive, he had made the mistake of sleeping a couple of times. For von Fidrmuc it was a pleasant fling with a pretty nonentity between his major affaires. For Dulcinella it was the major event of her life, and when her boss made it plain to her how little she really meant to him, she could think only of avenging herself. She had suspected for some time that much of her boss's work was to do with espionage, and had gradually come to realize that a lot of it was phony. A search of the office files revealed enough evidence for her to be sure of it. She decided that an effective way of hitting back at her uncaring lover was to report him to the Germans, and for this purpose she decided to go to the German embassy.

It was a stroke of luck for von Fidrmuc that the person sent to interview Dulcinella was Trudy Körner, recently arrived at the embassy, ostensibly as a junior attaché but actually as an operative of the RSHA section of the SS. She listened to the girl's indignant story, looked through the papers she had brought with her, and agreed that the whole thing was a scandal and that action should be taken. These were certainly her sentiments at the time. They confirmed her own view that the Abwehr was not only a treacherous organization but a monstrously inefficient and fraudulent one too.

She counseled the girl to say nothing to anyone else, but to come back to see her the following day, when she would report what would be done about her boss's outrageous trickery. She gave the girl a rendezvous at a restaurant in the city for the following day. Then she passed along the whole story to the RSHA in Berlin.

It could not have come at a better time. She had communicated directly with Kaltenbrunner, and he in turn consulted Huppenkothen and Hoffmann. They were in the last stages of arranging for the Druid's departure for England. They were looking around for a completely trustworthy control.

When the Portuguese girl turned up for her rendezvous the following day, Trudy Körner was as sympathetic as ever. Steps were being taken, she told the girl. There was only one thing.

Would she be willing to repeat her story to one of the Abwehr officials in Lisbon, so that he would hear from her own lips how her boss had been cheating him?

They drove in Trudy's car to a house in its own garden in Estoril, and when they got inside, there was Paul von Fidrmuc, looking crushed and frightened. (He was not faking, either.) He had been told by Trudy exactly what to do, and the moment she left the room he was down on his knees, tearfully begging forgiveness of the girl, pleading with her, promising her everything, including marriage. Ten minutes later they were in the adjoining bedroom, making love. "Put your heart and soul into it," Trudy had said, "and make sure she responds." In the late afternoon, the door of the bedroom opened and von Fidrmuc beckoned. Dulcinella was sprawled across the bed, asleep, as Trudy came in. Motioning to the Sudeten, Trudy took one of the large pillows and thrust it over the girl's head, holding it there securely while von Fidrmuc held on to the naked body thrashing beneath. It took what seemed to the man an agonizingly long time before the limbs finally went still. Trudy removed the pillow, stuck the tongue back in the mouth and adjusted the set of the face, and stood back.

"Now let us get her out of here," she said.

V

They left the body on the beach near Cascais, and there was a paragraph in police reports a few days later. Portuguese newspapers did not go in for explicit sexual details, so that it was only implied that the girl might have died of a heart attack while "undergoing great emotional stress." Her companion, whoever he might have been, the police report said, had probably panicked and decamped when he found that the girl had died.

There was a routine police visit to Paul von Fidrmuc's office. He was able to demonstrate that the girl had ceased to work for him at least two weeks before. He had proof he had spent most of the time at the German embassy on the day the girl had supposedly died.

By that time, von Fidrmuc was only too well aware that he was working for the RSHA. From now on, he would continue to feed his phony information from his nonexistent spies to the Abwehr in Berlin. But the Ostro Network would now have a genuine spy working for it. The Druid would be feeding back information by a special Sicherheitsdienst code, and when he did so, von Fidrmuc must give it priority over everything.

And in no circumstances whatsoever must he admit to anyone that there was such an agent as the Druid, or for whom he was working.

He had no choice but to accept the conditions. Not that he found them particularly onerous. In his new role, he had acquired not only a real spy but a new mistress. Trudy Körner had sized him up and found him desirable. And it gave her an additional hold over him.

VI

Late in May, 1942, von Fidrmuc got his first message from the Druid in England. The message began:

HAVE AUTHENTICATED FOLLOWING DETAILS FORTHCOMING ALLIED LANDING IN FRANCE. NATURE OF OPERATION: LIMITED TO ONE DIVISION STRENGTH. NOT REPEAT NOT FULL SCALE INVASION. TARGET: DIEPPE AND WEHRMACHT FIELD HQ AT QUIBERVILLE. TROOPS 2ND CANADIAN DIVISION. COMMANDER GENERAL CRERAR. CODE NAME: OPERATION RUTTER. DATE OF OPERATION: MIDSUMMERS DAY. WHATS ABWEHR REPORTING ABOUT THIS? ORDER OF BATTLE FOLLOWS. . . .

The message ended:

FOR YOUR INFORMATION JOHNNY ARRESTED. DO NOT REPEAT DO NOT INFORM ABWEHR.

CHAPTER 5

Disaster at Dieppe

I

IT WAS NOT PART of the Druid's mission to transmit the ordinary trivia of intelligence to his controls in Lisbon and Berlin. There were at least twenty Abwehr agents in Britain supposedly reporting back every phase of activity inside enemy territory, including rearmament programs, bomb damage, civilian morale, military plans, and the weather, and he had been told not to try to duplicate them. Of course, if information came into his possession which would enable the RSHA to compare, and therefore test the quality of, similar reports to the Abwehr, it would be given special scrutiny. The opportunity to do so came in the early summer of 1942, when the Druid unwittingly became involved in the planning for Operation Rutter. This was the Allied attempt to land in German-occupied France, and it subsequently became known to the world at large as the Dieppe raid. It was one of the costliest disasters of the war, and the Druid helped to make it so.

On a cool, cloudy morning in May, 1942, the Druid left his rooms in Chelsea, strolled up Sloane Street and across Hyde

Park to a rendezvous in Wigmore Street. He was feeling good about everything, because, as even the English were beginning to admit, the war was going well for the Reich and badly for them. Over the BBC and in the morning papers, the war news, though censored, could not conceal the fact that National Socialism and its Axis allies were everywhere triumphing. The Americans were still groggy in the Pacific from the slugging they had received from the Japanese at Pearl Harbor. In Russia the Wehrmacht was churning back the Red Army and manuring the steppes with Bolshevik blood and bodies as it pushed forward toward the Caucasus. In the Western Desert of North Africa the English had already lost their fortress of Tobruk and were now being threatened in Cairo and Alexandria by the soldiers of Rommel's Afrika Korps. If the Führer's luck held, there would be German armies in Persia and along the Suez Canal by Christmas, with the road to India open to them. How long then before Germany linked hands with its Axis partner in Asia? And how long before the English finally gave in, and the Welsh, the Scots, and the Irish would find themselves free men again?

He passed a painted slogan on the wall: "OPEN 2ND FRONT NOW!" and noticed that passersby quickly averted their faces when they saw it. It had been put up by the Communists, demanding that the English take the pressure off the embattled Red armies in Russia by invading the Germans in France; and the Druid smiled to himself, realizing that the English felt guilty at their failure to come to the aid of their Russian allies. No wonder they looked so miserable! Since the Luftwaffe had left to go East, where they were attacking Moscow, Leningrad, and Stalingrad, the English did not even have the shared sense of mutual danger from bomb raids to uplift and enliven them. All they had were shortening rations, empty shops, and bad news for breakfast. It made them look shabby and glum, and the Druid wondered how long they could put up with it.

At the Wigmore Hall, the Zandvoort Players were already in rehearsal, and the Druid slipped into a back seat and listened as they ran through their repertoire. They were playing the second of Beethoven's *Rasoumoffsky Quartets* and playing it impeccably, but he agreed with his superior at CEMA that it was hardly stuff to give the troops, especially Canadians. How was he going to persuade them to liven things up? He looked them over with a mixture of admiration and contempt, which was the way he always felt for the refugees he had so far encountered in London, so full of skills that were utterly useless in wartime, and so pathetically determined to pursue them. Why couldn't they adapt themselves, like ordinary people? But then, he reminded himself, they weren't ordinary people—these were German Jews, and his mother had never failed to point out to him how arrogant and selfish they were.

He waited until they came to the end of the *Rasoumoffsky* and then clapped his hands from the depths of the hall.

"My friends," he said, in his silkiest tones, "I must congratulate you on your marvelous technique. Beethoven would have been proud of you! But tell me"—he was walking forward now, and addressing the elderly violinist who headed the quartet—"would you have in your repertoire something like 'The Merry Widow'? Or even a little Gilbert and Sullivan?"

All four of them immediately broke out into a babble of excited German. He pretended to be unaware of the fact that the fiddler was calling him "a dumb English shithead."

I I

It was not, after all, in Bristol that they eventually gave their concert, but in a tent in a field not far from Ryde, on the Isle of Wight. The event was only thinly attended, and the Druid soon realized that even if the Zandvoort Players had come up with a Stephane Grappelly version of "Tiger Rag," instead of the pallid adaptations of "Moonlight Sonata" and "None but the Lonely Heart" which they did play, they would hardly have struck a spark off their audience. The officers and men of

the 2nd Division, Canadian Army, were browned off. For the
past two months they had been practicing landing drills off
the Isle of Wight coast, and each time things had gone wrong:
landing craft had turned over, drowning a couple of men; rendezvous with the Royal Navy had not been kept; boats and
men had got lost. And they were gloomy about the future,
because they knew what was going to happen to them.

It was in the officers' mess after the concert, sipping a whisky
with a young lieutenant, that the Druid heard the news that
decided him to break his radio silence. His host was a deep-
tanned, muscly member of a French-Canadian regiment who
had volunteered for overseas service at the age of nineteen and
worked his way up through the ranks. He was moody and
monosyllabic until he realized there was something special
about the Druid's voice, and elicited the fact that he was
Welsh, and it was as if this unleashed the floodgates. "I hear
they don't let you speak your own language in Wales either,"
he said in a thick Canuck accent, and added: "You know, my
uncle once told me that in the last war, the English fought the
Huns to the last Frenchman. In this one, they've lost the
French, so they're fighting to the last French-Canadian instead!"

He laughed at his own joke, swallowed his whisky, and
proceeded to unburden himself. He asked the Druid if he
knew that Molotov had been in London recently threatening
Churchill that the Russians would give up the war if the British didn't open up a second front soon. It had scared the shit
out of Winnie, and he had had to promise to do something at
once. That's why he had given the go-ahead for Operation
Rutter. In the next half hour, the Druid gathered that on
Midsummer's Day the Canadians were due to go ashore in
France, and to judge by the French-Canadian's outpourings,
they would be doing it simply to save Winston Churchill's face
and England's reputation. One of the lieutenant's complaints
was that they weren't even going into France to liberate the
French, which would have been all right with him, since they

were his brothers, but just to show the Huns—and the Russians —that the English still had a punch in them. It was all propaganda, to stop the Allies from nagging the English about the second front, and that, in his opinion, was no justification at all for getting himself killed.

Much later, he looked owlishly over his glass at the Druid and said, "You didn't ask me where we're going ashore in France."

The Druid said he didn't want to know.

"It's Dieppe," the Canuck said.

"My mother once went there on a day trip," said the Druid.

The Canuck's eyes warmed with sudden sentiment, and he reached across and pressed the Druid's hand hard. The Druid did not pull away, but gazed back, a friendly half-smile on his face.

"I like you, *mon ami*," the lieutenant said. "Let's get together again when I come back."

"Let's do that," the Druid said.

"*If* I come back," the lieutenant said. "*Si le bon Dieu le veult!*"

III

The signal was a single letter of the alphabet penciled in a corner of a telephone booth on Victoria Station, and there were several treffs, or rendezvous points, each specified by a different letter. The Druid preferred Aldwych underground station at the rush hour, when there were so many people around—for East Enders were still coming up to spend the night sleeping on the platforms, despite the end of the bombing—that it was all but impossible to be kept under surveillance.

But when Johnny arrived the first thing he said was "Make it short, laddie—they've put the dogs on me." He changed abruptly to Welsh and added: "Someone snooped when I was in Swansea and reported I met someone there—and they're trying to find out who it was. But don't be afraid, I will not be telling them, even when they bring me in."

The little Welshman grinned.

"You are not to worry," he said. "When they're not quite sure what I am doing, they usually arrest me, put me away for a time. They've done it before, and it is not too uncomfortable. I'll survive. And," with sudden earnestness, "that's what I'd like you to tell Trudy. They're not going to hang me. She mustn't fret when there is no news from me. I'll be back again. And tell her I'm always thinking about her, and we won't be separated forever."

The Druid was scanning the crowd of milling people, suddenly sickened by the smell of unwashed bodies.

"I will tell her," he said. "Rely on me."

Johnny asked, "What was it you wanted of me? You've got news?"

The Druid shook his head. "It is no longer important. Look after yourself. I must go."

"Take a train," said the little Welshman as one swept through the tunnel into the station. "I'll go back up. I can see my tail watching which way I'm going to jump. He can't handle the two of us."

They waited until the doors were closing, and then Johnny cried "*In!*" and the Druid leapt. The last thing he saw as the train took off was the imperturbable little man picking his way along the platform. Just before the train dived into the tunnel, he caught a glimpse of a tall man with a mustache standing by the exit sign and staring frantically into the carriages. But they were going far too fast for the Druid to have been seen.

That night he assembled his radio transmitter for the first time since his arrival in Wales and began sending a message: "DRUID CALLING. DRUID CALLING. HAVE AUTHENTICATED FOLLOWING DETAILS ALLIED LANDING IN FRANCE. . . ."

He had hoped that Johnny would send the message for him. From now on, he realized, it was he who would have to take the risk.

I V

Among the activities CEMA sponsored was a series of art shows which were sent around the country to army camps and factories, to show off to the largely uncaring masses collections of paintings, drawings, and sculptures which had been lent to the organization by assorted private owners, galleries, and art dealers. Shortly after the Druid joined them, his fellow-workers informed him they were giving a party to the donors as a way of thanking them for their cooperation. "It's as good an excuse as any for a booze-up," one of the girls said. He was quietly told that any liquid contribution he could make to bolster CEMA's drink cellar, which was hardly well filled, would be welcome. He thereupon consulted May at the Gluepot. She told him where to go in the black market in Soho, and for a sum which even the Druid considered extortionate, he returned with six bottles of Scotch. The girls greeted him as if he were a Klondike miner carrying bags of gold dust.

As it turned out, one of the guests at the party proved himself to be almost as generous a provider of alcoholic scarcities. The traveling exhibit included in its collection two little cartoons by Goya from the *desastres de la Guerra* series. Aside from the fact that they hardly seemed appropriate for showing to British soldiers who might at any moment be going into battle, they were devastatingly effective, and the Druid wondered who was their fortunate owner. When he made discreet inquiries, he discovered they were part of an even more impressive collection in the possession of an expert on Spanish art by the name of Thomas Harris.

Harris was obviously a popular type, because the moment he showed himself at the party nearly every CEMA employee dropped everything—and everyone—to rush up and greet him with rapturous cries of "Tommy, darling Tommy!" One of the things the Druid had noticed in wartime England was that very few women wore perfume, and therefore usually smelled of soap or less pleasant bodily odors. Tommy Harris, on the other hand, was surrounded by a small cloud of expensive scent as he came into the room, and the Druid reflected wryly that he must, like Kaltenbrunner, bathe in after-shave lotion. He noticed that Tommy Harris was carrying a small suitcase which he now proceeded to open, and all the girls began cooing at the contents. They proved to be three bottles of excellent dry sherry, a couple of bottles of passable port, and three bottles of Madeira— "for the old ladies," he cried, with a giggle, "of both sexes!" He loudly confided that the drink came "from my private bodega. Jerez de la Frontera has come to Chesterfield Gardens!" A girl sidled up to the Druid to whisper that Chesterfield Gardens was where Tommy lived ("He gives the most super parties"), and she went on to confide that "he's in intelligence, you know, though what he does is very hush-hush." She laughed. "You'd be shocked if I told you what he sometimes gets up to! Though I don't mean that about his intelligence work," she hastily added. "It's the parties I'm talking about. They really are *something!*"

They watched as the pink-cheeked and exuberant Mr. Harris went up to the bar, opened a bottle of his own sherry, and poured out two generous glasses. One of them he handed on to a young man standing beside him, who, the Druid realized, must be Harris's companion. In contrast to the older man, he was doe-eyed, sallow-complexioned, and almost sullen in expression. The Druid wondered where he had had his suit made, because it was cut with a distinctly Continental or Latin flair, with one of those jackets made for wearing across the shoulders like a cape. As he moved toward the bar himself, the Druid gradually realized that Harris and the young man were speaking together in Spanish.

"Why do I have to come to these dreary parties?" the young man was saying.

"Now be a nice boy and drink up your sherry," Harris replied soothingly. Then his voice changed although his amiable expression did not as he added: *"Because if you don't, you little rat, I'm going to put you right back in your cell and turn the key on you!"*

He flicked his button-bright eyes in the Druid's direction as he finished speaking, and a faint frown of suspicion crossed his face. Continuing to speak in Spanish, he suddenly addressed the Druid.

"Would you be such a talented as well as so handsome a young man," he asked, in exaggeratedly flowery fashion, *"that you actually speak and understand this lovely language?"*

"If that's Spanish you are speaking," the Druid said, "I'm afraid I can't help you. The only other language I speak is Welsh. Sorry."

"Dear boy, please don't apologize," Harris said, a warm smile wreathing his features. He was speaking in English now. "Do you really speak Welsh? It is the language of the poets, and since I have some Welsh blood in my veins, I'd be a very proud man if I could speak Welsh too."

The Druid indicated the two Goya cartoons hanging on the far wall. "I'd be prouder if I owned those," he said.

"Ah, yes, those little things." He gazed at them for a moment, and then regarded the Druid thoughtfully. "Are you interested in art, then?"

The Druid explained that his subject was music, but that he adored looking at pictures, and that one of his ambitions—so far unrealized—had been to visit the Prado one day.

"When the war is over, maybe," he said.

Harris was still looking at him. Now he seemed to make up his mind.

"In the meantime, perhaps I can whet your appetite a little," he said. He fumbled in his inside pocket, and took out a card. "I have some little numbers at home you might like to see.

Better than those," he added, indicating the Goyas. "Rather more, er, impressive." He handed over the card. "Why don't you come along to this address next Thursday afternoon. Shall we say four-thirty, in time for a sherry?"

The Druid was aware that Harris's companion had been watching and listening, and now he saw his hand go out and press the other man's arm.

"Keep your hands off that pretty boy!" he whispered fiercely, in Spanish.

"Shut your mouth or I'll put you back where you belong!" Harris whispered back, also in Spanish, the smile never leaving his face.

Then in English he said, "Next Thursday, then?"

"I can't wait," the Druid said.

After they had gone, the girl who had confided in him came up, grinning.

"Did I hear him asking you to one of his parties?" she asked.

"Not a party," said the Druid. "He's offered to show me some of his pictures."

"Oh, my!" said the girl. "You'd better watch your step!"

V

AFUS[1] REPORTING NOTHING REPEAT NOTHING ABOUT OPERA-
TION RUTTER OR LANDINGS DIEPPE OR ANYWHERE ELSE. SEND
CONFIRMATIONS SOONEST. HAVE ALERTED WEHRMACHT BUT
LOW LEVEL PENDING MORE FACTS. COULD JOHNNYS ARREST
BE PART ENGLISH BLUFF CAMPAIGN?

Plainly the RSHA had checked his message about the forth-coming Dieppe operation and found it specious. But what could he do now to beef up his information? When he traveled with the Zandvoort Players these days, it was to apathetic musical societies in the Midlands or open-air concerts in the

[1] AFU, *Agentenfunkgerät* (agent's secret radio transmitter in enemy territory).

East End of London, far away from the English Channel and the 2nd Canadian Division.

Midsummer's Day, miserably wet and windy, came and went, the day when the Canadians were due to hurl themselves against the German defenses at Dieppe; and all that day and the day following, the Druid listened to the BBC in London and the Nazi propagandist Lord Haw-Haw from Hamburg, hoping that some word would come that the assault had begun. Nothing.

What had gone wrong? He could have sworn that the young French-Canadian lieutenant had not been deceiving him.

Then about a week after Midsummer's Day, the Druid got another message from his control:

> TWO AFUS NOW REPORTING ENGLISH PLANNED SOME SORT OF OPERATION AT DIEPPE MIDSUMMERS DAY BUT CANCELED OWING TO WEATHER. ONE AFU SAYS CODE NAME WAS OPERATION ROTTEN WHICH PROBABLY CORRUPTION FOR RUTTER. ALSO REPORT OPERATION NOW COMPLETELY ABANDONED. OUR APOLOGIES FOR DOUBTING YOU. BETTER LUCK NEXT TIME.

The Druid radioed back:

> WHY DID AFUS REPORT OPERATION ONLY AFTER NOT BEFORE IT WAS CANCELED?

His control replied:

> GOOD QUESTION. HOPE AND BELIEVE YOULL GET THE ANSWER TO THAT ONE. GOOD LUCK AND HEIL HITLER!

The Druid had given the young French-Canadian his address at CEMA when they had parted on the night of the Zandvoort Players concert, and one day early in August there was a call for him. He recognized the dark Quebec accent at once.

"I haven't much time to talk," the voice said. "They're limiting us to three minutes apiece, this being one of the special areas. I'm just calling to say hello and report I'm still in the land of the living."

114

"When are you coming to London?" the Druid asked quickly.

"I had hoped to come this week," the lieutenant said. "But plans have changed again, and I don't expect to get leave at least until September. They sure fuck you about in this fucking army. *Au revoir, mon ami.* I just want you to know I'm still trying to keep my feet dry."

There was a click and the line went dead, and the Druid slowly, thoughtfully, put the receiver back on its hook.

That night he radioed his control:

STRONGLY BELIEVE OPERATION RUTTER REVIVED. URGE YOU REALERT WEHRMACHT. WHAT ARE AFUS REPORTING?

Control:

AFUS MUTE. BUT TAKING CHANCE WARNING WEHRMACHT HIGHEST PRIORITY.

There was another message later:

OKM[2] SAY RN[3] SIGNALS KEEP MENTIONING OPERATION JU-BILEE. WHAT DO YOU KNOW?

The Druid:

NOTHING. BUT COULD HAZARD GUESS. HAVE WEHRMACHT TAKEN PRECAUTIONS?

Control:

DON'T WORRY. THEY'LL BE WAITING.

On the morning of August 19, 1942, the 2nd Canadian Army Division went ashore at Dieppe in a raid known to its planners as Operation Jubilee (the name substituted, "for security purposes," for Operation Rutter). There were 6,108 soldiers who took part in the landing. By the end of the day, 2,853 of them had been killed, wounded, or captured, and the rest were in retreat.

2 OKM, Oberkommando der Marine (German Navy).
3 RN, Royal Navy. The Nazis had broken their code.

Few of those who took part in the raid were left long in doubt about the state of the German defenses. It was quite obvious from the start that the Wehrmacht knew they were coming, and had made all the necessary preparations.

It was the Druid's first success. But as he read the censored accounts of the disaster in the British newspapers, and listened to the unalloyed cries of triumph from Lord Haw-Haw over Radio Hamburg, one thought continued to nag at him.

Why had the AFUs stayed mute? With all those agents operating in Britain, why had not a single one of the Abwehr's spies mentioned anything at all about the Dieppe operation? Could they have been deliberately silenced—and if so, why and how?

The Double Cross Committee was only too aware of the answer to that question, and very angry about it.

CHAPTER 6

Double Trouble

I

ABOUT A WEEK after the bad news from Dieppe reached London there was a meeting of the XX Committee at MI5 headquarters in the War Office in Whitehall. The XX (or Double Cross) Committee was the body which sponsored and controlled the activities of the Abwehr spies who had been captured and "turned" against their Nazi masters, and its members decided what false or deceptive information the suborned agents should send back to Germany. They were an assortment of brilliant men, high in total cerebral capacity: ex-colonial civil servants, professional intelligence officers, career military men, co-opted professors and other academics, the odd lawyer, scientist, and scholar, and an official from the Special Branch at Scotland Yard. Socially speaking, they belonged to the British upper-middle class, conformist, loyal to His Majesty King George VI, good, solid ex-public-school boys all.

There were, however, two other men at this particular meeting whose background was not dissimilar but whose attitude toward life in general and the British war effort in particular was altogether more equivocal—though "worldly" is the word they would probably have used. One of them was Kim Philby, the liaison officer between MI5 and MI6, the two principal branches of the SIS, who had come armed with some questions he wanted to ask. The other was the "Spanish art dealer" Thomas Harris. It was well known in the SIS that Harris and Philby were friends, and had been since the early days of the war, when Harris had pulled strings—he had excellent connections—to get Philby into MI5 and then into the Iberian counterespionage sector. They obviously had many things in common, including a fondness for Spain and the Spaniards, a passion for Spanish art, and a love of good food and drink (though Harris liked wine and Philby any kind of booze). What their colleagues could not guess was that they shared more esoteric interests, including mutual ideological obligations.

Thomas Harris always had a disconcerting effect on the members of the XX Committee when he turned up at one of their meetings. He brought into the room such an air of cosmopolitan, sophisticated self-confidence, such an atmosphere of supercilious yet well-controlled arrogance, that his superiority to them clung to him like an aura and assaulted their senses almost as pungently as his expensive toilet lotion. He made them feel like awkward schoolboys pretending to be grown-ups. If Philby was present at the same time, Harris had a habit of turning to him with a twinkle in his bright eyes which seemed to suggest that they were two aesthetes mixing with their inferiors, and they must grin and bear it with fortitude. Yet the committee members, while not resenting Harris, could hardly help but be in awe of him. He really was such a special character. He was not only fabulously rich but also so knowledgeable and quicksilver clever. He was certainly one of the principal reasons why the Double Cross System of manipulating the Abwehr's spies had—until now, that is—worked so well.

One of the jobs which Harris had undertaken for MI5 since the outbreak of war had been the interrogation of captured spies, first at the reception center at St. Albans and later at a more professional headquarters at Latchmere House, Ham Common, on the outskirts of London. This ugly suburban mansion, cut off from the road by a high wall, had once been a private nursing home for the mentally disturbed, and there was really little change in the treatment of its inmates once MI5 took over, except that they no longer came voluntarily for treatment. The staff took pride in the fact that none of the Abwehr spies, male or female, who were brought there emerged from an interrogation without revealing some of their secrets, and that went for the so-called uncooperative ones who were subsequently shot or hanged. But where Harris succeeded over his colleagues was in persuading the captives he questioned not merely to confess but also to expatiate. He had almost Svengali-like qualities and could be hypnotically encouraging, and though, unlike some of the invigilators, he never threatened violence nor indulged in it, he was capable of instilling great fear in his charges as well as affection.

One of his first successes was with a member of the Spanish embassy in London, a certain Don José Brugada Wood, who had diplomatic privilege and was therefore impervious to any British sanctions except expulsion. But Tommy Harris, once he had been given evidence that Don José was part of an anti-British network operating out of the Spanish embassy, set about changing his allegiance, and quickly ingratiated himself with the Spaniard. He did it with such success that soon Don José, who had charge of the Spanish diplomatic bag between London and Madrid, was slipping in information which, he knew, would be passed on to the Abwehr once it reached Spain, and was deliberately deceptive.

Don José was added to the roster of Double Cross agents and referred to henceforth under his code name of "Peppermint," and he was soon revealing some aromatic facts about the underground activities being indulged in by members of his embassy. He told Harris, for instance, that the principal espionage agent both for Spain and for the Abwehr in Britain was the press secretary, Señor Alcázar de Velasco, who concealed his deep anti-British sentiments and moved in rarefied political circles in London. He was trusted by quite important politicians close to Prime Minister Winston Churchill, and extracted invaluable information from them, which he subsequently passed on to his Abwehr control in Madrid under the code name of "Guillermo."

But how to get rid of the dangerous Señor de Velasco? To expel him without giving the Spaniards adequate reasons would only offend them, and to produce evidence would uncover Don José's double role. Harris began a series of complicated maneuvers whereby de Velasco became convinced that his espionage activities had been discovered by the British, and that one of his seniors in the embassy who was jealous of him was secretly arranging for his diplomatic immunity to be abrogated, so that he could be arrested, tried, and, maybe, hanged for espionage. He panicked and fled the country.

He left behind as the new head of the Spanish espionage ring a young journalist named Luis Calvo, who was London correspondent of the Madrid newspaper *ABC*. Calvo was a handsome young man who had joined the Spanish Fascist party, the Falange, at an early age and dreamed of seeing Britain crushed by Hitler and Gibraltar returned to Spain, in a Europe dominated from the Urals to the Atlantic by Nazi Germany and its Axis partners. Don José was soon confiding that Calvo was sending regular reports, several of them of military importance, through the diplomatic bag to Madrid, especially those which would have otherwise been stopped by the censor. One of these days, he warned, the young journalist might stumble on something big. He had already chosen his own code name with which to work with the Abwehr. He called himself "Arabel," after his mother, Arabella Calvo.

It was decided to arrest Calvo and bring him to Latchmere

House for questioning. A strapping South African major with a patch over one eye and a livid scar across his cheek strode into the room dangling a rope, which he quickly looped around the young Spaniard's neck and pulled hard.

"That is how it feels when they begin to hang you for spying," he rasped.

Slowly slipping off his jacket and shirt, the South African towered over the cowering young man, the muscles rippling across his burly chest and enormous arms. One of them swung up and smashed the back of a hand heavily across the Spaniard's face. Calvo went spinning across the room.

"But the time when you hang is a long way away," the South African went on. "In the meantime, you've been brought to this place so we can have a little fun. *My* fun. You've had *your* fun."

Tommy Harris had been watching through a peephole. By the time he entered the interrogation room, Calvo was on his knees and pleading for mercy.

Interposing himself between the abject Spaniard and his tormentor, Harris angrily ordered the South African to leave, physically pushing him through the door as he pretended to resist, shouting, "He isn't even bleeding yet! Let me teach the little toad a lesson!"

Once they were alone, Harris looked down at the crumpled, sobbing figure, and said softly in Spanish, *"Don't worry about that brute, my unfortunate friend. I don't know whether I can save you from the gallows, but at least I can protect you from people like him."*

He went over and put his hand gently on Calvo's luxuriant crop of black hair, and at once the Spaniard grasped Harris around the knees, pressing himself to him in a passionate gesture of supplication and submission.

"I'll do anything, anything!" he sobbed.

They stayed like that for long moments, and then Harris reached down and drew the young man to his feet.

"Why don't I show you where you can get cleaned up?" he

said. *"And then perhaps we can have a* fino, *a meal, and a little talk together."*

II

From this incident had emerged the most successful operation of the Double Cross System. Arabel of the Abwehr became "Garbo" of the XX Committee (the code name was chosen personally for Calvo by Tommy Harris), and henceforward he was Harris's personal protégé, often staying for prolonged periods in his Chesterfield Gardens home, accompanying him to parties (which is where the Druid had first seen him), and acting as front man for a series of espionage activities which became more and more indispensable to the Abwehr. Soon, thanks to Harris's fertile imagination, Garbo became controller of a network of agents working in strategic points throughout Britain, from whom he obtained information and forwarded to his Abwehr control in Madrid. Some of it was true and important information which, Harris insisted, would reinforce Garbo's position with the Abwehr even if it did some harm to British security. Much of it was so timed that the Nazis would not be able to exploit it. Other items were deliberately deceiving, though not sufficiently so as to make the Abwehr think Garbo was intentionally tricking them. It was all part of a campaign to build up Garbo and his network for the pregnant moment when Tommy Harris and the XX Committtee would be able to use the young Spaniard to feed the big lie to the Germans at a moment when it was most calculated, once they acted on it, to bring them disaster.

But why had Arabel/Garbo been gagged during the Dieppe operation? And why had all the other Double Cross agents been silenced?

"Surely we could have thought up a cover plan?" Harris remarked, once the committee began to discuss the Dieppe disaster. "Garbo could have given them a yarn that would have thoroughly confused them about time and place. It might not have rescued the operation—which seems to me to have been a mistaken one, anyway—but at least it might have saved the lives of a few of those unfortunate Canadians. As it is, Garbo's control in Madrid wants to know why they didn't get a peep out of him." He looked around the table. "Any other controls complaining?"

Colonel T. A. ("Tar") Robertson, who was chairing the committee, nodded glumly.

"It was a mistake," he said flatly. "We acknowledge it was a mistake. But it was also orders from higher up. We asked [Lord] Mountbatten and [Lord] Swinton weeks ago whether we could start feeding them stuff, from the moment Operation Rutter was first approved. The Huns were already hypothecating a raid on them by us. They knew what the Russians were saying about a second front. It was logical of them to presume we would do something, even if it was only a *coup de main*. Then, too, it suited Hitler's book to spread rumors we were going to invade Fortress Europe, so that when we did make a landing, even if it was a successful in-and-out raid, he could claim he had thrown us back." He nodded at Harris, who was staring at his manicured nails. "So the thing to have done was confirm what we knew the Huns had guessed, and then, as Tommy suggests, to have confused them as to when, where, and in what strength it was coming. But it was taken out of our hands. General Montgomery was in charge of Operation Rutter to begin with and he thumbed it down. Then the Canadians were approached and they vetoed it too. Both said it was too dangerous. Monty never has understood the uses of intelligence, and the Canucks are—well, just plain ignorant of its value. So we were told to close down Double Cross for the duration of the op. I'm sorry." He sighed and shrugged his shoulders. "I promise you, Tommy, it won't happen again. This time it really wasn't our fault."

Harris glanced across the room at Philby. There was no twinkle in his eye on this occasion.

III

A few hours before the XX Committee meeting, Kim Philby had had a rendezvous with his Communist control, Ernst, on Paddington Green and the anonymous streets surrounding it. The session had not been a happy one. If anything, the Russians were even more devastated by the Dieppe failure than the British, since they had honestly hoped that it would take some pressure off them on the Eastern front. Even if a full-scale invasion had never been intended, they had at least hoped for three or four weeks of activity of sufficient strength to alarm the German High Command. Instead it had all gone to pieces in less than a day. They were extremely anxious to know why it had been botched so badly.

What bothered Ernst was Moscow's dark suggestion that the British had deliberately sabotaged the success of the Dieppe operation. Had they set a trap for the 2nd Canadian Division and sent them off across the Channel knowing full well that the Germans would be waiting for them?

Philby had been genuinely surprised at the suggestion.

"Why on earth should you think that?" he asked.

The myopic little Communist turned his thin yellow face, with its fuzz of brown stubble, up toward the Englishman. A sad smile hovered on his pale lips.

"You do not think the English are capable of such treachery?"

"My dear Nicky," said Philby, who liked to use his control's real first name when they were alone, "I have good reason to know that the English are quite willing to sacrifice their own baby brothers and sisters to save their own skin. But what good does it do them to get able and willing Canadians unnecessarily killed when they might be kept as sacrificial lambs for more useful occasions in the future?"

Ernst said softly, "It could be their idea of a convincing way to show my government how difficult it is to land in Europe, and why the English are delaying the opening of the second front."

Philby said, "And kill all those Canadians deliberately? I know he is a wicked old bastard, but I don't think even Winston Churchill is capable of that."

"Then why did the British warn the Nazis that the Canadians were coming?" Ernst asked.

"What are you trying to say?"

"I am reporting what my government tells me. We have our spies in Germany, even right inside the Nazi machine. And those spies tell us that just before the Dieppe operation someone—someone here—warned the Germans that the Canadians were coming."

"I don't believe it," Philby said.

"But my government does," said Ernst. "And that is what matters." He added: "We had better do something about it."

The memory of that conversation came back to him as Kim Philby looked around the row of typical British faces seated on the opposite side of the XX Committee table. Not for the first time, he was irritated by the self-satisfaction which his eye detected in the expressions worn by his colleagues. What a complacent bunch they were! So sure of themselves, so absolutely certain that by their cleverness and guile they had the Nazi intelligence network all sewn up. What was it John Bevan (in charge of deception) had said to him one day?

"Like puppets on a string, dear boy! Every agent they've sent—and the Abwehr too—dancing to our tune!"

There was not a single one among them sensitive enough to hear the larger orchestra he could hear playing in the background, nor acute enough to suspect they might be the subjects of manipulation, too. He was aware that the academics among them sometimes gave him an old-fashioned look, as if he didn't quite belong; but that was because of his raffish, insouciant air, his habit of treating serious subjects frivolously. It would never have occurred to them to suspect he might be working for a larger network, and that, as far as he was concerned, the XX Committee, and the SIS itself, was no more than a wayside post office at Nether Wallop. How could he possibly be disloyal? Was he not one of them, woven from the same cloth, even if there was a trace of vulgarity in the pattern?

Philby calculated wryly to himself that if, one of these days, they did ever find out the truth about him, they would shake their heads and say: "Well, I always did feel there was a touch of the scapegrace there! But a traitor? Must have been his father's influence. Mixes with Arabs, you know."

His eyes moved to Tommy Harris, elegantly blowing smoke through his nostrils and looking like Krishna, wreathed in incense, regarding, half benevolently, half contemptuously, a throng of very ordinary mortals. What would they say about him if they ever discovered that he, too, had loyalties bigger than a stuttering monarch, a drunken premier, and the smuggest population of dupes in the so-called democratic world?

"What, old Tommy Harris a Bolshie? Why, I can't believe it! He's civilized, Tommy—likes wine, women—and boys, too! You can't convince me Tommy works for the Reds. Far too civilized!"

At the far end of the table John Newcob, the Oxford mathematician, sat with his chin propped up on his arms, looking more like a sad spaniel than ever. Newcob was the man who liaised between the XX Committee and the GCCS (the Government Code and Cipher School) at Bletchley Park, and Philby had a warm spot in his heart for him, not simply because he was so brainy and so modest about it, but because, like Philby, he stuttered when he was nervous and sometimes had difficulty pronouncing his "r"s.

As Philby had once remarked at the end of a heavy drinking

session in a Bletchley pub during which they had stammered their way through a raucous version of "Phil the Fluter's Ball": "Do you realize we are special people, John? To 'er' is human, but to lisp divine!"

"You have never stuttered a twuer word," Newcob had gravely replied.

But they were both in control of their vocal cords this morning. Philby looked first at the chairman and then at Newcob.

"I'd like to ask John a question about communications," he said. "Were any AFUs detected by Bletchley in the week or ten days preceding the Dieppe landing?"

Newcob did not look down at his records.

"If you mean were any messages passed to the Abwehr through Double Cross controls," he replied, "the answer is no. As we have just been told, they were ordered not to send."

"Nothing intercepted at all?"

Now Newcob looked down at his papers. "We did get part of one message from abroad—on, er, August 16—that would be three days before the landing. We only got about a quarter of the message and it was in a code we didn't know. We didn't get enough of it to try it on Enigma. The girl who heard it did think she recognized the style and thought it might be from a control we've dealt with before." He shrugged his shoulders. "But we didn't intercept in time. And, you know, it may not even have been meant for us, a beam gone awry or something. It wasn't on the usual wavelengths at all."

"No one here tried to reply?"

Newcob shook his head. "If he did, we missed him."

Robertson said, "What's up, Kim? Got a bee buzzing in your bonnet?"

Philby indicated that it was "just a little idea" he had had, and it wasn't important. But he noticed that Tommy Harris wasn't fooled by that. There was a speculative look in those all-seeing eyes.

IV

On an August afternoon in 1942, the Druid walked through Mayfair to his rendezvous in Chesterfield Gardens. He was making his first visit in England to a rich man's home, and it would be interesting to guess how he would compare it with his experiences in Germany. Life had been much simpler and more bucolic in Patagonia, and until he arrived with his mother at his grandfather's home in Bremen he had never set foot inside anything more substantial than a sheep farmer's homestead. Haus Walfisch, as his grandfather's place was called, had therefore been something of a revelation. It was a huge Hanseatic mansion on the shore of the River Weser, full of large, dark rooms, grim ancestral pictures, its raftered halls hung with flags and heraldic banners.

His mother had laughed softly when she had seen his first, quickly smothered expression of astonishment, and said, "I know! Very Teutonic, isn't it?"

But though he did not tell his mother, he was thrilled by the sheer medieval splendor of the place. When the Druid was shown to his bedroom, he found a great four-poster bed poised before a curved picture window which looked out on a well-groomed lawn sloping down to the banks of the Weser. A three-masted whaler, glinting with bunting and multi-colored paint, was tied up to the dock (permanently tied up, as it turned out), a huge swastika fluttering from the highest mast and the house flag of the Von Forbath Line waving at the stern. In an alcove by the window of his room was the stuffed figure of a sea lion, its red jaws open in a snarl, its gleaming tusks ready to slash, as it reared itself up from a slab of ice-cold marble. The gallery outside his bedroom door was hung with trophies and memorabilia of the hunt for big fish on the high seas: vertebrae and giant jaws of whales, the rose-pink carcass of a sperm-whale calf, harpoons, axes, grap-

ples, and spears. The sea, and its denizens, was the dominant
theme of Haus Walfisch, and always in the most dramatic
form. Herr von Forbath slept in a bedroom which he had
turned into the replica of a whaler captain's cabin, his bed a
huge bunk chained to the paneled wall, portholes for windows, and a ship's wheel which spun and swayed when you
leaned on it to look outside. An enormous stuffed ray fish
flew above the desk in his study, lit from above when it grew
dark, hovering like a giant bat. There were tarpon, alligators,
and turtles pinned to the walls of the great bannered dining
hall. And his mother's bathroom, originally designed for his
grandmother, now dead, was like an underwater cavern, taps
of gleaming gold over polished shell basins, with the bath its
centerpiece—a pool of heart-shaped, dovetailed mother-of-
pearl sunk into the floor and surrounded by mirrors which,
when you pressed a switch, changed to the walls of a giant
aquarium in which fish of every kind, exotic, tropical, Portuguese men-o'-war, octopuses, and stingrays, glided or lolloped
past in a kaleidoscope of changing lights. One of these days,
perhaps, he would have a mansion like it, on a clifftop in
Wales.

In the circumstances, the Mayfair home of Thomas Harris
could hardly be expected to measure up. There were a couple
of loud American GIs arguing with three girls at the corner
of Shepherd's Market as the Druid came down Curzon Street,
and two U.S. military policemen (or "Snowdrops," as they
were called, because of their white helmets) eyeing them
speculatively on the far corner. Chesterfield Gardens had had
some near misses during the blitz of 1941, and still showed
traces of it, and the elegant long windows of the rows of
houses had long since been boarded up against blast. The
street looked shabby and neglected. But once the door was
opened—by a young man who looked very much like a
soldier in mufti—there was a feeling of quiet luxury both
under the feet and on the walls. From above his head came

the sounds of Bach, and when he looked up the flight of stairs he saw the smiling face of Tommy Harris gazing down on him, glass in hand.

"If it isn't the minstrel boy himself!" he called. "Come on up and refresh yourself."

The Druid mounted the stairs, past some good Dürer etchings, and went into the lounge, where at once a young man about his own age, in battle dress and a lieutenant's pips on his epaulettes, rose from a couch.

"This is Paul," said Harris. "He just came up from camp—unexpectedly," he added, with the slightest edge in his voice. "He'll be staying a few days, I expect. This is Liberty Hall, you know."

"I can always go and stay with Brian," said Paul softly.

"No, no." Harris gazed at the two young men with a glint in his eye that made the Druid feel they were being examined like *objets d'art;* but then he saw the expression on the older man's face warm up, and he smiled.

"What a handsome pair you two do make," Harris said. "It's lovely seeing you, Paul. Really."

He went over to the sideboard and poured a drink for the Druid. It was the driest sherry he had ever tasted, puckering his lips as he sipped it. Harris was watching him. He was clad in a maroon-colored velvet smoking jacket, a pair of green slacks, and a bright red scarf tucked into a black shirt. He reminded the Druid of the visiting toreadors his mother had once entertained at her father's home in Bahía Blanca, the same flaunting of colors, the same inward strut.

"Not quite sweet enough for you, perhaps?" Harris asked.

"It isn't like the sherry we buy in Llandudno," the Druid said, and then smiled, sipped again, and added: "But I like it."

"Good."

The sense of strain remained, and was hardly eased by the way the other two began to prattle. Paul was a poet, it was explained, who had found himself transformed into an instructor in unarmed combat at an army camp in Sussex. He smiled deprecatingly as Harris let out this tidbit, and the Druid had trouble concealing his skepticism. Paul looked so delicate and slender that in unarmed combat one could have snapped his limbs like twigs.

The Druid looked across at his host and said, "You never told me what *you* do, sir."

"I?" said Harris. "I'm just a humble dealer in the arts. I broke my hip once, when I was a young boy at school, and that keeps me out of the services. So I just carry on. Someone has to keep the cultural flag flying while chaps like you"— indicating Paul—"indulge in your blood sports."

Paul snickered. "Don't be an old fraud, Tommy! Everybody knows what *you* do!" He turned a pair of innocent brown eyes on the Druid. Harris was watching him with just the trace of anxiety in his own, and the Druid realized the young man was aware of it, and was teasing him. "He keeps General Franco happy and prevents Spain from coming into the war on the Nazi side," he said. "And do you know how?" He paused, then went on: "By keeping up the market price of Spanish pictures, and making sure there's a steady trade in England for Spanish sherry!"

"I'll be knighted for it yet!" Harris said, in a relieved tone.

They heard the doorbell ring below, and then the sound of the door opening and loud, laughing voices.

"My God, an invasion," said Harris, rising. "I told you this was Liberty Hall!"

As he went to the head of the stairs, the Druid got to his feet himself and said he must go. But then Paul leaned across suddenly and put a hand on his shoulder.

"No, stay!" he said pleadingly.

V

It was several hours later, and the "invasion" had turned into a party. Tommy Harris's wife had appeared suddenly, and with her had come food, loads of it, more than the Druid had seen at any time since he had arrived in England, and bottle after bottle of French and Spanish wine. More and more people kept arriving. Some couples came, young men and women, a lot of them in uniform, but most of the guests were male and the Druid was not slow to notice that the majority of them were homosexuals. They began by greeting each other circumspectly and going off into corners to chat in whispers interspersed with sudden peals of laughter. But around about eleven o'clock a tall, fleshy young man came stumbling up the stairs dragging behind him a callow, teen-age soldier in the uniform of one of the guards regiments, and with the oafish grin on his face of someone who is practically awash with drink.

The young man leading him was far from sober himself; he let out a sudden yell which quieted some of the babble in the room, and then shouted, "Look, everyone, look what I've found!"

At which he dragged the guardsman toward him, clasped him under the armpits, and gave him a long, passionate kiss on the lips which lasted so long that, after a minute or so, the two of them slid to a heap on the floor. There was the noise of clapping and cheering from different parts of the room, and the sight of the couple locked in their passionate embrace seemed to release something in everybody. Wherever the Druid looked, he saw hands going around waists, people beginning to touch, caress, kiss, feel, and, over in the far corner of the room, his host leaning back, a contented smile plastered on his gleaming pink face as both a pretty girl and a tall, intense-looking young man poured confidences (or were they kisses?) into his ears.

"Don't look so shocked!"

A hand slid into his and he turned to see Paul leaning toward him, a reassuring look on his gentle face.

"You may not believe it," he whispered, pointing to the disheveled heap, "but that chap there—his name is Guy Burgess—is doing marvels for the war effort. Yes, he's queer. He's never bothered to conceal it. But he's wonderfully successful at the BBC, organizing propaganda. Works like a black to get all kinds of deception over to the Nazis. He deserves a little relaxation. As for our host." He chuckled. "Don't let old Tommy fool you when he says he's just a humble dealer. Poppycock! I doubt if there's anyone in the country doing more for the war effort."

"If you mean by supporting the Spanish wine industry," said the Druid, indicating the bottles, "I can see why you said that."

"Oh, that!" Paul shrugged it aside. "I honestly don't know how he manages it, and it must cost him a fortune. But no, that wasn't what I meant. I can't tell you what Tommy really does, but I can assure you there isn't anything more important."

"Do you *know* what he does?"

Paul grinned and squeezed his hand. "Even if I knew, I wouldn't tell you! Now take that puritanical look off your face, and tell me something about yourself." He leaned closer. "Have you ever had a girl—or a boy? And does this—this party really shock you?"

Guy Burgess and the guardsman had unlocked themselves by now, and the guardsman was in the middle of the room, swaying on his feet and doing a clumsy striptease.

"Yes," said the Druid, "it does."

A voice spoke behind him. "Then let me take you into the library, away from this revolting spectacle. I have been neglecting you, dear boy. I promised to show you my pictures."

It was Tommy Harris, his expression sober and concerned. The Druid loosed his hand from Paul's, and followed him into the library.

CHAPTER 7

Trouble with Ostro

I

By the summer of 1942, Paul von Fidrmuc was beginning to feel the strain. It was all very well for the Gestapo to insist that he keep his Ostro Network going from Lisbon on behalf of the Abwehr and, at the same time, run control of the Druid exclusively for the RSHA. But sometimes the complications stretched his nerves to breaking point. It would have been difficult enough if the Ostro Network's spies had been genuine ones, but the fact (which the Gestapo knew but the Abwehr didn't) that they did not exist except in von Fidrmuc's imagination taxed his nerves to the limit as he strove to keep all his cards in play.

Heightening his confusion and worry was the fact that his purely imaginary reports so often turned out to be more accurate than those received from other Abwehr spies in Britain—real ones, operating under other controls. Through his mistress Trudy Körner, who still kept her job at the German embassy in Lisbon, he had got a line into the main Abwehr office there, where a certain Kreme von Auenrode was in control of an important network of espionage agents in Britain. Trudy, who was nothing if not sexually adaptable, had formed a close friendship with Elizabeth von Auenrode, Kreme's attractive young wife, confidante, and secretary. Elizabeth was tolerantly contemptuous of her dandyish Austrian husband, a World War I officer a good deal older than herself, and she unblushingly unburdened herself about him and his activities, both domestic and professional, confident of Trudy's entire trustworthiness. She even gave her friend, to amuse her, some of the reports sent in by von Auenrode's agents in Britain, or mentioned when they were in Lisbon to report. And Trudy passed on the information to Paul.

When he read these reports, Paul von Fidrmuc was astounded by their quality. So often, he noted, these genuine spies showed remarkable enterprise and courage in worming themselves into the confidence of quite highly placed Britons, who let slip most invaluable information. But why, with these precious facts in their possession, did their English informants so often draw the wrong conclusions? Why did all the spies continually get the facts sensationally right but were steered by their informants to conclusions which were abysmally wrong? And why, with no genuine facts to help him at all, was he more often correct in his assessments than these men on the spot were? It is true that when the Druid reported, which was only rarely, he did so cleanly and clearly, and von Fidrmuc wondered why the Wehrmacht and the Luftwaffe were so slow in acting on his information. It was the Druid, for instance, who had given Berlin first news of the arrival in London from America of a general officer named Dwight David Eisenhower, and, at a moment when German reference books still located Eisenhower as a colonel in Washington, forecast that he could soon become commander of U.S. forces in Europe. But the Druid had had bad luck. At the time, he had reported that Eisenhower would be presented to King George and Queen Elizabeth at a reception at Windsor Castle, while simultaneously no less than three

Abwehr agents in London mentioned that King George was giving a royal reception "to visiting American officers" at Buckingham Palace in London.

It was three against one, and Goering had ordered the bombing of the palace. But, as delayed Court records had subsequently shown, the Druid had been right, and it was at Windsor Castle that the reception had been held.

The Druid was not proving so good at tracking down the Abwehr agents in Britain and reporting on them. But could there be a reason for that which no one had yet explained? Why had the Druid so far failed to make contact with the Abwehr's intrepid agents? It was this which troubled von Fidrmuc.

Von Fidrmuc told no one, not even Trudy, about these perplexing questions until the autumn of 1942, a few months after Dieppe, when the Allies took a crucial step toward changing the direction of the war. All through the summer he had been working and worrying about what the Anglo-Americans would do next, and the more he balanced his rag-bag of gossip and newspaper news against the enemy's need for a substantial operation, and the more he stared at the map of Britain in relation to the rest of the world, the more he was forced to an inescapable conclusion. The Anglo-Americans had to go somewhere—the American people had joined the Soviets in demanding action—and it had to be a place where some sort of victory was already being won and could be exploited. Where else then but North Africa? Rommel had been stopped at Alamein, in the Egyptian desert, and von Fidrmuc knew enough about the German strategic situation to realize that once halted, his vaunted Afrika Korps would never get to Alexandria, Cairo, and the Suez Canal. The gamble had been lost because Germany no longer had the war matériel, the planes, guns, ammunition, supply ships, gasoline, to give Rommel the muscle for that extra push that could have given him victory. Whereas, even the Germans acknowledged that men, guns, planes, and supplies were being poured into Egypt by the Anglo-Americans, and that when *they* pushed, Rommel would have to retreat.

And then? Why, was it not obvious that the Anglo-Americans would want to compound Rommel's humiliation by hitting him in his rear just when he was most vulnerable? All they needed to achieve it was to land in North Africa—where only the confused and ambivalent armies of the tattered and defeated Vichy French would be there to feebly resist them—and batter the Afrika Korps' rump at the same time as Montgomery's Eighth Army was smashing him in the chest and belly. The reward would be the whole of North Africa from Suez to Casablanca, and the Allies would control thousands of miles of territory containing airfields, roads for communications, and ports for launching armadas of troops for operations against German-held Europe on the other side of the Mediterranean.

It had to be North Africa! He fabricated circumstantial-sounding reports along these lines reaching the same conclusion from different angles, and assigned them to two of his fictitious agents, Ostro 1 and Ostro 2. He also wrote a report from Ostro 3, his notional American agent in Washington, describing an overheard conversation at a diplomatic dinner party at which a general, just back from a visit to Gibraltar, had reported a "fantastic" buildup of ships and matériel there, probably for use in North Africa.

He was about to turn these over to Trudy for handling when she returned from a session with her friend Elizabeth, bringing with her the latest batch of reports from the von Auenrode network in Britain. Von Fidrmuc read them through with growing fascination, for it was obvious that what he had conjured up in his fertile imagination was actually taking place in fact in England. The Anglo-Americans *had* started their buildup of forces, the Abwehr spies reported, and they *were* getting ready to move, for troop concentrations had been spotted, convoys had been seen preparing to assemble, and armament-laden trains had been checked as they moved to the ports. But then, to von Fidrmuc's stupefaction and dismay, these spies on the spot went on to predict a completely different objective for the Anglo-American forces from the one he had calculated. Several of them forecast that the enemy was preparing for a massive move against, of all places, Norway, which was ridiculous, considering the time of the year. And there were at least fifteen reports favoring a reinforcement campaign to bolster up Malta, the British-held island in the Mediterranean, just south of Italy, which was under heavy attack from Axis bombers and threatened with invasion by Nazi troops. But no suggestion whatsoever of a possible move against North Africa.

Von Fidrmuc was deflated. He would look an awful fool if he sent no fewer than three reports to ABT1 in Hamburg giving a forecast (completely invented as it was) so much at variance with von Auenrode's on-the-spot informants. On the other hand, he desperately needed to keep up the reputation of the Ostro Network to maintain his income and finance his gambling activities at Estoril, not to speak of Trudy's little extravagances. After some sweaty hesitation, he decided to risk breaking orders and try to seek confirmation of his prognostications. Without consulting the RSHA or mentioning it to Trudy, he sent a message to the Druid asking him for news of any forthcoming operations by the Anglo-Americans. The reply came back after several days. The Druid could not be of much help. But he did offer one clue. He had made contact with some sources in London who apparently frequently talked Spanish among themselves, unaware that he was completely fluent in the language. He reported that these days he had noticed they often made reference to something which sounded like a forthcoming event, perhaps a military operation. They called it "Flama." This was a Spanish word, the Druid unnecessarily pointed out, which meant "flame." Could "Flame" be the code name of the next Anglo-American operation?

In no circumstances would it get von Fidrmuc out of

trouble, but at least it was a detail to add as a circumstantial item to his report. He decided to scrap two of his fictitious messages, and send only one, from Ostro 2, predicting a North Africa move, adding that the code name of the operation was "Flamme," the German word for flame. One of the Abwehr control officers in Germany then duly forwarded it on for the consideration of the German High Command. But it was buried under the predictions from von Auenrode's network and other Anglo-American cover plans which had been flowing in, and Ostro 2's report, it turned out, never even got as far as Field Marshall Keitel's office. Consequently, when the Anglo-Americans did actually land in North Africa, in October, 1942, taking the Nazis completely by surprise, von Fidrmuc's uncannily accurate prediction was all but forgotten in the subsequent confusion.

Except, of course, by von Fidrmuc himself, who hastened to remind the Abwehr in Germany of Ostro 2's remarkable achievement. By chance it was seen by an Abwehr officer secretly working for the SS, and it was to one of his contacts there, Kriminal Inspektor Hugo Hoffmann of the RSHA, that he pointed out von Fidrmuc's prescient report.

The British were also considerably interested, as well as jolted, by the Ostro report. Von Fidrmuc communicated with ABT1 in Hamburg in the Abwehr code, and this was read by a British agent in Lisbon and decoded by the Government Code and Cipher School at Bletchley Park. They were duly impressed by Ostro 2's astuteness in forecasting the North African landing. But there was one particular item in his report which alarmed them. The word "Flamme" was mentioned as the probable code name for the operation, and "Flamme," translated as flame, was sufficiently near to the actual name chosen as to set alarm bells ringing at MI5. The code name of the North African landing had been Operation Torch.

How had Ostro 2 got so close to it? Where was he obtaining his information? From an agent still running loose in Britain? Had one of them escaped the dragnet, after all?

It was the Druid's luck that no one realized the word he had used in his report to von Fidrmuc was from the Spanish one, "Flama." Otherwise, someone in MI5 might have started asking questions of his Spanish-speaking colleagues. Thomas Harris, for instance.

II

The problem of Ostro 2 came up toward the end of a meeting of the XX Committee early in February, 1943, and for several members that was a relief, since the discussion preceding it had been exceedingly painful. It was true that so far as Operation Torch was concerned, the XX Committee had played a more useful and less frustrating role than they had in the days leading up to the raid on Dieppe. For one thing, they were not gagged—or, that is to say, not completely. The twenty-odd captured Nazi spies now working for the Double Cross System, plus their ten or so notional assistants, had at least been allowed to operate in a combined effort to conceal the real nature of Torch, and to confuse the Germans as to its timing and target. And they had largely succeeded. The landing in North Africa had—at least in part thanks to their efforts—completely surprised the enemy.

But the Double Cross campaign had, nevertheless, run into a considerable amount of opposition from the brass hats, who were desperately afraid the half-truths on which the Double Cross deceptions were based would tip off the Germans and enable them to guess where the landing was going to be made, with disastrous results. Through the network he had built up around Garbo, for example, Thomas Harris organized a series of messages ostensibly coming in from all parts of Britain which would reinforce the conviction among the Nazis that it was at Dakar, in West Africa, that the Anglo-Americans were going to land. It was a plausible supposition, since earlier in the war the Free French under General de Gaulle, with British help, had attempted to occupy Dakar and suffered a severe setback; and, from everyone's point of view, a successful operation there at this juncture would wipe out a defeat and hearten both the French and the British, in addition to making a good upbeat story for the Americans. To reinforce the Dakar story, the Double Cross Committee suggested that Nicholas Elliot, who was case officer for another persuasive double agent, Tricycle (Dusko Popov), should send him to Lisbon to let drop a likely West African story to his Nazi control.

But when the deception program was submitted to higher authorities for approval, the British Foreign Office had promptly vetoed it, on the grounds that rumors of a forthcoming attack on Dakar, which was still in the hands of the Vichy French, might enable the Germans to create difficulties in British relations with their one-time allies.

As one of the XX Committee wrote later: "No one could understand the thinking behind that ruling. One presumes that there must have been some. If the distribution of Special Intelligence in the Foreign Office was even barely efficient, whoever made that decision ought to have been on the list and ought to have known that, if the Germans had a way of making trouble between us and the French by means of their agents' reports, they had already had plenty of such reports with which to do it. . . . Very soon the French would know that the Germans were wrong, as we would in fact land, not in Dakar but in North Africa. The decision seemed still more senseless when one bore in mind that North Africa and Dakar were both equally French possessions."[1]

Nevertheless, Harris and Elliot were told to abandon their Dakar ploy. As a substitute, the Foreign Office suggested the Double Cross System should indicate Norway as the target instead, but this was such an obviously implausible deception, and elicited such skepticism from the double agents' Nazi controls, that it was abandoned. The rather more persuasive

[1] Ewen Montague, *Beyond Top Secret* (London: Peter Davies, 1977).

141

suggestion that hard-hit Malta was to be reinforced was the only substitute the committee could organize in the time available.

On the other hand, they did have one considerable success in cheating the Nazis, even if it was won at great cost in lives and shipping tonnage. A few days before the great Anglo-American convoy of 1,400 ships, filled with men and matériel, arrived off southern Spain and turned toward the Mediterranean, on its way to the North African landing, a message went out, purportedly from the British Admiralty, to another convoy of British ships proceeding home, empty, from a voyage to West Africa. The message gave broad indications in its text of what position the convoy would reach in forty-eight hours' time, and warned its convoy commander to watch out for German U-boats. In fact there were no German U-boats in the area at the time. But forty-eight hours later, there certainly were. For the message was sent in an Admiralty code which the Germans had cracked, and Nazi wolf packs waiting in the Atlantic to prey on Allied shipping were ordered at once to intercept the homebound convoy. They launched a series of running attacks which lasted nearly a week, and by the time they withdrew, fifteen ships had been sunk and nearly two thousand seamen lost.

But in the meantime, the North Africa-bound convoy got its 1,400 ships safely through the Straits of Gibraltar and reached the shores of North Africa without being sighted or attacked.

Did the Admiralty know that its code had been cracked by the Germans? Did it deliberately send the intercepted message? It had been Double Cross's most successful diversionary ploy of the campaign, but hardly one its members wished to dwell upon.

So they were glad to see Kim Philby once more among them, and listen to what he had to tell them. Since Philby was in charge of the Iberian sector of SIS, Lisbon, where Ostro 2's control operated, was under his jurisdiction.

III

Philby was just back from Casablanca, Morocco, where he had been attending the conference between Prime Minister Churchill and President Franklin D. Roosevelt. He had stopped off in Lisbon and Madrid and was therefore full of good stories. Did the committee know, for instance, that a Spanish agent of the Abwehr had got wind of the Big Two Conference, as it was called? He had cabled to Berlin the news that Churchill and Roosevelt would be meeting at Casablanca on January 13, and suggested a bombing raid or a parachute attack to kill or capture the two Allied leaders. All he got for his scoop was a heavy silence from ABT1 Hamburg. The office had translated the agent's message from its original Spanish—all of it, including the key word "Casablanca," which thus became "White House"! So Churchill and Roosevelt were having a meeting. What sort of an idiot was Agent K104 to suggest they should try to bomb them or harass them in Washington, D.C.?

The members of the Double Cross Committee tittered politely, since most of them had already heard the story, and then John Masterman, who now ran the Double Cross System, reminded Philby that there was the little matter of the Ostro Network. Like most of his colleagues, Masterman had by now become convinced of "the extent to which the Germans depended upon our controlled agents, and recent events had taught us too the gullibility and the inefficiency of some branches of the Abwehr."[2] All the same, Ostro was sending back disturbingly accurate news. Where was it coming from? Had a German spy somehow slipped through the net and started independent operations in England?

Masterman suggested Philby should get back to Lisbon without delay, find out who was running Ostro and who his

[2] Masterman, *Double Cross System*.

143

agents were, and then take steps to bring them under control. From Philby's point of view, it was a suggestion that could hardly have come at a more awkward moment. He had informed Ernst, his KGB control, that things were going well for him in the SIS and that his bailiwick now included North Africa and Italy as well as the Iberian Peninsula. He estimated that by some subtle lobbying and maneuvering, he might even succeed in bypassing his departmental superior and take his place as the head of a most important branch of the SIS. But it was a promotional campaign which would tax all his ingenuity and need his constant presence, jockeying for position, in the SIS offices in Ryder Street. He had no doubt that so far as Moscow was concerned, this was a campaign to which he should give full priority, for what could be more invaluable to them now and in the future than to have one of their agents high in the hierarchy of British intelligence?

On the other hand, Philby had no wish for anyone else to take care of Ostro. If there *was* an independent Nazi spy loose in Britain, he wanted to get to him—or her—before the SIS did. He would win no praise from Moscow for his promotion if, in securing it, he lost them possession of a successful Nazi network. But how was he going to handle both matters at the same time?

He told Masterman he would arrange to leave for Lisbon as soon as possible. In the meantime, could all the relevant documents on Ostro (intercepts, reports from SIS agents in Lisbon, and so on) be turned over to him? He would need a day or two to familiarize himself with them.

The necessary order was given.

I V

As he emerged from the XX Committee conference room, a commissionaire approached Philby with a message. It was to ask him to call round at his office in Broadway on his way back to his own office and have a word with Denzil Roberts. Philby and Roberts were, at that time, simply colleagues in the same intelligence game, but were coming closer through Roberts's girl friend, for her cousin was one of Kim Philby's favorite subordinates, mainly because he took the spy game as skeptically as Philby pretended to.

Realizing that Roberts would hardly summon him unless it was important, he walked across to Broadway at once and found the SIS man sprawled over a leather couch, his head buried in a large and very ancient volume which proclaimed itself *The Boke of Archaeologie* in illuminated letters across its tattered cover.

Philby had to spill cigarette ash across the pages to indicate he was there. Roberts smoothly switched hats and became the dedicated SIS man again. He presumed, he said, that Philby was already familiar with the case of Vera de Schallberg, the blonde Danish-German spy whose two unfortunate companions had been hanged two years before, but who had been given a respite and was now "in storage" in a women's jail. Quickly, Roberts added some details which his colleague might not know, including the story of Vera's training course on the island of Rügen and her strange encounter on a Baltic beach there with a young man spouting to the waves in an unknown language.

"She never did discover who he was," Roberts said, "except that the man's trainer called him 'the Monk' and that the Nazis considered him something special. For the life of her—and I mean that literally—Vera couldn't identify the language she heard him speaking." He paused and looked owlishly across at Philby. "Now she can."

It seemed that Vera, esconced in a Shropshire jail, had come across two fellow-prisoners in the yard where she took her daily exercise. They were chattering together, and as she drew near she realized that the language they were using was unintelligible to her. Only when she came near to them a second time did it dawn on her that she had heard a similar language before—declaimed rather more musically by the Monk to the waves off Rügen.

Later she had asked her wardress who the two girls were, and was told that they had been brought in under wartime regulations.

"Welsh Nats, that's what they call themselves," the wardress had remarked scornfully. "Caught trying to blow up a power station or something, the stupid bitches. We're going to have trouble with them too, you mark my words. A hunger strike or something, I wouldn't be surprised. They're refusing to answer any orders in English because, they say, it's the language of foreign occupation. And they're demanding to be taken back to Wales, or be given interpreters in Welsh. I know what I'd give them if I were governor!"

Vera had asked and eventually secured permission to get a message through to Roberts's girl friend, who had been up to see her.

"Welsh!" Vera said, the moment the SIS girl came through the door. "That's what I heard the Monk speaking on Rügen. He was a Welshman! And if you haven't got him already, it's in Wales that you're going to find him."

"I wonder," said Philby after listening to the story. "Yes, I suppose she's right. Where else would they be planning to send a Welsh-speaking agent but Wales?" He looked across at Roberts. "Have you talked to Arthur Owens?"

"We call him 'Snow,'" said Roberts reproachfully.

"And the Abwehr calls him 'Johnny,' and who the devil cares?" retorted Philby. "He's a Welsh Nat, isn't he? What does he tell us?"

"Nothing," said Roberts. "Snow is in jail, and he isn't saying anything except to tell us repeatedly that he doesn't know what we are talking about. For all I know, he may be telling the truth--for once. Anyway, when Snow decides not to talk, you'll never persuade him otherwise. He knows we're not going to hang him."

"Have you tried getting him drunk?"

Roberts winced as if at an unhappy memory.

"*In vino veritas*, you mean?" He shook his head. "That may be all right with ordinary drunks, but with Snow *veritas* usually turns out to be everything but what you really want to know, and to get him in that garrulous state takes more bottles than the petty-cash account can cope with."

They gazed together through the window at a double-decker bus carefully maneuvering its way around a gaping bomb crater in the middle of Victoria Street. Philby felt a gnawing at his own insides, indicating that he could do with a drink himself.

Roberts coughed delicately. "I wondered if Vera—" he began, then hesitated and started again. "I think I mentioned that Vera de Schallberg is the only person who has seen this Welsh-speaking character. She says she remembers him well, told Ann, in fact, that she would never forget him. Quite taken with him, she was, and I don't think there's any doubt she would recognize him at once if she saw him again. So—"

"Let me guess," said Philby. "So you think it might be a good idea if Vera were released, so she could start looking around Swansea or Cardiff or Conway Castle, or even Llandudno promenade, to see if she can't spot him egging on the Welsh Nats to revolt against the hated English?"

"Not quite," said Roberts, his lips tightening at Philby's levity. "I would like Vera de Schallberg released, yes—under proper conditions and controls, of course. And that's the real reason I've asked you round today, to get your backing and approval for an application to have the girl let out on probation." He glanced across at Philby and added: "Not that I want her to go grubbing around Wales to try to track down our friend. I don't agree with you about that. Why should the Nazis send coals to Cardiff, so to speak? The Welsh Nats don't need any Welsh-speaking outsiders around to keep them active. They're quite capable of thinking up their own mischief. No, I believe there's more likelihood that whoever's running him has sent him to London."

"And who *is* running him?" Philby asked.

"That's what we have to find out. I'm pretty sure it isn't the Abwehr. We'd have grabbed him by now." Roberts stared straight at Philby. "Will you back me up when I ask them to let Vera out?" As he saw Philby hesitating, he added: "It's more of a risk for her than it is for us, you know. She's already living on borrowed time. She knows she'll hang if she lets us down."

Philby grinned. "Okay. Why don't we let her find him for us, and then hang them both?"

Roberts looked quite shocked.

V

In the autumn of 1943, someone else was released from jail. The tide of war had turned and was now running in favor of the Allies, so Polly Wright managed to satisfy a panel of lawyers and upright citizens that sleeping with a German in Germany four years earlier no longer made her a threat to British home security. The notorious Regulation 18B was being relaxed, anyway, and she was not even asked to report to the police after she was let out of Holloway Prison. She spent an afternoon queuing at Marylebone Town Hall for a ration book, identity card, and clothing coupons, took a studio room and bath in a block of flats off George Street, and spent the next four hours lolling in the bath and shampooing her hair. That night she went to a concert given by the BBC Orchestra at the Albert Hall, and had another bath (of emotion, this time) as a program of John Ireland, Debussy, and Brahms washed over her. Since she knew practically every member of the orchestra, she did not go behind at the end of the concert, feeling some members might be embarrassed, especially her erstwhile husband. Instead, she waited for a bus and rode back to Regent Street and walked down Mortimer Street for a reviving drink at the Gluepot.

The first thing she saw, at the end of the bar, was the white profile of Lucille Long, sharp nose and glittering eyes framed against the black board of the partition. As usual, she was deep in conversation with a small group of men clustered around her, and Polly, still bruised from the experiences of the past two years, decided not to intrude.

She went up to the bar and was asking for a drink (May was not on duty that evening) when a loud voice shouted, "If you take any money from Mrs. Wright, I'll never patronize this lousy pub again!"

It was Lucille Long. She waited until a double gin-and-tonic had been poured, and then shouted again, "Now come on over here and tell us all about yourself."

Polly moved slowly down the bar, clutching her glass, trying not to appear conspicuous. She immediately felt herself grasped around the waist, pulled against Long's scrawny chest, and warmly kissed.

"Welcome home, Polly love," the composer said.

After they had snuffled against each other for a few moments, Long pulled away, looked at the four men with her, and announced, "This is one of my oldest and dearest friends, Polly Wright. She's just come back from a little vacation."

"An enforced vacation," Polly said. "And the weather wasn't good at all."

She felt the eyes of one of the men focused on her, and she looked at him. He was tall, young, good-looking, with astonishingly clear blue eyes.

Long said, "I gather you two have met before."

"That's right," said the Druid quickly. He smiled and looked deep and directly into her eyes. "Don't you remember?" he lied.

"Who could ever forget?" she said.

CHAPTER 8

Slips

I

THAT TOMMY HARRIS was inordinately fond of good food, good drink, and the pleasures of the flesh was not considered a vice or even a weakness by the friends who so often shared these precious wartime indulgences at his parties in Chesterfield Gardens. But they did chuckle among themselves over one of Tommy's little vanities. He was extravagantly proud of his powers of invention, of his ability to conjure characters and events out of thin air and give them life and substance, and he was often saddened by the realization that the world was never likely to learn what kind of brilliantly inventive work he was doing, and how invaluable it was to the war effort. He often complained of his enforced anonymity to those of his friends he could trust, most of whom were colleagues working either in the Double Cross System or other branches of the SIS: Kim Philby, Anthony Blunt, Guy Burgess, Donald Maclean, Nick Elliot, John Masterman, Graham Greene, Malcolm Muggeridge. Only the first four of them knew the full extent of Harris's many-sided activities—that he had a separate life with the KGB too, for instance—though Malcolm Muggeridge often suspected that he was, perhaps, not quite the straight-forward British intelligence officer he claimed to be. Alas, the world would never learn the real nature of his work, he complained, and would never read those quite wonderful passages of purple prose which he was regularly sending to the Abwehr on behalf of his spy and protégé, Garbo.

By the end of 1943, Garbo was having such a success in deceiving the Abwehr (under his Nazi operational name of Arabel) that the head of the Double Cross System was able to write: "The Garbo case went from strength to strength during the year. . . . Garbo himself turned out to be something of a genius. He was a master of a facile and lurid style of writing; he showed great industry and ingenuity coupled with a passionate and quixotic zeal for his task. Throughout the year he worked, on an average, six to eight hours a day drafting secret letters, encyphering, composing cover texts, and planning for the future. Moreover, in March he began to operate a wireless set, the purchase of which was arranged through his agent No. 4, who also recruited an amateur operator (featured as a Communist and supposed to be working for people he believed to be Spanish Reds). In fact, of course, he was one of our own operators. The Germans showed their trust by sending over for him the identical cypher then in use between certain German Secret Service stations. When later they changed, they entrusted Garbo with a new cypher based on the one newly introduced."[1]

By this time, Garbo had sent three hundred secret letters and well over a thousand radio messages to Lisbon, had organized a network of fourteen different agents in various parts of Britain, and had eleven well-placed "informants" in the government. All of them were fictitious, in fact, but Garbo made them and their information seem so genuine that the

[1] Masterman, *Double Cross System*.

Abwehr paid him more than any of their other agents in Britain, sending him £20,000 (about $70,000) in expenses and rewards.

It irked Tommy Harris that credit for this enormously successful masquerade was being given to the Spaniard Luis Calvo operating under the code names Arabel/Garbo, whereas he was simply the puppet in the hands of his master, who invented the plot, set the scene, and pulled the strings. The Druid by now had met the doe-eyed Luis, and had been told that he worked for a newspaper in Madrid. He speculated sometimes that Calvo might be an Abwehr agent, working through the Spanish embassy in London to get information back to Madrid and thence for Berlin. That would be a plausible explanation for his friendship with Harris, a good source of information with a sympathy for Spain and things Spanish. He was tempted to make closer contact with him; he needed a sympathizer now that Johnny was no longer around. But his instinct held him back. There was something about the Calvo-Harris association which smelled. One day he had noticed a letter to Thomas Harris (it turned out to be about a forthcoming art show) on a secretary's desk at CEMA and he offered to deliver it by hand on his way back to Chelsea.

When he was shown into the library at Chesterfield Gardens, Harris rose to his feet and came forward to greet him. But the Druid saw that Calvo was seated behind Harris at the desk, surrounded by sheets of paper, and that in the lamplight his face was dark with anger.

Calvo ignored the Druid's appearance and spat at Harris's back, in Spanish: *"I tell you it is too flowery! You make me write like a moonstruck girl!"*

"They like it that way," Harris replied, over his shoulder. *"I have invented a style for you."* He held out his hand to the Druid with a smile and said, in English: "My dear fellow, what a happy surprise. What can I do for you?"

"You also invented me, and I hate it!" he heard Calvo mutter.

"I brought this." The Druid handed over the envelope. "I didn't mean to disturb you."

"If you believe that, you will believe anything!" came a petulant whisper from Calvo, half to himself.

Harris showed no sign that he had heard the comment, but nevertheless, with gentle amiability, edged the Druid into the hall and then back onto the pavement of Chesterfield Gardens, giving only the most fleeting glance of reproach to the servant as he did so.

The Druid had obviously interrupted something. But what? Could it be that Harris was writing Calvo's newspaper dispatches for him? That seemed most unlikely. Could Harris be working for, and with, Calvo, helping him do a little espionage on the side for the Spanish—and the Germans? Somehow, he could not accept the Englishman in that role, not because he did not think him willing or capable of working for the other side, but because, in that case, Calvo would have been in the stronger position, capable of dominating and ordering Harris around, and only too evidently the opposite was so. But what other explanation was there? That Calvo and Harris were lovers? Maybe. But from what the Druid had observed at his parties, there was much more attractive talent—female talent—available to the Englishman among his own guests than this rather sulky, pasty-faced young Spaniard, and though sex might be involved, it would have to be something much stronger and compelling that bound them together. Again: but what?

He sent a message to his control in Lisbon asking for discreet inquiries to be made in Madrid and Berlin about the background and proclivities of a certain Luis Calvo. The reply came back from Hugo Hoffmann himself. It informed him that Calvo was the most successful agent the Abwehr had ever infiltrated into enemy territory, his achievements so invaluable that a campaign was being mounted in Berlin to have the Führer thank him personally—*if* he survived, of course, and when he returned to Berlin. In the meantime, there were rumors around the Tirpitzufer that he would shortly be made an "honorary German" in order that he might be decorated with the Iron Cross for his remarkable intrepidity.

The Druid queried:

ARE YOU REFERRING TO SAME PERSON? NAME IS CALVO REPEAT LUIS CALVO.

Hoffmann replied:

HANDLE WITH CARE. ARABEL IS ADMIRALS PET. DOES NOT BELIEVE WE CAN WIN WAR WITHOUT HIM.

The Druid was astounded. There was something wrong somewhere.

II

At one moment in the night, transported by the sheer ecstasy of having a man again, Polly Wright imagined that the one in her arms was her beloved Erich, and she cried out: *"Liebling! Liebling! Love me, fuck me, kill me!"* in German. She recalled later that the blue eyes above her blazed with sudden fury, the mouth opened and hissed the word "Whore!" (or was it the German word *"Hure"*?), and a pair of hands began pressing violently around her throat. Then abruptly the Druid pulled them apart and flung her to one side.

After a time she stirred, raised herself on an elbow, and said tentatively, "I didn't know you spoke German. You understood what I was saying, didn't you? I'm sorry. Did I shock you?"

He took his time answering, but presently turned over, smiled at her, and reached out an arm.

"Was that German?" he asked. "I thought you were speaking Yiddish or something. Gibberish, anyway. Shocked?" He laughed. "Come here!" and proceeded to surprise, if not shock, her. It was quite a performance, but not one which left her emotionally comfortable afterward, for there had been something altogether too clinical and calculated about it.

Later, lying there with his eyes closed, he said, "You *aren't* Jewish, are you?"

"Would it matter if I was?"

"No," he said. "I just wondered why they arrested you in Germany, just because you had a lover there. I thought it might be because of the race laws."

"It was," she said flatly. "I was English. England had gone to war and I'd become an enemy alien."

"Why didn't you marry him? That would have made you a German. Would you have minded that—turning your back on England, I mean?"

"He was married already," she said dryly. "So was I." And then added: "No, I wouldn't have minded changing my nationality. Not if it had meant staying with Erich. Anyway, England hadn't exactly done much for me even before they put me in jail. As for what I think of them now—" She stopped suddenly.

"You don't have to mind me," he said. "I hate the English too, for what they've done to my people. I'm Welsh, as you know. Where I come from, we think the English are as bad as the Nazis—even worse, maybe."

She looked at him to see if he was joking, and was startled when she realized he was not.

"And where *do* you come from?" she asked.

"A little place called Llanfyllin, in North Wales," he said.

"And what did the English do to you?" she asked. "Send your parents to a concentration camp? Rape your sister?"

He flushed angrily. "No, but they drove my people out of their homes, forced them to abandon their farms, made them go overseas because they had no freedom to live or to speak like Welshmen!"

"Now I know why there are so many Welshmen in London,"

she said, grinning, and thought for a moment that he was going to hit her. "Sorry," she added hastily, "I didn't realize you felt so strongly about things."

His blue eyes blazed at her, and then he too began to grin. "Take no notice of me," he said. "This Welsh blood of mine makes me get all worked up sometimes. But don't worry, I'm as loyal as the next man."

They were drinking a cup of tea and nibbling some toast she had made, with dried eggs scrambled over it, when she decided to risk the question.

"Why did you tell Lucille you knew me?" she asked. "You know bloody well we've never seen each other before in our lives until last night. How did you hear about me?"

His face had gone very pale. He licked his lips, put his hand over hers, squeezed, and said softly, "Did you mean it when you said you hated the English? You've every right, you know. More than I have. I wouldn't think of blaming you."

"I loathe the bastards," she said.

He looked relieved. He smiled at her.

"Shall I tell you why I hate the bastards too—the truth this time? And why I and the people who think like me would do anything to get back at them?"

"Oh, Christ," she said, "don't tell me you're one of those Welsh Nats!"

The Druid nodded. "Yes," he said, "and we're not going to stop until we've got the English pigs where we want them!"

As she stared at the glitter in his amazingly blue eyes, Polly Wright shivered. He was beginning to pull on her arm.

"Oh, God," she said, "as if I wasn't in enough trouble already!"

But she allowed herself to be drawn across the table until their mouths were touching. It only occurred to her later that he still hadn't answered her original question, and she still didn't know why he had come to the Gluepot to seek her out.

I I I

By the end of 1943 it was obvious that the Double Cross Committee would get suspicious if he put it off any longer, so Kim Philby announced that he was off to Lisbon to look into the Ostro problem. In the past four or five weeks, the GCCS had intercepted several messages from the Ostro Network to ABT1 in Hamburg, purportedly from agents inside Britain, and they were worrying. It was not that they contained devastatingly accurate news about British plans and operations; some of the statistics—about bomber and fighter production, for instance—were grossly wrong. But this was the period of the war when, the tide having turned, the British and the Americans had begun to plan seriously for the coming invasion of Fortress Europe. It would not be only loss of face for the Double Cross Committee but potential disaster for the Allies if it should turn out, just when signs of invasion preparations began to be manifest in every part of Britain, that three or possibly four genuine Nazi spies were on the loose, watching and reporting all the signs, perhaps becoming privy to plans and movements. Much would depend on secrecy to make the invasion a success and to deceive the Germans about when and where the landings would be made. For the Allies, it was the most pregnant period of the war, and they could not risk having Ostro's spies blowing the gaff on them. They had to be found and neutralized, and since they maintained no contact whatsoever with the double agents already captured and manipulated by the Double Cross Committee, they had to be traced back through their control—in Lisbon. It was Philby's task to find out the identity of this control and who and where were the agents he controlled.

It so happened that one of the Double Cross Committee's most successful double agents was in Lisbon at the same time as Philby. The daredevil Yugoslav playboy Dusko Popov (Tricycle) was now so well trusted by the British that he was allowed to pass freely inside and outside the country, and he had flown to Portugal to report to *his* Nazi control, Kreme von Auenrode. The Germans trusted Popov too, and considered him one of their most successful spies, so there was no question of Philby having any meeting with the Yugoslav in the Portuguese capital. But while in Lisbon, Popov had met up with an old college chum, a German named Johnny Jebsen, who worked for the Abwehr but was a none too secret anti-Nazi. Johnny brought alarming news.

As Popov wrote later:

Johnny discovered the existence of a special Abwehr ring in Lisbon called Ostro. The discovery temporarily upset our notions of having a monopoly on German spies in England.

"Ostro is run by someone called Paul Fidrmuc von Karmap,"[2] Johnny told me worriedly, "but I haven't much of a line on him. I don't know his background and I don't know if that's his real name, although I rather doubt it. He's running three agents, Ostro 1, Ostro 2, and Ostro 3. One and two are in the United Kingdom, Ostro 3 is in the United States."

"How long has Ostro been operating?" I asked. I was trying to figure how much damage the group might have done.

"Don't know. The Abwehr has been keeping Fidrmuc under cover. Even von Karsthoff [pseudonym of Popov's Lisbon control, Kreme von Auenrode] and Kamler [another Abwehr control in Lisbon] don't have any control over him. They have orders only to collect his information and send it . . . to Berlin."[3]

Popov duly reported this disturbing news to MI6, not knowing they were worrying about it already, and von Fidr-

---

[2] This was his full title.

[3] Dusko Popov, *Spy/Counter-Spy* (London: Weidenfeld & Nicolson, 1974).

muc's name was immediately relayed back to Philby in Lisbon. Now at least he knew whom he was looking for. His bosses in London naturally expected him to set the SIS's representatives in Portugal to the task of dogging von Fidrmuc's movements, to discover who he was and how he operated. What they did not realize was that Philby also informed his real masters, the KGB, of the nature of his mission. It did not take both services long to provide Philby with some extremely tantalizing information.

They told him, for instance, about von Fidrmuc's mistress Gertrude Körner, and revealed she was cheating on her lover —with another woman. And they also informed him that the other woman was none other than the wife of the chief Abwehr control officer in Lisbon, Kreme von Auenrode.

Philby was both amused and intrigued. Even more so when the SIS suggested some ways of exploiting this savory situation.

I V

For Christmas, 1943, the von Auenrodes gave a party at their small country estate at Sintra, a short distance from Lisbon, and since the Austrian was a gourmet of the old school there was no lack of good food and wine to satisfy the guests: vodka from Russia and Poland, Tokay and geese from Hungary, *Goldwasser* and other exotically colored liqueurs from Danzig, pâté de foie gras, wild boar, pheasants, and partridges from occupied France. There were quite a few Portuguese, Spaniards, and South Americans at the party, several of the choicer *poules de luxes* summoned from the Wonder Bar of the Estoril casino to dazzle and dally with the male guests, and a sprinkling of attachés from the German and other Axis embassies. Among the last was Gertrude Körner. Also at the party was Dusko Popov, the double spy, still in Lisbon reporting to his control on his activities in Britain.

Trudy had not brought Paul von Fidrmuc with her, since

the von Auenrodes had not invited him, and he would have been *de trop,* in any case, with Elizabeth von Auenrode around. It had been arranged for Trudy to stay the night so that, early the following morning, Elizabeth would drive her back to the embassy in Lisbon, where she would be picking up travel papers for a forthcoming trip. (The von Auenrodes had a rendezvous with Admiral Canaris in southern Spain in a few weeks' time.) They had, however, no intention of getting to the embassy until much later in the day, and drove, instead straight to the small villa which the Gestapo used for its varied activities, and which Trudy had arranged to be empty that day. They had a picnic basket of goodies from the Christmas party, and it would not have occurred to Trudy to be sensitive over the fact that the bed to which they would presently adjourn had once been the scene of a particularly brutal suffocation.

The SIS Portuguese specialists had been staking out the villa ever since the SS guard and the Portuguese maid had gone off together on Christmas morning. (As Cecil Gladhill, the SIS station chief, explained to Philby, the maid was a friend, and had let it be known that the Señora Körner was coming and wished to be alone because she was bringing someone with her.) They waited until the two women were well into their celebration, and then burst in upon them, announcing themselves as Portuguese police. The men acted suitably chastened when Trudy Körner angrily showed her papers and made it clear she had diplomatic status, but became officious again when Elizabeth von Auenrode could produce only an ordinary German passport. They proposed to take her into custody and make further inquiries, they said, since both women were unable to prove their right to be on the premises. Trudy looked alarmed at this, and Elizabeth panic-stricken. Was there no way of resolving this very awkward situation? The women reached for their purses and were sternly told to put them away.

But then the SIS assistant head of station, a suave half-Chinese, half-Portuguese from Macao, entered the bedroom and charmingly apologized to the two women "for this awkward interruption of your happy hour," as he put it. It was just possible, however, that all could be straightened out if a little information was exchanged. At this stage in the war, the Special Branch of the Portuguese police, which he represented, wished to have the fullest possible information about the activities of the various foreigners who were such welcome guests in his country. For example, Herr von Fidrmuc. Fräulein Körner had a relationship with him, did she not? He was supposed to be an exporter, but he did not seem to export very much. On the other hand, he did seem most prosperous, always so cheerful when he lost large sums of money at the casino. Where did it all come from? Were the rumors true that the British were spreading, that Herr von Fidrmuc was an intelligence agent, and that from Lisbon he was running a network of spies, several of whom continued to communicate with him from England? If so, who were they, and how did they communicate? The Portuguese authorities would like to know.

At which Trudy Körner burst into laughter. While Elizabeth von Auenrode stared at her in astonishment, she carefully explained to the slant-eyed man smiling so gently at her that von Fidrmuc was a hoax, a trickster, the biggest con man in the history of the intelligence game.

"He has no spy ring!" she said. "His Ostro Network doesn't exist. He makes up news from the newspapers and from the gossip he picks up, and then tells the Abwehr it came from his agents in England." She turned to Elizabeth von Auenrode. "And if you ever tell that to your husband or anyone else, I'll see that he finds out about us!" Then back to Slant Eyes. "So you see, he isn't any embarrassment to you at all. I can prove it. We have a statement from him, signed by him, at the embassy."

Slant Eyes shook his head skeptically.

"Why would you be willing to let him get away with it? What good is a false spymaster to you?"

Trudy glanced at Elizabeth.

"To keep the others on their toes," she said. "It spurs them on when they know they have a rival."

V

"Do you believe Körner's story?" Philby asked.

Gladhill nodded. "I didn't at first," he said. "Anything's possible in the spook world, of course. What I couldn't swallow was Körner and the SS accepting it. Then we got confirmation from the Abwehr boys themselves. Because you know what Elizabeth von Auenrode did? She went right back to her husband and told him all about it. She just couldn't resist revealing that von Fidrmuc was a fake. After all this time and all the worry they'd had, she was able to tell him that their big rival—the man who had always threatened their standing in the organization—was nothing but a clipper of newspaper items."

"And he accepted that?"

"Of course he didn't! Not right away. He wormed out of Elizabeth exactly how she had got hold of the story, what she'd been up to with Trudy Körner—all the gory details, I may say, which must have taken her quite a time to unburden —and then told her he'd forgive her. He didn't even order her to stop seeing Trudy again. But what he did do was go to see Trudy himself, telling her Elizabeth had confessed, and saying he wouldn't make any kind of fuss or scandal with the SS— because, of course, Himmler and Kaltenbrunner don't like lesbians one little bit—so long as she showed him proof that von Fidrmuc was a fake."

"And she proved it?"

Gladhill nodded vigorously this time. "Dug a document out of her safe showing Fidrmuc's signed and sealed admission that there was no such thing as an Ostro Network. Of course it wasn't the original confession. She'd sent that off to Berlin. But this was a witnessed second copy. It convinced von Auenrode all right."

"How do you know?" asked Philby.

"Because," said Gladhill, "the first thing he did when he got back to his office was send out a message to Dusko Popov, our very own Tricycle, to come over for a celebration. He had a magnum of champagne and a pot of caviar and he told him the whole story. They got pissed as newts between them, and I can't blame them, I must say. It's as much a relief to us as it is to von Auenrode, knowing the Ostro Network is a figment of Fidrmuc's imagination. Wait till they hear about it in Ryder Street! Let's get the message drafted right away, shall we? I'd like to see old J. C. [Masterman]'s face when he realizes we've got the Double Cross Committee off the hook."

"Let's do that," Philby said.

As a result of the message which they enciphered between them, Philby and Gladhill once and for all ended SIS anxiety over the Ostro Network.

As Dusko Popov wrote later:

Sending Kim Philby to Lisbon [and] by our combined efforts, we soon knew more than the Abwehr about Fidrmuc.

Ostro was a magnificent hoax. Fidrmuc was operating alone. Ostro 1, 2 and 3 were ghosts. They were what is known in the trade as notional. Furthermore, Fidrmuc never did any actual spying. He based his reports on rumours, on what he could cull from periodicals, and, foremost, on his fertile imagination. And for this he milked the Abwehr royally and ingeniously, accepting only part payment in cash, the rest being in art objects, which he sold at high profit.[4]

[4] Popov, *Spy/Counter-Spy*.

163

But if Gladhill, Popov, von Auenrode, and the Double Cross Committee were convinced that the whole scare had been nothing more than a false alarm, Kim Philby was not so sure. Something still nagged at him, though he could not quite pin it down. And then, just before he was due to return to London, he had a conversation with a KGB control in Lisbon, who handed him a message from Ernst, his case officer in London. The message said:

IF OSTRO IS FAKE, ASK HOW HE GOT SO CLOSE TO TORCH OPERATION? WHO GAVE HIM CODE WORD FLAMME? OR IS HE FAKIR NOT FAKER?

That was it! Ernst's implied rebuke was timely, because it was von Fidrmuc's uncanny prescience over the North African operation which had been worrying Philby too. His KGB colleagues agreed with him that it was time they went to have a consultation with Paul von Fidrmuc personally about the exact nature and quality of his Ostro operation.

Philby had in his possession some photographs which, he surmised, might be of some aid to him in furthering the purpose of the conversation. They had been taken by the SIS before they finally burst in on Trudy Körner and Elizabeth von Auenrode during their romantic rendezvous at the SS villa. They did not leave much doubt about the exact character and nature of the encounter between the two women. And Philby suspected that von Fidrmuc, who was known to have old-fashioned ideas about relations between the sexes, might not take too kindly to the pictures which Philby proposed to show him, and might be far less forgiving toward his mistress than von Auenrode had been toward his wife.

It was in the first week of January, 1944, that the opportunity came. Kreme and Elizabeth von Auenrode had left by car for Madrid, on their way to their rendezvous with Admiral Canaris. (The meeting place was subsequently changed to Biarritz, France, when the Spanish unexpectedly indicated that the Abwehr chief's presence could cause them embarrassment.) Trudy Körner had been urgently recalled to Berlin for consultations at SS headquarters. There were strong rumors running around Lisbon that dramatic changes were taking place in the Abwehr, and that the SS was about to move in. Philby and his KGB advisers calculated that von Fidrmuc, already worried about his status in the organization, was likely to be in a jittery state. Especially as he had no one around to consult. They had confirmation of their surmise when it was reported that the Sudeten was visiting the casino every night, and gambling more heavily than ever.

V I

Kim Philby always liked coming to Lisbon, and as head of the Iberian sector of the SIS he had a valid reason. As he sat sipping his whisky in the Wonder Bar of the Estoril casino, he reflected that it looked more like the film set for a spy thriller than ever. In one way or another, practically every person in sight was mixed up in the intelligence game. Vasco, the Portuguese barman, kept his ears open for gossip and sold it to the appropriate embassy the following morning. The high-priced house tarts were of various nationalities, but they remained indiscriminate in their choice of clients, were expert at going through their clients' pockets in the early hours, and had no compunction in selling whatever secrets they found to an enemy embassy, provided it was willing to pay more than a friendly one. Portuguese businessmen, Spanish journalists, South American traffickers in drugs and women, all sold intelligence on the side. And, in addition, there were the professionals. At a table in the corner of the bar, Gladhill, the SIS station chief in Lisbon, was drinking with a colleague from London, Ian Fleming, and both of them were watching their secret collaborator Dusko Popov passionately embracing a dark-eyed

Spanish beauty, who, they all knew, worked for the Abwehr.[5]
A young American was quietly drowning his sorrows in drink
along the bar, looking as if the roof had fallen in on him.
Philby was aware that it had done just that. The Yank was a
newly arrived operator from the OSS (Office of Strategic Services) gung ho to do something to win the war, who had broken
into the Japanese embassy a few nights earlier and stolen a
code—only to be ordered sternly by Washington to put it
back at once, before the Japs discovered its loss and changed
it. The Americans had already broken the code and were reading the Japanese messages.

Then there were the Germans, most of them these days too
busy watching each other to watch the enemy's agents. Ernst
Kamler, a relative newcomer for the Abwehr, was being closely
observed by Gustav Schröder, an operator from the RSHA,
and both of them were being furtively examined by a mysterious character named Dr. Heinrich Kösler, who ostensibly
spied for the Germans but might have divided loyalties since,
as the SIS and the KGB knew, he was a Jew. Then there were
the KGB operators, a couple of Polish cloakroom attendants,
three Portuguese croupiers, and two Hungarian *poules de
luxes,* none of them Russian but all of them, as Philby knew,
with loyalties transcending class, creed, position, breeding, and
nationality.

Only Paul von Fidrmuc (Philby wryly reflected) seemed
utterly unlike a professional spy. His beautifully kempt gray-
flecked hair, his brown clean-cut features, his admirably tai-
lored dark suit, his strong hands with their long, manicured
fingers, all proclaimed him an ex-officer and a gentleman, with
a pedigree undoubtedly taking up a page of the *Almanach de
Gotha.* Philby could picture him in princely dress moving
among his aristocratic peers at the Congress of Vienna, or
leading a gallant cavalry charge across a forest clearing on
the outskirts of Pressburg. He held his cards, surveyed his op-

[5] Fleming later used Popov as his model for the spy novels featuring
the intrepid British agent James Bond.

ponents, and played his chips with an elegance and aloofness learned from generations of gambling parties in royal ante-chambers, and his *sang-froid* when he lost, as he was doing tonight, was remarkable. The only clue to his state of mind was the nerve jumping in a vein on his temple, and it took another skilled gambler, like his sweaty Greek opponent or the suave and watchful croupier, to guess that von Fidrmuc was losing because he was not concentrating, and that there were other things on his mind.

It was two o'clock in the morning before he finally gathered up the last of his chips. There were so few that he did not bother to cash them in, but threw them in a gesture to the croupier, and then rose to go. Passing through the bar, he took in the motley gang of assorted agents with the slightest wrinkle of his aristocratic nose, but did not acknowledge any of them, though Philby guessed that he had seen and recognized every one. He drove an Alfa Romeo and it had been brought to the door by an attendant and was waiting for him. Philby paid his bill and followed, driving back to Lisbon in a beat-up Jaguar loaned him by an attaché at the British embassy. He was in no hurry. He knew von Fidrmuc would be waiting for him. The KGB would make sure he did not go anywhere unobserved.

Presently he parked his car on a corner behind the Praça do Comércio and walked to the cozy little house where von Fidrmuc lived and ran his import-export business. He rang the bell, stepped back so he could be plainly seen under the overhead light by someone studying him through the peep-hole, and waited patiently for the door to open. When it did so, von Fidrmuc, in a dressing gown, was facing him.

"I have no gun," said Philby. "I have no one with me. But I would like to talk to you."

He had spoken in German, but it was in English that von Fidrmuc replied.

"Come in, Mr. Philby," he said. "What could you possibly want with me at this unearthly hour?"

VII

It must have been quite an encounter. Rarely during World War II did two such sharp, worldly, and expert professional spies come together in such a confrontation. Here were two men whose whole careers as secret agents were based on bluff—on their ability to deceive, outwit, and outmaneuver their superiors in two of the world's most vaunted intelligence systems. For twelve years, at least, Kim Philby had persuaded the SIS in London that he was a loyal, right-minded Briton spying bravely for his King and country, never allowing his British employers to guess he had a far stronger and more fanatic allegiance to the spy network of the Soviet Union. For six years in Lisbon, Paul von Fidrmuc had built up a masterly edifice of deception, persuading the Abwehr he controlled a network which, in reality, existed only in his imagination, living on his wits and getting munificently paid for it in a world where one slip could mean his death. Two urbane men of the world staying alive by perilous confidence trickery, and showing hardly a sign of nerves in the process.

As Philby later explained to his KGB control, Ernst, the winner of this confrontation would inevitably be the one who gave away the least, and, unfortunately for "von Fid," as Philby called him, it was the Briton who held all the cards. They sparred for a time, as rival agents do, and exchanged odd scraps of intelligence which they guessed the adversary already knew. Had he heard, Philby asked von Fidrmuc, that the French ambassador's mistress had not only been found selling secrets to the Gaullists, but had also got herself pregnant by the U.S. naval attaché? And did Philby know that the Turkish third secretary and the assistant barman at the Wonder Bar had both consulted the same doctor about a dose of VD, and had one given it to the other, or had both of them got it from the wife of the Hungarian press secretary?

Philby accepted a second glass of whisky and then casually

remarked that the British knew von Fidrmuc was a phony and his Ostro Network a fake. Certain circles in the Portuguese police had apparently stumbled on his little secret. Hadn't Frau Körner told him about it? She had paid them a nice little sum in American dollars from the German embassy secret funds to keep quiet about it, but you know how greedy the Portuguese were becoming these days. They had decided their discovery was worth a little more than Frau Körner had given them, and the British, once they knew what they were getting, had agreed with them. So what was von Fidrmuc going to do about it?

The Sudeten carefully lit one of his Russian cigarettes and screwed it into its jade holder. He took a delicate sip of his cup of steaming tisane. He smoked and sipped.

"Do?" He shrugged his shoulders. "Why should I do anything?"

Because, said Philby, the SIS had ways and means of blowing the gaff on von Fidrmuc and letting the Abwehr know about Ostro. Once Canaris had learned how he had been cheated, life wouldn't be very comfortable for von Fidrmuc in Lisbon any more—if there was any more life left for him.

The Sudeten smiled, still unperturbed. "My people would never fall for it. They would know it was a British trick."

Ah, but what if Frau Körner confirmed it? As, Philby pointed out, she had already confirmed it to the Portuguese police.

"I don't believe it!" Von Fidrmuc was becoming annoyed. "She has no reason to tell such a ridiculous story."

At which Philby took out of his wallet the embarrassing series of photographs of Trudy Körner and Elizabeth von Auenrode taken during the most compromising moments of their encounter at the villa. For the next few moments, the Sudeten studied the anatomical contortions of his mistress and her girl friend, and Philby noted with satisfaction that, for the first time since their meeting, the telltale vein in the other man's temple had started jumping.

Finally, he took one of the pictures, holding it by his polished nails as if it were a piece of garbage in a pair of tongs, and said, "Did Frau Körner tell *her* what she told the police?"

Philby looked at the sweat-laden, ecstatic face of Elizabeth von Auenrode, and nodded.

"Then why should I worry about what you British are going to do?" asked von Fidrmuc. "That little tart will already have told her husband, and he will have passed it on to the Abwehr. It's all up with me, anyway."

"I think not." Philby was confident now that he had his man. "Why should von Auenrode tell Berlin? He's in enough trouble already, and your playful little friend Trudy can, I feel, be trusted to take care of him if he talks. And why should he, anyway? If he gets rid of you, they send a replacement— and new worries and new rivalries to plague his life. Whereas, now he knows about you . . ."

There was a long pause while von Fidrmuc digested the unpalatable facts. Philby watched him staring down at one of the more explicit pictures on the table, and there was an expression of ineffable distaste on the Sudeten's patrician features. Finally, he sighed.

"I've never got used to that sort of thing," he said. "Have you?"

"No," Philby said.

He sighed again. "All right. I seem to be in the market. The question is, what do you want to buy? In return for your silence about Ostro, of course."

"Who gave you the news about Operation Torch?" asked Philby. "If I remember rightly, you called it 'Flamme'. That's too near to be a wild Ostro guess. How did you come by it?"

As Philby told his Soviet control later, all sorts of things must have been going through von Fidrmuc's mind at that moment. Panic, of course, at the thought that the SIS could blow his comfortable wartime niche in Lisbon. Fear, also, over what was going to happen to him in the near future if, as now seemed only too likely, Germany lost the war. But sheer blazing anger and disgust, too, at Trudy Körner for what she had been up to behind his back—and maybe that was the strongest emotion of all, and the reason for his sudden decision.

"You may be interested to know," he said abruptly, "that the Ostro network isn't *entirely* a fake. I have one spy working for me in England." He smiled. "The Abwehr doesn't even know he exists. He's been in England since 1941, and you haven't found out about him either. He really is something special, and the only trouble is that he's Trudy Körner's baby. The SS sent him."

He paused and looked slyly across at Philby, as if he guessed that the Briton was desperately trying to keep his mouth shut, trying not to ask: *Who is he?*

"He is a most able and successful agent," von Fidrmuc finally went on, "and, in a way, in spite of Trudy, I'm proud of him."

He paused again. Philby was almost bursting.

"His code name is the Druid," the Sudeten said at last. "I'll tell you all about him—in return for certain guarantees."

Philby waved an arm. "Oh, I don't think there'll be much trouble about that," he said. "Providing you don't want us to guarantee that we won't win the war."

CHAPTER 9

Takeover

I

As IT HAPPENED, Philby moved in on von Fidrmuc just in time.
Another day or so, and it would have been too late. For on
February 13, 1944, Adolf Hitler's faith in Admiral Canaris and
the Abwehr was finally shattered by a series of intelligence
blunders in Spain, and he agreed with Heinrich Himmler
that the whole organization, including its overseas espionage
network, should be turned over to the RSHA. The SS were in
control, and they knew all about Ostro anyway.

Trudy Körner came back in triumph to Lisbon to inform
Elizabeth von Auenrode that her husband was being posted
at once to Vienna, but hinted that Elizabeth need not go with
him. Trudy had a job lined up for her at the German embassy
in Lisbon, and asked her to stay. To her surprise and anger,
Elizabeth elected to accompany Kreme von Auenrode to Austria. For her sexual comforts, Trudy Körner found herself
thrown back into the arms of her erstwhile lover von Fidrmuc.
However much she might have sighed, the new/old arrangement was at least politically convenient.

Nor did she have to keep any SS secrets from von Fidrmuc. They shared the knowledge of the Druid's existence, which she had concealed from Elizabeth; and even if von Fidrmuc's Ostro Network was now blown to the British, neither they nor anyone else outside a small circle in the RSHA knew they had an SS spy operating inside Britain. Or so she thought. (For von Fidrmuc kept one secret from Trudy. He did not tell her about Philby's visit—or his own confession to him about the Druid.)

The moment in Berlin that she learned that Ernst Kalten-brunner had taken over control of the Abwehr and that Walter Huppenkothen had moved into an office next to Canaris at the Tirpitzufer, Trudy had brought up the question of the Druid's future activities. Should he now be asked to cooperate with the Abwehr's spies in Britain? Should Arabel and Cato and Fritz and all the rest of the network be told that, ever since 1941, a Nazi comrade had been among them? It was Hugo Hoffmann, sensing danger in his bones, who persuaded them otherwise. He was all for preserving the Druid's status as a lone wolf, emphasizing that any revelation of his existence outside the secret circle could start all sorts of trouble—resentment among Abwehr personnel in Germany, possible anger and rebellion among the agents in Britain, and danger to the Druid himself.

Paul von Fidrmuc was entirely in agreement with this decision when Trudy informed him of it. He did not tell his mistress that his reasons for preferring the Druid's continued isolation were quite different from those of the SS. His were bound up with Kim Philby's visit, and what had passed between them.

It was a moment when everyone in the foggy world of espionage was keeping secrets from so-called friends as well as acknowledged enemies. When Philby had talked to von Fidrmuc and made promises to him about his postwar future, Philby had deliberately failed to mention he was acting on behalf of the KGB and not for the SIS. And when he got back to England, he made no mention whatsoever to the SIS that he had had a session with von Fidrmuc. So far as his British superiors were concerned, the man was simply the imaginative chief of a nonexistent spy network whose fantasies had now been revealed—and his danger discounted.

On the other hand, not only the SS knew the secret of the Druid's presence in England. Von Fidrmuc had revealed it to Kim Philby, and he had passed it on to the KGB.

Would they now warn the British about him? Or, as Philby guessed, keep it to themselves? For the Druid, it was the most dangerous moment of his mission, and there was no one around to warn him.

II

The Anglo-American planners had given the code name "Overlord" to the invasion of Europe, which was due to take place some time in the summer of 1944, and "Neptune" was that part of it in which the combined navies of the two nations participated in getting the armies safely onto the enemy shores. The job of the deception forces attached to General Dwight Eisenhower's Supreme Headquarters Allied Expeditionary Force (SHAEF) was to conceal not the fact that an invasion was coming—the Nazis already knew it was inevitable—but just when, where, and in what strength. For this purpose, the double spies captured by the British and turned against the Nazis were mobilized in a combined attempt to underscore the deception and confuse their former Nazi masters about the intentions of the Allies.

"From the beginning of 1944," wrote J. C. Masterman, "all our activities were swallowed up in the one absorbing interest of the grand strategic deception for the Normandy invasion. The climax which we had hoped for from the beginning was approaching and all other aspects of the work sank into insignificance—at least for the time. It will be remembered that we had always expected that at some one moment all the agents would be recklessly and gladly blown sky high in carrying out the grand deception, and that this one great coup would both repay us many times over for all the efforts of the previous years and bring our work to an end.[1]

As a result of Dusko Popov's consultations in Lisbon with his Nazi controls, it was known that the Abwehr particularly trusted three of their espionage networks in Britain: one run by a Polish officer named Captain Roman Barby-Czerniawski, known to the British as "Brutus" and to the Germans as "Armand"; one operated by Luis Calvo, who was, as we know, "Garbo" to the British and "Arabel" to the Germans; and Popov, "Tricycle" to the British and "Ivan" to the Abwehr. Their reliability so far as the Nazis were concerned had been carefully built up by the care and ingenuity of their case officers, who had allowed them to send over solidly accurate, and sometimes quite risky, information in an effort to bolster their reputations. The idea was that when they did come to send over false news to the Nazis, to put them off the scent about D-Day and the invasion, they would be believed, and the bait swallowed and acted on.

But then, in the spring of 1944, something happened which threatened the success of the whole plan, and it had, ironically enough, nothing to do with espionage. Dusko Popov's old German college chum Johnny Jebsen was arrested in Lisbon by Gestapo officers looking into Abwehr records. They discovered that, like many another Abwehr member, he had grossly falsified his expense accounts when traveling on missions for the agency, and had also been involved in some large and very murky deals in black-market currency. The trouble was that not only was Jebsen an anti-Nazi but he also knew both Popov and Luis Calvo were double spies. In an effort to buy his freedom, or while being questioned under

[1] Masterman, *Double Cross System.*

drugs or torture, he might reveal the fact that two of the Abwehr's spies in Britain had been "turned," and that would blow everything.

It turned out that Jebsen, who was smuggled back to Germany from Portugal in a tin trunk by the Gestapo, and subsequently beaten to death by them, never did betray his connections. Meanwhile, however, the situation was considered to be so fraught with dire possibilities that the Double Cross Committee, after several hours of deep discussion, decided to abort a planned new visit by Popov to Lisbon and take him and his network entirely out of the game. The decision frustrated and angered the Yugoslav. Thomas Harris, who was also present at the meeting, felt called upon to suggest that the Garbo circuit suffer the same fate, rather than risk hazarding the D-Day deception program, and he was close to tears when he arrived back at Chesterfield Gardens to convey the bad news to his Spanish puppet Luis Calvo. His sorrow turned to joy the same evening, however, when Arabel/Garbo's control signaled from Madrid that, in recognition of his sterling work under most persistently dangerous conditions, the new SS masters of the Abwehr had agreed to back a recommendation that he be awarded a medal by the Führer. Obviously, Jebsen had kept silent—at least about Calvo.

They were still in business! Tommy Harris's instinct was to celebrate, and a few days later he summoned all his many friends to a party.

III

The Druid was going up in the world, musically speaking. He no longer trundled the Zandvoort Players on their dogged round of recitals to Wigan, Thetford, Oswaldtwistle, and Carlisle, nor even had to coax unwilling orchestral players to spend their free time lecturing and demonstrating their talents to factory workers around London. One of his superiors, noting his willingness for hard work, impressed by his enthusiasm for music, and charmed by his manner and lilting Welsh voice, had recommended him to a sister organization as a liaison with the Music Department of the BBC. He now had an identity card enabling him to enter several departments of the broadcasting organization, was able to attend BBC concerts in studios and at the Albert Hall, and was on nodding terms with several conductors and drinking terms with several of the players. In the Gluepot one day, the critic Ralph Hill, who had given him his first introduction to CEMA and now treated him like a favorite son, forecast big things for him in the postwar musical world if he played his cards right.

"There's no telling where you might end up," he said. "The field is wide open. I'm sitting on a committee drafting a proposal for a new council of the arts once the war is over. It will have supervisory powers over everything—theatre, opera, music, museums, art galleries, the lot. There's a K in it for whoever gets that job, and lots of gongs for those who assist him. Stay with it! You can go a long way."

The RSHA had ambitions for him too.

He had been informed by now of the SS's takeover of the Abwehr, and there had been exhortatory messages from both Kaltenbrunner and Huppenkothen urging him to be first and most authoritative with news of the Anglo-American invasion plans. "Wales and the services of one particular Welshman will not be forgotten when the day of victory comes!" signaled Kaltenbrunner. "Germany never forgets her friends."

Hugo Hoffmann was less declamatory but no less dramatic. "Situation has not changed," he signaled. "You are still on your own. Stay that way."

The Druid had found it so simple to settle into life in London, and in the musical and artistic circles where he moved so freely and easily, that he was jolted when a crisis came up, as it did about this time. Polly Wright was anything but demanding, and she never showed any resentment when days passed and they did not meet or go back to her studio flat to make love. There was a tacit understanding that the demands of his job, plus, of course, his association with the Welsh Nationalists, whatever they were, took up most of his time. He was sure she had no suspicion that he was only seeing her at all because otherwise she might speculate about him, and share her speculations with her friends. As it was, she seemed content, never complained of being neglected, and asked no questions.

He always knew where to find her. So long as the pub was open, she would be in the Gluepot, propping up the bar. One night when he arrived just before closing time, he found her huddled in a corner with a young man who, to judge by the sound of his voice and the wild waving of his arms, was drunk. The Druid had heard talk about a Welsh poet named Dylan Thomas, who worked for the BBC, and here he was. He halted in mid-flow as Polly sighted the Druid approaching and waved and smiled to him. He swung round with his pendulous lips pouted in resentment, his plump cheeks pink with annoyance.

"Who dares to interrupt the bard?" he thundered.

"Only a fellow-Welshman would dare," replied the Druid, holding out his hand.

He turned to the bar and asked May for a round of drinks, and when he rejoined them, glasses balanced in his hand, he found Thomas's piggy eyes angrily regarding him.

"Say something in Welsh!" he said belligerently. "Let us hear this minstrel boy!"

With an apologetic shrug to Polly, the Druid began to recite a little poem by Emyr Humphreys:

> "I was born on the softer side
> Of a mountain crag by Llanfyllin . . ."

which he had learned as a child at his grandfather's knee. He let the musical words sound their fullest and most bell-like tones, and saw first pleasure and then puzzlement cross over Thomas's features.

When he had finished, Thomas said, "And where did you

178

learn your Welsh, cocky?"

"At my grandfather's knee," the Druid said.

"Where, in what country?"

"Where else but Wales?" the Druid said.

"Where else but Wales he says!" retorted Thomas. "I don't believe a word of it, my peacock! If you learned that in Wales, then your grandfather was born in Barcelona! I don't speak Welsh myself, but I have an ear for it like a divining rod, and it cannot be deceived. There's a Spanish sound in that Welsh you speak, my cockalorum, and señoritas lurking in your family closet. Have you looked up the bones in your skeleton cupboard? There's castanets among them, I'll swear!"

The Druid forced a grin. "Then they must have come over with the Armada," he said.

"Time, gentlemen and ladies, please!" called May from behind the bar.

"Just one more quick round, my sweet and darling May!" cried Thomas, turning quickly toward the counter.

Polly Wright was looking quizzically at the Druid.

"Saved by the bell," she said, half to herself.

I V

Unlike most of the other European nations overrun and occupied by the Nazis, the Danes had no government-in-exile in London. The king and his administration had stayed behind to sweat it out with their people, and what Danish freedom fighters there were around in Britain had been hived off into the armed forces of Free Norway, where they shared similar Scandinavian language and common traditions. It was in the uniform of a Free Norwegian that Vera de Schallberg found herself outfitted in the spring of 1944, when she arrived in London from her jail in Shropshire. To keep her out of trouble or access to information, she was given a dull job helping in a supply depot in Hammersmith. Her immediate superior, a burly blond sergeant from Stavanger, shared his countrymen's susceptibilities to pretty women, and had a hard time keeping his hands off his slim and extremely attractive assistant, but he had been warned that meddling or harassment would mean instant transferral to a ditchdigging job with the Pioneer Corps, and that dread prospect quenched any temptation he might have otherwise had to take a risk. He kept the girl slogging at her job from eight in the morning until five in the afternoon, but otherwise her time was her own. She lived in a dormitory behind Olympia, reported three times a week to an office in a side street off the Pimlico Road, and was glad to be free and alive.

She knew exactly what she had to do. But in a city which was now literally teeming with young men, all in uniform, of a score of nationalities, how on earth was she going to pick out one—even if she was positive she would never forget him? How could she (and how could the British) even presume that the Germans had sent him over here? Yet she had a hunch that, despite the mild manners of the British intelligence men who had freed her, the prospects of her surviving the war were by no means good if she failed to find the Monk, as she still continued to call him.

It was Ann, the tall and friendly girl from the SIS, who did her best to try to help her. She gave her the names of three different Welsh service clubs in London where soldiers and civilians were wont to gather for social evenings; and she learned to play housey-housey (bingo) with lonely Cardiff businessmen; drank warm brown beer with two corporals from the Welsh Guards who taught her how to swear in Welsh; and danced an exhilarating boogie-woogie with an American GI, who, it turned out, was named Emlyn Davies, had strings of relatives in the Welsh valleys, but lived in a colony of expatriates in Lancaster, Pennsylvania. But not even the guardsmen spoke anything but Welsh cusswords and none of them, or anyone else she saw, bore the faintest resemblance to the beautiful young poet she had seen only once in her life, on a

Baltic beach on Rügen, but would never forget.

And then one night she went with a Dutch girl to a concert given by the BBC orchestra under Adrian Boult at the Albert Hall. The place was packed for a program of Delius, Vaughan Williams, and Tchaikowsky, and they were lucky to get two seats on the front row of the top balcony. It was just toward the last surging crescendo of the "Pathétique" that she happened to glance down at one of the boxes along the opposite side of the auditorium, one which had a glass partition in front of it so that the BBC could use it for making announcements during the program. She saw first the BBC's broadcaster seating himself before the microphone, getting ready to announce the end of the program. And then a door behind him opened and a young man came in, moved toward the announcer, and leaned forward to say something to him.

"It's the Monk, it's the Monk!" whispered Vera excitedly. Everybody around her hushed her to be silent.

Ignoring them, she bounced to her feet, brushed past her startled companion, and then climbed first up to the top exit and then down staircase after staircase, to the level of the orchestra boxes, hoping she would arrive in time. But by the time she finally made it, the audience was already streaming through the exits, the last of the applause was dying down, and in the BBC's box a mechanic was unscrewing the microphone. She peered desperately through the thickening mob, but it was hopeless.

Next morning the telephone rang in Kim Philby's office, and it was Denzil Roberts on the other end. There was the faintest tinge of excitement in his prim, thin tones.

"I say, do you know what?" he said. "Vera thinks she has seen him."

"Who?" Philby asked.

"Why, the man she calls the Monk, that's who. The Welsh heartthrob."

Philby's heart missed a beat.

V

There were three officers in army battle dress in the Gluepot that evening, and the Druid wondered at once what foreign force they could possibly belong to. It did not for a moment occur to him that they might be English; they were too flabby, looked too unfit, and, in one case, at least, too old. Yet they had British service ribbons up, recording the fact that they had seen action in the Middle East and Italy, and the youngest of the three even sported parachute wings on his arm, indicating, the Druid knew, that he had completed a course in airborne combat. All of them were talking at once, loudly and confidently, and they were positively flashing their money around, flipping a note across to May every time she poured them a gin or a whisky, to persuade her to make it a double.

"Bloody war correspondents!" said Polly Wright. "Supposed to be over here for the invasion. If it doesn't happen soon, they'll drink the place dry."

Now he could see the insignia—*War Correspondent*, in gold thread on black—threaded through their epaulettes, and the sight of them was like a talisman to him. Here were a trio who would know where they were going, and probably when.

"Know them?" he asked.

"I know one of them," said Polly Wright. "The old one with the gray hair. That's Dickie Capell. Used to be the *Telegraph* music critic. Now he's a war correspondent! Can you imagine? All he knows about war is the *1812 Overture!*" She looked at him. "Want to meet him?"

He nodded and she began to move down the bar.

"At least," she said, grinning, "you won't have to buy them a drink."

In fact, the first thing he did was offer them a round, and had his hospitality returned several times over. It seemed that this was something of a reunion for the three newsmen.

The last few months had seen them dispersed to different war fronts, in Egypt, Algeria, and Italy. Now they were together again, and there was no need to explain what prospect it was that had brought it about.

"The vultures are gathering," said Capell solemnly, and a rictus of distaste crossed his gentle face.

"*And* it's about time," said the youngest of the trio. "God knows we've been waiting long enough."

He caught the deliberately puzzled expression on the Druid's face, and burst into laughter.

"You don't know what we're talking about, do you?" he said.

"Aw, he can't be that thick," said the middle one. "We're here for the invasion, chum. Everybody knows that! It's no secret. Jerry's been talking about it for months. The only thing the Hun doesn't know is where it's going to take place, and when."

"My guess," said the youngest, "is the Pas-de-Calais. Only hope they don't drop me and my lot on Cap Gris-Nez. I'd hate to get the sharp end of Blériot's Memorial up my arse."

"And I think it's going to be Bordeaux," said the middle one, "with a clean, straight run through central France to the Rhine."

"No doubt," said Capell, "with magnums of Château Margaux to fuel you on the journey." He turned to the Druid. "Yes, it is true we are here for the invasion. But as you have no doubt gathered from this idle chatter, none of us has the vaguest notion when and where it will take place."

"Come off it, Dickie," said the youngest one. "You can't tell me you don't have a theory. You must have tried to work out where it's going to be, just like the rest of us. How about an airborne landing on Beethoven's birthplace in Bonn? Or would you prefer Bayreuth?"

"I have a feeling," the ex-music critic said mildly, "that Shakespeare could give me a better clue than the German composers. What about *Henry the Fifth*, for instance? 'For

God, for Harry and Saint George!' Doesn't that little speech come during an invasion of France? Before Harfleur, wasn't it—in Normandy?"

There was a pause, and then the youngest one said, "Let's have one for the road, shall we?"

Capell turned to the Druid.

"They tell me the Americans have made a new recording of the Bruckner Number Six. Have you heard it, by any chance? Monteux and the Philadelphia, I believe. An arduous experience to have to listen to it, I always think. Just like climbing Mount Everest."

As they were walking home, the Druid asked Polly if she had a copy of *Henry the Fifth*. She laughed and said he had better go to Marylebone Public Library next morning and ask for the volume of Shakespeare's plays.

VI

Though the days of the Luftwaffe's blitz on London were long since gone, the British capital was still feeling the sting of Nazi bombs. A series of what came to be known as "scalded cat raids" had been unleashed, with small flights of fast Heinkels nipping in to drop loads at random. The Druid reported back to his control that the effect of the raids, though not heavy in toll of life, limb, and property, was psychologically most effective. He urged more of them. "The British are just not in the mood to take any more," he signaled, to which Berlin, through Lisbon, signaled back: "Don't worry. More much more is coming." Among the missiles the German planes were dropping was something the British called a "butterfly bomb," which came down with a flutter, looked harmless on the ground, was extremely hard to defuse even by the most intrepid bomb experts, and was good for blowing off an arm, a leg, or taking out an eye. The daughter of a regular at the Gluepot had picked one up out of a gutter and would now have to go through life—provided she survived the war, of course—minus an eye, her left breast, and three fingers. Ironically, though the course of the war had irreversibly changed in the Allies' favor, the endurance of the British civilian population was just about at the breaking point. The Druid reported that more of the English were listening each night to Hamburg radio to hear what Lord Haw-Haw was saying; and the dire threats he was repeating, in his haughtiest tones, were that the Führer was about to unleash a secret weapon on London whose effect would be horrendous. The broadcasts, the Druid signaled, were better than the weapon itself, which he doubted could be as deadly in fact as it was in theory. "You will not be disappointed," the message came back.

In the circumstances, the Druid admitted the right of the British to look tired, gloomy, and fed up with the war. They were underfed, they were harried by ever-increasing shortages, red tape, and regulations, harassed by bombs, and snowed under by hordes of American troops who hogged every taxi, filled every restaurant table, and grabbed every available girl in London. If the Druid had hated the English as the exploiters of his people, it had always been an ingrained reaction, bred in his bones. But his loathing for the American soldiers in London came from his guts, and was exacerbated every time he walked down Piccadilly and got jostled aside by the hordes of GIs, sneered at because he was young and not in uniform, even ridiculed by the tarts soliciting the soldiers and eager to show their contempt for mere civilians. "Look at the nancy boy trying to steal our pitch!" they would cry as he walked by, and some muscly Texan would stroll over and jostle or goose him into the gutter while everyone jeered. It would be worth winning the war not just to secure the independence of his people, but also to put the Yanks in their place; he suspected they would prove responsive subjects for insult and humiliation, and relished the role he might play in it.

One morning Tommy Harris looked into the Druid's office

and asked if there was a cup of coffee available. He was covered with soot and soaked to the skin, and it seemed he had been up all night helping a colleague. There had been a raid in the night which had hit the West End of London and Westminster, shattering windows in the House of Commons and Westminster Abbey, and starting fires along St. James's Street. The Partridge Gallery, which specialized in old masters, had been among the buildings hit in St. James's and old Partridge had sent out an SOS to his fellow-dealers to rally round and help him save his Rembrandts. The auxiliary firemen helping to fight the blaze failed to appreciate the importance of their intervention, continued to pump water into the galleries where the priceless paintings were hanging, and called the police when the volunteers insisted on breaking into the building.

"We all ended up in the cells at Savile Row Police Station," Tommy said. "Have you ever tried to convince a British police sergeant that a Tiepolo doesn't like being hosed down with water, and that a Rubens positively hates the damp? Or made the mistake of declaring that the life of one of those paintings is worth more than us and the firemen put together? He didn't take kindly to that at all." Harris struck a pose and looked reproachfully down his nose. "'Yuman loife moy be cheap these doys, sor,'" he quoted, "'but Oi reckon it's still a bit more valuable than canvas and point. Anywoy, wot are yew gents worrying abart? Very dark all those paintings, Oi'm told. Won't do them any 'arm to get a good wash. Moight loighten them up, and enloighten the people who come to see them, you moight say. Ha-ha-ha!' Coffee, dear boy! I need coffee!"

He sat on the Druid's desk and chatted away as he sipped at a restorative cup of execrable office coffee.

Presently he said, "By the way, I'm giving a little party on May 2. It happens to be the birthday of Kim Philby, one of my closest friends, and he's bringing his new wife along for a little celebration." He dropped his voice to a whisper. "Confidentially, she's not his wife at all, really. There's another one around somewhere—some foreign girl in his murky past—but she's disappeared. But the official separation's just come through, and what with the birthday and all, it's a good excuse. You will come, dear boy, won't you? It'll be the last chance before everybody gets too busy."

"Thank you. I'd like to come," the Druid said. "But too busy with what?"

"Why, the invasion, of course!" Harris said. "Once that starts and the reprisals begin, London isn't going to be a place for holding parties. Haven't you heard about Hitler's threats? London will be laid waste! The Thames will be red with blood!"

"I prefer not to think about it," the Druid said.

The dealer reached down and patted his hand. "Don't worry. I expect we've got a few things up our sleeves, too."

"I wish I were sure of that," the Druid said.

CHAPTER 10

FUSAG

I

FOR THOSE in the know, London was a curious place to be in during the weeks leading up to the invasion of Fortress Europe. Gradually it began emptying of troops as the formations were called out of the city to their assembly points and all leave was canceled. It was announced that large blocks of territory, including the whole of the Channel coast and twenty miles inland from it, would henceforth be barred to all except those who normally lived there and others on strictly authorized business. The Druid reported to Lisbon the sudden crop of territorial prohibitions, but pointed out that his BBC pass could still get him through most military barriers. He also noted the departure of the troops.

"Piccadilly Circus is no longer the third circle of Hell," he reported, in an unusual betrayal of his feelings. "The hated Yankee troops who made it such a pesthole have been called back to camp, and English civilians can once more walk freely on their own pavements. Even the prostitutes no longer spurn them as customers. I do not need to emphasize the significance of this. The troops are being readied for the slaughter and it cannot be long delayed."

Berlin relayed an immediate message back through von Fidrmuc:

ASSEMBLED WHERE? FOR ACTION WHERE AND WHEN?

In his own fashion, the Druid now began to pity the English civilians who were left in London, for he knew something of which they were still ignorant. For the moment they relished having the capital to themselves again, together with their pubs, their shops, their restaurants, and their taxis, and when they forgathered for a drink in the evenings, they even allowed themselves the luxury of feeling guilty. They knew quite well where all the troops, including the loud and assertive Yanks, had gone. They knew that the invasion was coming. And they began to talk with apprehension of the bloodshed which the soldiers would soon be facing, and of their own guilt at being here, safe in London, when it happened.

The Druid felt like telling them: *You don't need to feel guilty. London is going to be just as dangerous as the beaches, any moment now.*

Because he knew, through the RSHA, that Hitler's secret weapon was about to be unleashed at last, bringing death and destruction upon them. Lots of them had heard rumors, of course, and he was surprised at how many had heard the threats voiced by Lord Haw-Haw over Hamburg radio. But he was also irritated because they jeered at Haw-Haw as a Nazi propagandist and refused to believe a word he said. Well, they would find out, and he couldn't wait to see their faces then. If they had any faces left to see.

In the meantime, he wondered about Thomas Harris. He had a strong suspicion that even if the British public remained ignorant of the imminent menace of the Führer's secret weapon, there were circles high up in the government, and almost certainly in British intelligence, who were aware that it was no bluff, and that a sword of Damocles was hanging over their heads. Like him, they must be asking themselves the agonizing question: which would come first, the invasion of Europe or Hitler's bombardment of London? And he was pretty sure that one of those in the know, and troubled by it, was Tommy Harris. What did he *do* that he was in possession of such rarefied knowledge? Could there be an explanation in his close association with Admiral Canaris's favorite spy, the ineffable Spaniard Luis Calvo?

The Druid was aware, of course, that one of the reasons he had been sent to England was to look for double spies. He had known all about the Gestapo's suspicions of the Abwehr right from the beginning. But the RSHA's takeover of the Abwehr's functions and facilities had reassured him, especially since it had been made plain to him from Berlin—by Huppenkothen even if not by Hoffmann—that a closer look at the Abwehr network in Britain had shown no signs of betrayal or deception. The agents in place were not only clean, they were also most reliable, their information having proved factual and invaluable time and time again.

But what stuck in his throat was the knowledge that the endorsement went for Luis Calvo too, and it seemed all wrong. Yet how could he prove it? To make a false accusation, even to raise a suspicion, would be called downright sabotage by the network's friends. Because, of course, if he cast doubts on Luis Calvo's proven loyalty and reliability, he was casting doubt on all of them. Was he suggesting all the Abwehr's agents in Britain had been captured and turned? He could imagine the angry indignation such a suggestion would arouse among the Abwehr control officers, and cringed at the thought of the recriminations which would be heaped upon his head.

And yet, and yet. Where did Thomas Harris come in? And how much did he know of Luis Calvo's activities?

I I

In the last week of April, the Druid used his pass to go down to Bognor Regis, in West Sussex, where his old friends the Zandvoort Players were giving a recital, which would be recorded and later broadcast over the BBC. The audience consisted mostly of airmen and airwomen from the RAF station at Tangmere, a few miles down the road, and the Druid noted with amusement that his former charges now included numbers like "Deep in the Heart of Texas" and "Blue Moon" in their repertoire, and did not even look sheepish or disgusted about it.

The train bringing him down had stopped at Three Bridges for military policemen to come aboard and examine identity cards and travel warrants, but once in the restricted area he sensed no impairment of his movements. On the excuse that he wanted to visit the cathedral, he spent the night in Chichester, and traveled the following day by bus to Portsmouth and Southampton, from which he took the train back to London. After his trip, he suspected more strongly than ever that it was into Normandy, straight across the Channel from the area in which he had been moving, that military operations would soon be taking place. He had seen constant military activity on the roads and in the harbors, where the waters were teeming with all kinds of craft, busily loading supplies. He encoded a long report setting out his theory that Normandy would be the main thrust of the coming landing, and included an approximate counting of all the military trucks, conveyors, tanks, armored vehicles, barges, floating cranes, dredgers, destroyers, tugs, tank landing craft he had seen (admittedly much of it from a distance). He received almost immediately a query passed on from Berlin:

ENUMERATE DIVISIONAL BADGES WORN BY TROOPS SEEN.

He replied by giving regimental badges. He had seen no divisional insignias at all.

There was no further comment on that, only a message asking him to make a similar exploratory trip to eastern England and Scotland this time, and to report on what he had seen. It would take time to arrange, but he set about drawing up an itinerary. He was puzzled about why he was being asked to make such a journey.

III

He would have not been puzzled for long if he had been aware of what the Double Cross Committee's spies had been sending back to the Abwehr over the past two weeks. It was all part of the deception plan to conceal the real thrust and intent of the forthcoming invasion, and the whole strength of the committee's roster of double spies was bent on persuading the Nazis that a completely different order of battle existed from the one actually standing by.

As J. C. Masterman's official account of the deception campaign put it: "The plan, in broad outline, was to create two army groups, one real (21st Army Group) and one notional (First United States Army Group or FUSAG). When the 21st Army Group went overseas (into Normandy) FUSAG would be left consisting of the U.S. Third Army (real) and the British 4th Army (notional). In the final stage, when the U.S. Third Army had gone overseas, on or about D+30, FUSAG would be left with only notional formations."[1]

The object of those notional (or nonexistent) elements of FUSAG was to convince the Germans that Normandy was only a feint, and that the real invasion force was being held in abeyance until the Nazi armies had been drawn into the Normandy trap—after which FUSAG would then be hurled into

[1] Masterman, *Double Cross System.*

France at the Pas-de-Calais, 200 miles away. So every German spy involved in the Double Cross System was busily sending back to his control at the Abwehr details calculated to build up a completely false order of battle for the Anglo-American forces, giving them twenty-six or -seven more divisions of troops than they actually had, and putting the bulk of the Allied army—in Nazi strategists' calculations, at least—miles away from where the Druid had actually seen it.

"In the early stages before D-Day," Masterman wrote, "the map for the real order of battle showed the main weight of our forces in the Midlands, the west and the southwest; the false order of battle showed the main weight in Scotland, the east and the southwest."[2]

What the RSHA wanted from the Druid were confirmatory details concerning the First U.S. Army Group about which the Abwehr's spies were telling them so much. They guessed that FUSAG was the card the Allies were trying to keep up their sleeve, and they were eager to trump it.

It would have panicked the Double Cross Committee if its members had known that a Nazi spy outside British control had been asked to report urgently on troop dispositions north of London. For an independent observer had only to look around Scotland and eastern England to discover that there was no such thing as a First U.S. Army Group. There was the Third Army, true, under the command of General George S. Patton, but that was slated to reinforce Normandy. There was no 4th British Army, and nothing like twenty-seven divisions in reserve. And if FUSAG didn't exist, how could the Allies be holding it back for what was threatened as the *real* invasion of Fortress Europe, by way of the Pas-de-Calais? Such a revelation could destroy the whole D-Day deception plan.

[2] Ibid.

IV

Early one evening in the last week in April, 1944, the Druid was walking across Sloane Square, on his way back to his apartment, when a long-legged girl rose from a bench and made her way toward him. She was wearing khaki battle dress, and he noticed, when she came up close, that the word "Norway" was sewn across the top of her sleeve. She was a little breathless and there was a high flush on her cheeks which made him immediately wary.

"Excuse me to bother you," she said, "but I have lost Swan Court and it continues to elude me. Could you tell me, please?"

He pointed down the King's Road and said, "Just follow your nose, turn left at the Town Hall, you can't miss it."

She was walking on when she had a thought, and, turning to him, asked, "You are going same way? Perhaps we could accompany?"

He agreed that he was, and she fell into step beside him, all the while chatting in an endless stream: about how Denmark and Norway were comrades in misfortune, now that both their countries had been overrun by the Nazis, of how she had been working in a bank in London when war came, and had felt forced to get into uniform because of the terrible things Germany was doing to her country. Did he know her country? She had been born in Odense, where Hans Andersen had also been born. He told her gravely that he had been born in Wales, where many great storytellers had also been born, but that, alas, he had never been outside the United Kingdom.

They reached the corner of Chelsea Town Hall and he pointed down the street to the entrance to Swan Court.

Just before they parted, she gave him her most winning smile and said, "How strange that you have never been out of England. I was sure we had met before—somewhere." She looked him straight in the eyes. "Not in Germany, perhaps?" Then, in a sudden quietly spoken sentence in German: *"You are the exact image of a young man I saw when I did my training at Camp Four on Rügen. I called him 'the Monk,' because he was always in isolation, but I know more about him now and I believe his code name is the Druid. Are you not the Druid?"*

She stopped suddenly, laughed prettily, and said in English, "Oh, excuse, please! I sometimes forget what language I speak!"

She held out her hand to him, and the one grasping hers was firm and very cold. Seemingly unaware that he was staring at her, she thanked him with her most dazzling smile, and walked down the street toward Swan Court. She did not look round, but she had a feeling that he was still standing there, still staring after her, long after she had disappeared.

The man from the SIS was waiting for her when she reached the apartment.

"It is the Monk. I have no doubt about that," she said. "A little older, a little less beautiful, but the same. He understands German. I could see it in his eyes the moment I called him *der Druide.*" She slumped down in a chair, crossed her elegant legs, and pulled a cigarette out of the packet in the top pocket of her jacket. The SIS man leaned over and lit it for her.

She looked troubled.

"Do I have to go on with this?" she asked.

"You are still working your passage," he said.

"His eyes are so marvelously blue," she said.

He laughed. "If I may say so, yours are remarkably blue, too."

"He never even noticed them." She blew out a puff of smoke. "I just hope I frightened him out of his wits, and he's now taken off while there's still a chance."

"Oh, he won't do that," said Kim Philby confidently. "You'll be seeing him again, you can be sure of that."

V

The head of the OSS in London, David Bruce, brought a bottle of precious Jack Daniels whiskey. General Dwight D. Eisenhower's aide, Captain Harry Butcher, triumphantly handed over a bottle of Tio Pepe ("from the cellar Mrs. Churchill presented to my chief," he proudly declared), not seeming to realize that in this house of superb *finos* Tio Pepe was *vin ordinaire*. There were two jars of caviar from a diplomatic courier just in from Persia, a ripe round of Camembert which had somehow found its way from German-occupied Normandy, and some German schnapps smuggled out of Norway by a couple of Norwegian commandos.

Not that Tommy Harris needed such reinforcements. No one knew quite how he did it, but there was always enough food and drink to take care of everyone, and its quality was prewar. Usually, Harris confined his parties largely to SIS types and old colleagues from what he called "Guy Fawkes College," the sabotage and dirty-tricks department of MI6 to which he and several of his friends, including Kim Philby, had formerly belonged. But tonight the guest list had been broadened to include members of Allied diplomatic staffs, and representatives of intelligence organizations attached to the so-called "free armies" with their headquarters in London. David Bruce and Harry Butcher were somewhat taken aback to see a couple of officers of General de Gaulle's Free French security service knocking back wine and Camembert in the corner, for the Americans were quarreling bitterly with the French at the moment. Tommy Harris, who relished a piquant situation, insisted on introducing them, and then left them muttering monosyllables at each other, until a ravishing Polish countess in well-cut uniform strolled across and switched their minds from politics to sex.

Kim Philby was circulating. He had left his "wife," Aileen, on a comfortable chair, her hands modestly over her obviously swollen belly, for she was very pregnant, and made the rounds, a tall glass of what looked like neat whisky in his hand, a pleasant smile on his face, and a stuttered word of wit or welcome for everyone. He gave the impression that he liked parties and people, and there was much clapping of male hands on his shoulders, and many female embraces. There was only the slightest tension in him when the Druid came up the stairs and Tommy Harris went across to greet him. It was the first time Philby had seen him, but he knew at once who he was. Vera de Schallberg was right: his eyes were a most devastating blue, and he was easily the handsomest man in the room. He was dressed in a neat blue suit, the edge of its office respectability taken off by a dark, informal shirt and a red tie, and as Tommy Harris took his hand in both of his and drew him forward, Philby saw those eyes sweep the room like an icy-blue beam. He half closed his own as he stared through the haze of cigarette smoke, and had a vision of this young man in SS uniform, with swastikas up. Philby was not given to doubting the instructions of the men who ruled his life, but he suddenly had a freezing pang of apprehension, and the feeling that here was someone too dangerous to leave around.

It was not until much later that, following instructions, Vera de Schallberg arrived.

V I

Connoisseurs of espionage and secret agents are sure of one thing: Kim Philby's career as a double spy for the SIS and the KGB would not have been half as successful had it not been marked by strokes of good luck. Time after time, when he needed to bring off an intelligence coup, or dodge disaster and exposure, a fluke, a coincidence, a bureaucratic error, a thoughtless remark, or a rash and premature accusation gave him the opportunity he needed either to pierce a dark secret or to wriggle out of a trap. He would not be alive and well in Moscow today had it not been so.

In the case of the Druid, luck stayed with him. It was sheer good fortune that he had eventually, if reluctantly, agreed to go to Lisbon to investigate the Abwehr control, Paul von Fidrmuc, and his Ostro Network. Otherwise, his colleagues might have discovered what only he and the KGB now knew (among the Allies, anyway): that not all Ostro's spies had been figments of von Fidrmuc's imagination, that one of them was real, and in Britain. Then there was his luck with his colleague Denzil Roberts. He was the only other member of the SIS who had suspected that an independent Nazi spy was loose in Britain, and it was he who had enlisted Philby's help in getting Vera de Schallberg released to track him down.

It could have been most awkward if Vera had gone on reporting her search to Roberts, and means would have had to be taken to prevent it. But then suddenly the powers that be had decided Roberts's services were needed overseas, and he and his girl friend had been posted to Algiers, Cairo, and points east. Vera had been passed over to Philby's care, and his departing colleague would never know—Philby would see to that —whether there actually was an independent Nazi agent on the loose in Britain. The secret of the Druid's existence would stay with Philby and the KGB. That was the way Moscow wanted it.

Ironically enough, it was at least half an hour after her arrival that Vera and the Druid came face to face. From the other side of the room, Philby watched Harris bring the two together, and in the next thirty seconds he no longer doubted the young man's qualifications for his job. Vera gave him a smile both slightly mocking and provocative, leaving it to him to indicate whether they had ever met before. He gave no sign whatsoever that he had ever done so. On the other hand, his evident pleasure at meeting such a pretty girl was so natural and easy that no one would have guessed that he had anything else on his mind. Nevertheless, for the rest of the evening, whenever he glanced across, Philby noted that the Druid hardly left the girl's side, fetching her drinks and food, keeping her amused, and, finally, when she glanced anxiously at her watch, indicating that if she must go, he would go with her.

Tommy Harris protested that the party was just starting to take off, but bowed before the girl's insistence that she had a curfew to keep.

"Ah, me," said Tommy Harris when he came back from seeing them off, "I had plans for that boy. What can he see in that dyed Scandinavian floozie?"

It was a week before Vera de Schallberg reported back to Philby. She had seen the Druid four times in the past seven days, she said, and suspected he had followed her back to Olympia or to the depot in Hammersmith on two other occasions. On their second outing they had gone to a cinema in the West End, and, walking home, she had told him she had an uncle who was a Danish merchant in Lisbon, and that she wrote to him occasionally. On the following evening she had shown him a photograph of her uncle, and it so happened that his Lisbon address was on the back. The Druid must have recognized it as one of the accommodation addresses used by his own control, Paul von Fidrmuc. On the fourth night, he had taken her to a small hotel in Earl's Court and they had slept together. Later she had "confessed" to him that she did a little work for the Germans, that she had trained at a camp in Germany before coming to England, and that her letters to her uncle in Lisbon contained secret-ink messages. She had mentioned that before leaving Germany she had been given a code name, and that she was known to the Abwehr as "Viola." Then she had got very frightened over what she had told him, burst into tears, and begged him not to betray her secret.

"I just want Germany to win the war," she had sobbed. "All my friends and all our family money is in Germany. And I love the Führer!" She looked across at Philby: "Which is true—though not the last," she said naïvely.

"What did he tell *you?*" Philby asked.

She shook her head, still puzzled and surprised.

"Nothing. I talked about Camp Four at Rügen, but he

199

showed no interest at all. I asked about when he was a little boy, about growing up, things like that. He was rather rude," she said primly. "Said how could I possibly understand what it was like to be a Welshman?" Then a half-smile crossed her face. "I think I should tell you that when I say things in German, he pretends he doesn't understand and asks me to translate the words into English, which makes me embarrassed." She giggled. "He says things, too—in Welsh. But I don't think he means them. I think he says them to deceive me, to make me think he is excited."

About three weeks later, Vera called a number Philby had given her and said she was in a call box. Could he arrange leave for her? The Druid was going on a trip to Edinburgh, Newcastle, and York, and had asked her to go with him.

"He has become much warmer," Vera said. "I have a feeling he has begun to trust me."

That was almost certainly because the Druid had checked her code name with von Fidrmuc in Lisbon, and had it confirmed—on Philby's orders. (But Philby did not tell her that.) Instead, he said he would fix it with the Norwegians, and told her to report to the RTO (the Rail Transport Officer) for travel vouchers. After which he sent an emergency signal to his KGB case officer, Ernst, and late the following evening went to see Tommy Harris.

VII

Tommy Harris and his MI5 colleague Anthony Blunt were working, heads together, over the desk in the library of Chesterfield Gardens when Philby came in. The radio on one of the shelves was relaying the lofty, patronizing tones of Lord Haw-Haw broadcasting from Hamburg. The two men had glasses of red wine in hand, and Philby helped himself to a whisky. He lifted his drink in a salute. They shared a loyalty which transcended their allegiance to the king and country for whom they worked, but it was rarely that they came together, and almost never did they talk about the ideology which bound them. So Blunt made signs at once that he was leaving, and Philby made no effort to persuade him to stay.

"Let's turn that damn thing off, shall we?" he said, after Blunt had gone, and went across to the radio. He looked around the dimly lit library, nodding approvingly at the Goya prints staring down at him from the walls. "Where's Garbo?" he asked, adding, in a mock-Swedish accent: "Gone off to be alone?"

Harris did not smile. "If you mean my little Spaniard," he said, "he is tucked safely away where he can't do any harm." He added, with a touch of asperity: "The times are far too fraught to have him around. Garbo has work to do. We have to keep our friends there"—nodding at the radio—"informed about what is going on in these islands. We wouldn't like them to be caught with their trousers down, would we?"

Philby said, "Which is one of the reasons I'm here. Tell me, Tommy, what would anyone be likely to find out about our invasion forces if he made a trip to Scotland, northeast England, and Yorkshire?"

"Nothing," said Harris.

"Why not?"

"Because there's nothing to see. We don't have anything up there worth a damn except a sprinkling of training camps and assembly depots. Everything we have is crammed into southern England, waiting for D-Day."

Philby said nothing. He seemed deep in thought.

"Come on, Kim," Harris said, "you wouldn't be here if you weren't worried. What are you trying to tell me? That someone is going around the North poking about for invasion troops? Who? I thought we had every Nazi agent in the country under our control. If we haven't, we're in trouble. Do you know what Garbo's been telling the Huns for the past two weeks? That the army waiting in southern England for D-Day is less than half the story. He's been sending them details—

division numbers, tank statistics, armored transports, every-thing—of a far bigger army waiting up North to begin the real invasion, once the Huns get involved with the first wave. We've even had Deception plant radio operators all over Yorkshire, Teesside, and the Lothians, sending phony messages to each other to make the Huns think there's a vast force of troops up there. My God!" He got up and faced Philby. "If anyone told the Huns there was nothing up there, he could ruin the whole plan? Are you serious? Have we missed one of them?"

"That's what I'm trying to find out," Philby said.

"My God!" Harris said again, and took a gulp of his wine. "That's been our biggest nightmare, the thought that there might be a free agent out there. It's the one thing that gives us all kittens." He looked hard at his friend. "All our efforts coming to the boil at last, and you choose this moment to scare the shit out of me? Are you serious, Kim? What have you heard? Does the committee know about this? And the boys in MI5?"

"No," said Philby.

"Then shouldn't we tell them, pronto?"

Philby shook his head. His voice hardened.

"This is our affair, Tommy. Don't say a word to anyone, particularly not to the committee. Is that clear?"

Harris said, "I hope to God you know what you're doing."

The lightness came back into Philby's tones.

"Don't I always?" He glanced at his watch. "It's time I went." He sighed theatrically. "Aileen waits up for me, you know."

They walked down the stairs together.

CHAPTER 11

D for Double Cross Day

I

ON THE DAY before he left for Edinburgh, the Druid went down to Victoria Station to make a routine check in one of the telephone booths in the forecourt. It was months since Arthur Owens, the little Welshman the Germans knew as Johnny, had been taken off to fester in an English jail, but once a week the Druid had continued to follow routine. Where Johnny was concerned, you never knew. This time the Druid's devotion to training paid off. As his eye flicked over the board beneath the telephone receiver, he saw the letter "S." At once he took an Underground to Charing Cross Station, sought out another telephone booth, and called a number.

A voice said in Welsh, *"Give me your number. I'll call back."*

It took nearly twenty minutes before the bell sounded in the booth, but then there was the Welshman on the end of the line, breathing like a wheezy old man, his voice hoarse with phlegm, whisky, and fatigue, but with the cheerful note still faintly there.

"Hallo, laddie. How's the minstrel boy?"

"You sound as if you've been running," the Druid said.

Johnny croaked with laughter. "I don't have to run to sound like this these days. That's why those buggers let me out, I think. Tell me, how are you doing?"

"I'm still *in situ*," said the Druid evenly.

"Yes, but you can't be telling them anything they want to hear, can you? A right fuck-up those boys have made, they really have. And it doesn't look as if it's going to get any better."

"You ought to have more faith," the Druid said.

"In what?" wheezed Johnny. "The only thing I've always believed in was the land of my fathers, and even that gets to look more like an English province every day. No wonder our lads back home are getting downhearted. You know the English aren't even arresting the Nats these days? They say we're no longer a threat to their security."

"A few bombs in the right places would soon alter that," the Druid said.

"Oh, come on, who's going to send us bombs?"

"You know who," said the Druid.

There was a bout of bronchial coughing, and then Johnny said, almost in a whisper, "Is there any news of Trudy? Have you heard from her?"

"Several times," the Druid lied. "She is still in Lisbon, and has asked about you—often. Can I give her a message?" There was a long, breathy pause, and the Druid said, "Nothing? She'll be disappointed."

"Oh, God!" Johnny said, and the Druid realized that he was sobbing. "What can I tell her, with this bloody war going on and on? I'm never going to see Trudy again! I'll be dead before it's over!"

"Calm yourself." His tone crispened, and, looking out of the booth, he decided to end the conversation. "Is this the only reason you left me a message? To tell me you feel sorry for yourself? I have no time for whiners."

He could hear Johnny gulping back his tears.

204

"Don't go! I do have a message for you. Two days after they sprang me from Pentonville, I had a treff with the Spanish contact. A letter came through the bag. It's at post Number Six. Another thing." He was rushing now. "When you see Trudy, tell her how much I love her. I want you to tell her that yourself, do you hear me, laddie? So keep out of trouble. Whatever you do, don't let the narks grab you. They're all over the place now. And listen—don't get mixed up with other agents, no matter what they tell you. I didn't warn you before, but I do now. Steer clear of them. They've all been turned, every one of them!"

The Druid asked very calmly, "Does the name Viola mean anything to you?"

"Oh, Christ, laddie, keep away from her," Johnny gasped, "she's already got two poor bastards hanged!"

The Druid carefully put down the receiver, slipped out of the booth, and disappeared into the crowd.

Just before the official closing time at sunset, he strolled into the grounds of the Royal Hospital in Chelsea and picked up the note from the agreed hiding place. Back in his flat, he gave it the treatment. It was from Hugo Hoffmann.

> I have sad news to impart, and I thought it best not to send it through Ostro. In the English terror raid on Bremen two weeks ago, Haus Walfisch was hit and destroyed. Your grandfather was killed instantly, but your mother survived long enough to be taken to the emergency hospital, where she succumbed to her injuries four days later. It may make it easier for you to bear if I tell you the doctors consider her death, bravely faced, was a blessing, for she would otherwise have been a chronic invalid. The Reichsführer SS has been informed and sends his deep sympathy to a brave soldier and good friend of the Reich. Neither you nor Wales will be forgotten, and your sad loss will be avenged. . . .

There was a short note about the Abwehr:

Under its new control, Pauli [code name for Kalten-brunner] feels things are going well. Despite internal upheaval, intelligence information from England continues to be thought excellent, and we have had early warning of English bluff attempts when landings begin. The OHL [German High Command] has been alerted and knows first invasion will be a feint. You will be asked for intelligence through Ostro when and where full-scale landings will be made. I for one will particularly appreciate confirmation of your Abwehr colleagues' reports. . . .

He added:

For that purpose, I am sending you copy of special code no. 7 used by V319 [Arabel/Garbo] to communicate. Following are times and wavelengths . . . should give you opportunity to check without personal contact. Good luck and *Heil Hitler!*

For the rest of the night, the Druid sat staring at the fading lines of secret ink on the paper before him, jotting down an occasional note, but committing the main lines of the code to his memory. It would have been impossible to guess from his face that he was heartsick over the death of his mother. The first streaks of dawn were filtering through the chinks in the blackout curtain before he went into the bathroom-kitchen, shaved, made himself tea, and dressed for the new day. Half an hour later, dressed in a fire watcher's battle dress, a briefcase under his arm, he walked down the King's Road to Chelsea Underground and took the train to King's Cross Station—and his rendezvous with Vera de Schallberg.

II

And this is where the mystery begins.

A corporal in the RTO office at King's Cross Station on the morning of June 2, 1944, processed the travel warrant of a certain Private Vera Schallberg (Norway) for Edinburgh, and had every reason to believe she subsequently took the morning train to Scotland. But in fact, though she was a particularly tall and striking blonde, not likely to remain unobserved by the male comrades in arms who were crowding onto the express, no one remarked her either on board or disembarking at York, Newcastle, or Edinburgh, the three stopping places. (Nobody noticed the Druid, either, but then, he was a civilian male, much less likely to awaken the interest of fellow-passengers.)

Nine days later, the Norwegian Army headquarters in London received a routine note from the sergeant in charge of the depot in Hammersmith that Private Schallberg had not reported from leave, and she was posted AWOL. Subsequently, the police were informed, but since lots of things were going on in London by that time, in addition to the fact that the capital was full of deserters from all the Allied armies, nobody went out to look for her, or even wondered where she had got to. It was not until nearly a month later that a file clerk in the Special Branch at Scotland Yard came across Vera de Schallberg's name on a list, and remembered she had once been arrested as a spy. The fact that she had (a) secured her freedom, and (b) managed to get herself attached to the Norwegians galvanized him into calling up MI5, and the counterspy organization said they would look into it.

No one will ever know whether or not they did so. The papers on the subject have long since been classified secret for all time by the British government. Fanciful speculations about Vera's fate have been discouraged, and, when pressed, have been neither confirmed nor denied.

Is she alive or dead? No one is officially saying a word.

The only certain thing is that since June 2, 1944, when she turned up at King's Cross Station for her meeting with the Druid, Vera de Schallberg has never been seen again. Was the Druid responsible for her disappearance?

Well, perhaps. But not quite in the way one might imagine. For there are strong rumors—which again no official source will confirm or deny—that after Vera came back from her trip to Scotland with the Druid, she was picked up by MI5 and interrogated. As a result of those interviews, the story goes, she was arrested and subsequently charged and tried for espionage in time of war. And hanged.

Why? For refusing to talk about where she had been—and with whom?

III

On June 6, 1944, paratroopers and glider commandos from the British 6th Airborne Division dropped on the bridges of the Caen River and Caen Canal in Normandy. At the same time, shock troops of the U.S. 82nd Airborne Division landed around the port and peninsula of Cherbourg, on the other side of the *département*. In between these linchpins, the Anglo-American armies swarmed ashore in a massive landing over seventy-five miles of Normandy coastline, and, at long last, after four bitter and frustrating years, the British and their allies were back in Europe.

The Druid got back to London on June 8, and read in the morning paper the first dispatch from Normandy from a paratrooper war correspondent. INVASION HAS BEGUN: FIRST DISPATCH FROM WAR FRONT was the headline over it. The Druid read it through carefully, and was puzzled. The correspondent wrote purplish prose about the bravery of the airborne troops who had stormed the Caen bridges to capture and hold them, but neither in his first dispatch nor in others that followed was there mention of any serious German opposition. Yet one of the most powerful armies the world had ever known was gathered in northern France, under the command of Field Marshal Erwin Rommel, waiting for this very moment. Why was this gigantic war machine not moving into Normandy to drive the Allies back into the sea? They were less than two hundred miles away. What were they waiting for?

For twenty-four hours, the Druid stayed in his flat, listening, waiting. His own set was silent, because what was there of any importance he could possibly send his control at this point in history? Of his journey to Scotland and northern England there was absolutely nothing to tell. In Berlin they were concerned with the outcome of the war, and would hardly welcome his trivia.

And then, on June 9, three days after the Allied landings, the Druid forced himself to go to his office. He took care of his correspondence and went over to a meeting at the BBC. When it was finished, he found himself walking into the Gluepot, and there, drinking at the end of the bar, was Polly Wright.

"Well, look what the wind's blown in!" she said sourly. "I thought you'd gone out there to storm the Normandy beaches and win the war for us single-handed!" She saw the look on his face, and quickly added: "Sorry. Why don't I keep my big mouth shut?"

She was the last person he wanted to be with. He felt drained, downcast, dispirited, even nauseated by the sight of her, of any woman. But he dragged his sagging spirits together and bought her a drink, and she raised her glass.

"Let's drink to Dickie Capell," she said. "He's over there in Normandy, poor old sod! It oughtn't to be allowed, a man of his age." She sipped her drink, gazing reflectively at the Druid, sensing his preoccupation. "But he was right, wasn't he, the shrewd old bugger? Those young'uns thought it would be the Pas-de-Calais. But Dickie remembered his Henry Five, and where are they now? Harfleur and Arromanches, that's where!" She changed tune abruptly. "What's up, love?"

It was nothing, he told her. He was tired after his trip. The audiences for the concerts in Edinburgh and Newcastle had been apathetic, and in York the flautist had banged his lip in the blackout and couldn't play. She suggested he should come home with her and relax. She would grill him a steak a GI had given her. But he pleaded the need to write his report, and made his way back alone in the gathering darkness to

Chelsea. It was still comparatively early in the evening, but the streets were practically deserted, and the few passersby looked tense. It was now ten days since the first "gas mains" had begun exploding in London, and everyone now knew that they were flying bombs which Hitler had begun launching against the capital. The Druid had to admit he was disappointed with them. He had expected something much more horrendous as a terror weapon, and he did not even look up when he heard the putt-putt-putt of a V-1's approach in the sky, nor cringe when the engine stopped and the load of explosive plunged into the earth. Maybe some people were terrified, but, he suspected, not many. Lucille Long in the Gluepot had described them as "cosmic cigars farting across the sky," but there was nothing really cosmic about them. If the Führer was beginning to hurl thunderbolts against Britain, they would need to be made more cataclysmic.

When he got back to his flat, he assembled his radio to be ready for transmission. He had already encoded a message for Lisbon, with instructions that von Fidrmuc should pass it on urgently to Berlin, but he hesitated, for he knew he was less informative than truculent and querulous. He had written:

WHY IS THE WEHRMACHT HOLDING BACK? DON'T THEY BE-LIEVE THIS IS REAL THING? BUT IT IS. ALL MY SOURCES HERE ARE SURE OF THIS. . . .

He had quoted the remark of a "typical Londoner" (it had actually been a barfly in the Gluepot) who had sneered at the German generals for "missing the boat" and added: "If old Hitler doesn't kick Rommel's arse soon and move him out of Calais, it's going to be too late."

"CHURCHILL IS REPORTED DELIGHTED AT GERMAN INACTIVITY," he had ended his message. It was an outburst of sheer frustration at the way the military situation was being handled, and he was still not sure whether he would send it. While he pondered, he spun the dial to the band Inspector Hoffmann had indicated was the one used by Arabel (the egregious Luis Calvo) to communicate with Madrid. What was that little rat sending his control about the invasion? It was half an hour to his airtime, and he hung on with growing impatience, until at long last the call sign began stuttering out of his set: "ARABEL CALLING! ARABEL CALLING!"

For the next ten minutes he scribbled busily, copying down the blocks of figures and numbers. Then he reached for his memory key and began the task of decoding.

An hour later he was still staring at the paper in front of him with stunned astonishment. It was hard to believe what his eyes told him he had copied down. For here was Arabel, the man described to him as the Abwehr's favorite agent, praised by the Führer for his intelligence work and the widespread and knowledgeable quality of his network, reporting on D-plus-3 on the progress of the Anglo-American landing. And what was he saying?

ARABEL CALLING ABSTELLE IV:

REQUEST FOLLOWING ROUNDUP REPORT BE URGENTLY SUBMITTED OHL [German High Command] FOR IMMEDIATE ATTENTION.

SOURCES DO NOT REPEAT DO NOT BELIEVE NORMANDY LANDING IS MAIN THRUST OF ANGLO-AMERICAN INVASION.

V372 LIVERPOOL REPORTS LARGE CONCENTRATIONS U.S. ARMORED TROOPS STILL HELD HIS AREA. V373 ESTIMATES AT LEAST 35 DIVISIONS ARE AWAITING ORDERS IN SCOTTISH LOWLANDS AND TYNESIDE. V377 TRAVELING BY TRAIN SAW ELEMENTS 20 DIVISIONS IN STRETCH 15 MILES SOUTH OF YORK. FOLLOWING ARE DIVISIONAL INSIGNIAS IDENTIFIED . . .

BASED THESE REPORTS I ESTIMATE AT LEAST 50 DIVISIONS TROOPS STILL BEING HELD BACK IN EASTERN NORTHERN ENGLAND AND SCOTLAND. SO FAR NOT SINGLE SOLDIER FROM FUSAG [4th U.S. Army Group] HAS BEEN ENGAGED.

STRONGLY SUGGEST NORMANDY LANDING IS PURELY DIVER-

SIONARY. REAL LANDINGS BY FUSAG WILL TAKE PLACE SHORTLY
PROBABLY PAS-DE-CALAIS AREA.

ENDS ARABEL. ACKNOWLEDGE! ACKNOWLEDGE!

Suddenly the full implications of the message flooded in on
him. This was not just sloppy work on the part of an inefficient
agent. It was lies. It was deliberately and carefully calculated
to deceive, and, if acted on by the German High Command,
would let the Anglo-Americans walk into France almost un-
opposed.

They had to be warned at once.

He reached for his pad and began frantically composing
and encoding a completely new message. Then he sat down at
his set, found the band, and began to send:

DRUID CALLING! DRUID CALLING! ACKNOWLEDGE!

Almost at once, the reply came:

OSTRO HERE! OSTRO HERE!

He wasted no words:

FOR RSHA BERLIN URGENT INFORM OHL AGENT V319 ARABEL
IS IN ENEMY HANDS AND ALL INFORMATION FROM HIM
SHOULD BE IGNORED.

HIS REPORT 50 ANGLO-AMERICAN DIVISIONS WAITING NORTH
ENGLAND AND SCOTLAND IS FALSE. I HAVE JUST TOURED AREA.
THERE ARE NO RESERVE TROOPS AWAITING ORDERS THERE.
THERE IS NO SUCH ARMY AS FUSAG. I SAW NO DIVISIONAL SIGNS
HE MENTIONS. STRONGLY BELIEVE ARABEL AND ALL OTHER
AFUS ARE PART OF ORCHESTRATED ENGLISH BLUFF TO PER-
SUADE OHL THAT REAL INVASION HAS NOT YET BEGUN.

STRONGLY EMPHASIZE THIS IS REAL THING AND SHOULD BE
TREATED AS SUCH. IT IS NO DIVERSIONARY OPERATION. PAS-DE-
CALAIS IS ENGLISH BLUFF NOT NORMANDY. SUGGEST OHL ACT
ACCORDINGLY BEFORE IT IS TOO LATE.

DRUID ENDS. ACKNOWLEDGE!

Back came Lisbon:

OSTRO ACKNOWLEDGES! MESSAGE RECEIVED IN FULL.

The Druid rose to his feet, turned out the light, and pulled back the blackout curtain. In the stillness of the night he heard the eructation of a V-1 flying bomb making its way across the London rooftops. Then it went silent, and the whole of the city seemed to freeze. Until, seconds later, there was the thump of an explosion and life went on again.

The Druid cursed softly in Welsh. He was increasingly disappointed with the Germans. The Führer deserved better of them than this.

Finally, he undressed and climbed into bed, feeling suddenly exhausted. But he could not sleep. He lay still all night, staring out the open window, listening to the patter of a light rain and the occasional putt-putt of an incoming V-1. Fervently, he prayed that his telegram would make more of an impact when it hit Berlin than these absurd flying firecrackers were making on London!

IV

In Lisbon next morning, Trudy Körner and Paul von Fidrmuc were cantering along a bridle path in the Monsanto Park when the Sudeten swung round in his saddle and said, "The Druid came through last night about the fighting. I have sent it on to Berlin."

"What does he say?"

"It's as we suspected," von Fidrmuc said blandly. "They're bluffing. They're trying to force Rommel to reinforce the defenders in Normandy, and then their main armies will make the real landing in the Pas-de-Calais. The Druid sent a warning. We shouldn't fall into their trap. We should hold our forces in reserve."

Trudy laughed. She had no suspicion he was lying to her.

"Aren't you glad we gave you the Druid to handle?" she asked. "I remember your face when we first told you about him—and how we'd found out about Ostro! We scared the wits out of you, didn't we? Now you are handling the brightest and bravest agent in the network, and one of these days the Reichsführer is going to reward you for it—I'll see to that!"

He blew her a kiss. "You are too good to me, *Liebling*."

The greatest pleasure von Fidrmuc got out of the Druid situation was lying about it to Trudy. Every time he made love to her these days, he wondered how she would have reacted had she guessed the truth—that his frenzied new passion and virility, which so greatly excited and enamored her, was due to one fact only. He was cheating on her, deceiving her. Not with another woman, but with British intelligence! And he got more kick out of it than he had running the Ostro Network in the early days, when he had conjured spies out of his imagination to fool the Nazis. It was even greater fun—because it was more of a gamble—than his hitherto favorite sport of playing for high stakes at the table.

At first he had resented it when the English agent Philby had turned up with the pornographic pictures of Trudy panting like a bitch in heat as she swarmed over Elizabeth von Auenrode. He had been appalled and shocked, his moral standards affronted, his *amour propre* profoundly offended. But then a slow anger had begun burning in him at the thought of the two women in sexual conspiration to humiliate and diminish him. As Philby had shrewdly calculated, he now thought there could be nothing more pleasurable than to get back at the arrogant mistress who had done this to him. What better way to do it than sabotage her favorite project, Operation Druid?

So he had consented to cooperate with the Englishman. Not without demanding—and getting—concessions in return, of course. He would be handsomely paid. When the war was over, and Germany had lost—as he was now convinced it would—he would be reprieved from any prosecution which might be instituted against former enemy intelligence agents. The Englishman had given his solemn promise that von Fidrmuc would not only be spared but would also be helped to re-establish himself in the postwar world.

And since then he had been back in the great game, and relishing it, doing what he always did best—deceiving the Nazis. And they didn't suspect a thing. He still continued to forward Berlin's queries and instructions to the Druid in England. But it was what he did with the reports the Druid sent back that made all the difference. Instead of sending them on at once to the RSHA, he reported their arrival to one of Philby's contacts in Lisbon. A treff was arranged and the message studied. Sometimes it was allowed to go on unchanged to Berlin; in other cases the message was subtly changed, or its sense completely reversed.

And last night the Druid had sent a message which made all von Fidrmuc's subterfuge worthwhile. It contained information that could blow the Allies' plans sky high, and radically alter German's strategy and tactics. It revealed the true nature of the Anglo-Americans' double bluff in Normandy, and if Hitler were to learn about it, he might well issue orders that would radically alter the whole course of the war.

For a moment von Fidrmuc had been tempted. For here was news worth its weight in gold and diamonds a thousand times over. He had clutched the Druid's message to his chest wondering whether he dare try to sell it to the highest bidder. Maybe the Abwehr would buy it, just to demonstrate its superiority over the Gestapo? But no, now that Canaris was in eclipse and Kaltenbrunner had taken over, that was too risky. How about passing it on to the Yanks—to the OSS—for a suitably magnificent amount of dollars, so they could boast of pulling a fast one over the British SIS? He reluctantly decided that the Englishman would not be pleased about that at all, and suspected that when Philby was not pleased his displeasure could be exceedingly painful to the one who had caused it.

So finally he had called up the agreed contact, and a treff had been made. The treff on this occasion was a coppice in

Monsanto Park and the contact who took the Druid's message was a motorcyclist in cap and goggles. The substitute message, completely altering the purport of the Druid's information, had been slipped into the mailbox of von Fidrmuc's office two hours later, and he had dutifully radioed it on to Berlin. It was of course exactly opposite in meaning from the message the Druid had sent.

He sighed as he transmitted the last group of letters, and waited for confirmation from the RSHA. He suspected he would never handle such an explosive piece of intelligence again. And he hadn't even received a bonus for turning it over to the British! True, he had suggested, as he handed it to the contact man, that he deserved a little extra for this particular merchandise. And, looking at the hard black eyes behind the thick motorcycle goggles, he had said, "Will you please convey that message to your master?"

The contact man had spat at his feet, and muttered what almost sounded like a "No!" in Russian.

Now what kind of a turn-down was that?

V

On June 11, 1944 (D-plus-5), Reichsführer SS Heinrich Himmler directed Ernst Kaltenbrunner, provisionally in command of the Abwehr, to send a message of congratulation to "our bravest, most resourceful, and most successful agent in enemy territory," and, to the joyful astonishment of the Double Cross Committee in London, it was to their own tame double spy Arabel/Garbo that the felicitations were addressed. His Madrid control radioed:

ATTENTION ARABEL!

REICHSFÜHRER SS HEINRICH HIMMLER HAS DIRECTED HIS WARM APPRECIATION TO ARABEL. ALL REPORTS RECEIVED IN LAST WEEK FROM ARABEL UNDERTAKING HAVE BEEN CON-

FIRMED WITHOUT EXCEPTION AND ARE TO BE DESCRIBED AS
ESPECIALLY INVALUABLE.

It was a solid confirmation from the enemy that the British
had succeeded, and the Germans had fallen for their deception
about the Normandy invasion. Though Anglo-American troops
continued to pour into the Cherbourg Peninsula and the Normandy bocage country, Arabel's repeated warnings that a Pas-
de-Calais attack would soon be coming had stalled the mighty
Nazi war machine in just the place where it was not needed.

J. C. Masterman, of the Double Cross Committee, wrote in
his report: "It appears that the Germans believed to the end
of the chapter that the Pas de Calais attack was intended and
would have been delivered if the Normandy attack had not
been more successful than they had expected. Evidence of the
movements of German troops entirely supports this view. Thus
immediately after the receipt of the message of 9th June [from
Arabel] . . . some seven German divisions which were to be
expected to be sent to the Cherbourg area were retained in the
Pas de Calais area for a fortnight after D Day . . a fatal strategic error on the part of the German command."[1]

But if the Double Cross Committee was swollen with heady
pride over the success of its deception plan, the Druid was
stunned. He too had monitored Himmler's message to Arabel,
and he found it hard to believe. How could they fall for such
an obvious trickster? Why was the German High Command
allowing itself to be so transparently deceived? Had he not
told them the truth?

To von Fidrmuc in Lisbon he radioed:

OSTRO! OSTRO! HAST WARNED BERLIN ARABEL IS BLOWN RE-
PEAT BLOWN? HIS PAS DE CALAIS REPORTS ARE FALSE REPEAT
FALSE. ACKNOWLEDGE!

Back came the reply from Ostro:

YOUR WARNING CONVEYED.

[1] Masterman, *Double Cross System.*

The Druid:

TO WHOM?

Ostro:

TO SD RSHA[2]

The Druid:

NOT GOOD ENOUGH. NEED PERSONAL ACKNOWLEDGMENT HUPPENKOTHEN OR HOFFMANN WITH SPECIAL RECOGNITION GROUP.

Ostro:

SORRY. HUPPENKOTHEN ABSENT HOFFMANN INDISPOSED. ACCEPT PERSONAL ASSURANCES MESSAGES GOING THROUGH.

The Druid:

CLOSING DOWN! CLOSING DOWN!

He pulled in the aerial and then sat for a long time over the set, brooding about what could have happened in Lisbon—or was it Germany? He had no doubt whatsoever that he had been betrayed, and though he was by no means panicked by it, he was well aware that emergency measures would have to be taken. After a time, he began carefully dismantling the transmitter and stuffing the parts in the old backpack hanging in one of the cupboards. He unplugged the battery, which he always kept on charge under a cover beneath the bed, and stuffed it in the pack. When he was finished, he flung the pack across the bed, well aware that he had come full circle, and that the bulky mass of canvas, ready to go over his shoulders, symbolized the end of his mission. This was the way he had come, and this was the way he would go.

It was his bitterest moment. At the most crucial time, just when he had the best-kept secret the English possessed and

---

[2] Sicherheitsdienst Reichssicherheitshauptamt: Security Department, Security HQ, SS.

was ready to pass it over to his masters, he had been cheated —by a traitor. He had no doubt whatsoever now that von Fidrmuc had sold him out. But what could he do about it? By the very nature of his mission, he had no fallback position to take. He could not call on his fellow-agents, for they would betray him, just as they had already betrayed Germany and themselves. Like Vera de Schallberg, they were all traitors, and he could not deal with all of them. There was Arthur Owens (Johnny). Thanks to his obsession with Trudy Körner, he could still be partly trusted. But where was Johnny? In jail again? On the run? Or drunk?

He felt let down. Even the German armies and their stupid generals had failed him. Hitler's secret weapon was a fizzle. It could not be long before von Fidrmuc informed his new pay-masters that the Druid had tumbled to his treachery and had closed down transmission. Then they would come looking for him.

It was about eleven-thirty in the evening when he slipped out of the apartment, and made his way up to the King's Road. He had a loaf, a can of Spam, some biscuits, and a thermos flask of hot tea in the top of his pack, and all the radio parts were well wrapped in socks and shirts and underwear. If any-one stopped him, he had a valid reason for being out. He had a week's holiday and was off on a hiking vacation, and his papers were in order.

Near Sloane Square Underground he found a telephone booth and dialed the number Johnny had given him. If Johnny was around, maybe he still had a lifeline. Johnny had a control in Hamburg. Through Hamburg, he could maybe get a mes-sage through to Huppenkothen or Hoffmann.

His spirits were on the rise again. He would cheat the Eng-lish yet! He waited eagerly, impatiently, as the telephone went on ringing. "Hallo," a voice said, at last. And then, in Welsh: *"What is it you could want with me?"*

"Gwladfa!" the Druid said. It was a Welsh word meaning "Free Wales," but in this case it was a cry for help.

CHAPTER 12

Grandfather's Land

I

"HE'S GONE," said Philby. "Left a message with his secretary to say he had a holiday coming, and that he was taking off for a week." He shook his head. "I don't think so. I think he's flown the coop. He knows Ostro has been turned. He knows his lines have been cut. I think he's off and running."

"In that case," said the KGB man, "we had better move quickly, before he tries something foolish and your colleagues at the SIS catch him and put a rope round his neck."

"Oh, they won't do that," said Philby cheerfully. "We don't hang Nazi spies in England these days. We just turn them into devoted employees of MI5, with guaranteed postwar jobs and pension rights."

"Not this one, I think," Ernst said. "That is why *we* have to deal with him—and the sooner the better."

Kim Philby had arrived from Lisbon by flying boat that morning, after a tour of his ever-expanding parish, and he had much to report. It was indicative of where his loyalties lay that he had postponed writing his account for the SIS in favor of making contact at once with his KGB case officer. For the past two hours he had been pouring it out, with names and news for Moscow from Rome, Cairo, Algiers, Madrid, and Lisbon.

It was while he was in Lisbon that he had learned from von Fidrmuc that the Druid had signed off. He had been amused to observe that the imperturbable Sudeten was not a whit disturbed by his agent's abrupt closedown. Philby had assumed he would warn Berlin that the Druid had gone off the air, and hint that quite possibly he had been captured. But that was not the way von Fidrmuc worked. The Druid had become a considerable source of income for him. The SS had paid well in expenses and rewards for their agent's services, and paid through von Fidrmuc. They would now be encouraged to go on paying. In place of the real Druid, a fictional one would take his place, kept alive only in the Sudeten's imagination. He would continue to receive questions and instructions from the RSHA and profess to pass them on to London. He would also concoct the replies and invent other messages from time to time—with a little help from Philby and his friends, perhaps? And he would keep the Druid alive and operating for just as long as the SS would swallow it.

"After all," he said loftily, "I am not exactly an amateur at this game."

"You are a true professional," Philby said. "But watch out for Fräulein Körner."

"Did you not know?" said von Fidrmuc, with just the slightest smirk. "Fräulein Körner has been called back to Berlin to answer some questions about her expenses. Now I wonder," he added innocently, "who could have tattled to the SS about that?"

Just before Philby left, von Fidrmuc opened a drawer and handed the Englishman a small book, and he saw that it was a passport.

"I thought you would be amused to learn," he said, handing it over, "that our friend the Druid isn't a Welshman at all.

They sent his effects here after his mother was killed in an air raid in Bremen. This was among them. And look, his mother was German and he was born in Patagonia. What kind of a Welshman does that make him?"

"The dangerous kind," said Philby dryly.

Von Fidrmuc looked across at the Englishman with a sly expression in his soft brown eyes.

"What kind of a passport do you hold, Mr. Philby?"

"British, of course," Philby said.

The Sudeten's voice suddenly grew petulant. "Then why," he asked, "do you have so many colleagues around here who are always scolding me in Russian?"

II

"A Patagonian Welshman!" said the KGB man softly, leafing through the passport. "He must be like our ethnic Ukrainians —more German than the Germans! And where does a Ukrainian German wish to be when he is in trouble?"

"Like now, for instance?" Philby asked. "Not in Mother Russia's arms, anyway."

"I beg your pardon?"

"I was making a joke, Nicky," Philby said. "I see what you mean," he added hastily. "An ethnic German yearns for Germany. An ethnic Welshman would make for Wales. I think you're right. But where in Wales, for God's sake?"

"If I remember correctly," the KGB man said, "the English have a Welshman who is one of their double spies. 'Johnny,' do they call him?"

" 'Snow' to us, 'Johnny' to the Huns, real name Arthur Owens," Philby said. "Last time I heard about that drunken old rascal, they'd clamped him in jail again. Couldn't trust him, they said. But if he's out again, it's an idea. He might know about the Druid, and if we pay him enough he could even lead us to him. Set a Taffy to catch a Taffy, eh?"

"I beg your pardon?"

"Never mind, Nicky," Philby said.

III

As it happened, Johnny had been released from Pentonville Prison a few days earlier, the Double Cross Committee having decided—for the third time since the war began—that the Welshman could not do them much harm, even if he was still regarded as "unreliable."

When Philby turned up, he was in his favorite pub, the Unicorn in St. Pancras, halfway through his fourth bottle of Welsh dark ale—the barmaid kept them in store for him while he was "away"—and in no mood to do favors for anyone from the SIS.

"The druid?" he asked truculently. "Who the hell are you talking about? There hasn't been an Eisteddfod since this bloody war started, and anyway, the last prewar druid joined the fucking silly army and got himself killed at Cassino, the stupid sod! What are you talking about?"

Philby was unperturbed. He slipped fifty pounds in nice new one-pound notes into Johnny's pocket and promised there was more where that came from, and the Welshman eventually took the SIS man's number and said he would talk to his friends in the Welsh Nats and generally scout around.

But he did not tell Philby the Druid had already been in touch with him. Nor had he any intention of doing anything that would betray the young man to the security services. Why, the Druid was his one and only link with Trudy! Without him, he would be totally cut off from the one single human being who meant anything to him.

And once more, this is a point where the Druid's movements can no longer be checked with certainty, and where some sort of reconstruction is necessary. When you are dealing with men and women in the intelligence services—rival intelligence services—which of them are you to believe, especially if they tell different stories? Are they deliberately attempting to direct your suspicions or surmises along the wrong route, despite their passionate hand-on-the-heart proclamations that they are telling the truth?

It is sometimes hard to know. Over a long period, the author maintained a lively correspondence with Kim Philby in Moscow, and when some of his letters were printed in a previous book,[1] there were many comments on the frank and open way Philby wrote about the intelligence activities with which he had been concerned. On the other hand, professional counterintelligence men pointed out several paragraphs in which Philby, while apparently disarmingly honest, was deliberately fudging or falsifying facts or laying false clues. The more plausible an experienced espionage agent's story sounds, the more suspiciously it should be regarded. Nothing that Philby writes or says in Moscow is not first vetted by his senior colleagues in the KGB. At the same time, ostensibly honest spokesmen and contacts in the British intelligence services are not to be trusted, either. They have a vested interest in preserving the deserved reputation they earned during World War II for the efficiency of their counterintelligence and deception services, and for them the Druid is officially a myth or a will-o'-the-wisp. The French security services are somewhat more skeptical and tell several stories (some of them entirely imaginary). The CIA has always been jealous of the SIS and will say anything (provided it can't be pinned on them) to denigrate its well-earned wartime reputation. And the modern intelligence services of West Germany have their own pet theories about the Druid, most of which suggest he was an even more loyal German than he was a Nazi (or a Welshman) and that he may well have fooled everybody except Germany in the end.

[1] *Dulles: A Biography of Eleanor, Allen, and John Foster Dulles and Their Family Network* (New York: Dial Press/James Wade Books, 1978).

From all these disparate stories, memories, recollections (and suspected inventions of interested parties), the author has reconstructed what follows. Some of the former members of the Double Cross System have helped him piece it together.

I V

The English had made the Welsh Nationalist Party a proscribed organization during World War II, and about forty of its members had been jailed as a precaution during the early days of the war under Regulation 18B. By 1944, they were all free again, but forbidden to forgather or make propaganda for their cause, and their underground organization had been penetrated by agents like Johnny and an ex-police inspector, code-named "Goronwy," who pretended fervent support for the cause but in reality were controlled by the Double Cross Committee. Their attempts at sabotage had been betrayed before they could do any harm, though they still occasionally set fire to an English-owned business in Rhyl or Llandudno or Pwllheli, or poured acid on the bearings of English ships sailing out of Swansea or Milford Haven.

And they continued to meet, at lonely farmhouses in the Welsh hills, where they damned the English as the persecutors of their race, their homeland, and their language, and spoke emotionally (in Welsh, of course) of the day when their people would achieve *Gwladf*a, a national home, and there would be a free Wales and a free Welsh people at last.

Johnny thought the whole bunch of them were romantic idiots, but naturally did not say so aloud. It was typical of their naïveté, in his opinion, that they somehow continued to put their trust in him, though he had betrayed them repeatedly to the police and to the Double Cross Committee. He guessed their confidence in his integrity stemmed from the surface reassurance of his flowing locks and fluent Welsh, and the fact that he looked like a wizard and sounded like a bard.

Whatever it was, they looked up to him, foolish yokels that they were.

The Druid had asked to meet the "hard core" of the party, and Johnny had refrained from replying that the hard core was full of Celtic mush, and sent out the necessary signals. They would gather at a rendezvous in the hills in a few days.

In the meantime, he had his own treff with the Druid.

On Wednesday market day in Criccieth, in the last week in June, he sat behind the wheel in the car park and pretended to read the Liverpool *Post*, until he saw the Druid striding along the seafront toward him. His shoulders were square and firm despite the weight of the pack, his fair hair was blowing in the stiff breeze, and his face was flushed from exertion and the sun and wind. He looked grim, purposeful, but monstrously fit, as if he had been driving his mind as well as his body, and the body had stood up to it better.

Johnny started the engine as the Druid slipped in beside him, and waited while he eased the pack onto the shelf behind him. Then he drove along the shore and turned inland toward the hills and began to climb.

"Where've you come from, laddie?"

"I've walked from Llanfyllin," the Druid said. "It's a long haul. I haven't walked that far since my father and I once climbed the Chubut Valley into Chile. This is a good country. It makes Patagonia look shabby. I'd like to have a farm here, one day."

"I'm from the south myself," Johnny said, adding, almost apologetically, "Merthyr Tydfil. Not like here at all. This is where your people came from?"

"It's my great-grandfather's land," the Druid said. He gestured across the blue hills. "The family raised sheep around here, and when he wasn't raising sheep, my great-grandfather went the rounds of the villages, preaching in the chapels and teaching in the schools, preaching and teaching in Welsh, and attacking the English landlords. That's how they came to arrest him—when he started the rent strikes against the

English, and told everyone to speak no word but Welsh."

He groaned, and said more loudly, "We haven't got any nearer to it since, have we? In Llanfyllin itself I had a hard time making myself understood, and that used to be the cradle of the Welsh language in my ancestors' day!" He pitched his voice higher in imitation of a villager: " 'Oh, it doesn't pay to speak the Welsh around here these days, sonny! No future in the language whatever! Look you, why don't you speak nice and slow in English, and I'll have a try to see what you're trying to tell me!' I was trying to tell him he ought to be ashamed not to speak the language of his fathers!"

Johnny said soothingly, "It'll change one day, laddie."

"Not if the English win this war!" said the Druid. "The Germans have promised me we will have our freedom, pledged themselves to give us *Gwladfa,* our own parliament, our own language, our own say in our own destiny. But the Germans aren't going to be able to do it because they aren't winning this war!" He turned round in his seat to face the little Welshman. "And do you know why they aren't winning this war? Because they've been betrayed, because you and I and all the others they sent over here—we have let them down, allowed ourselves to be tricked and confused by the English, we who were sent here to help them so they could help us! I'm ashamed to be a Welshman for the abysmal way in which we have failed!"

"The war's not over yet," Johnny said, but without much conviction. "But there's certainly not much we can do about it now."

"Only one thing," the Druid said grimly. "And that's the reason why I've asked your help."

The little Welshman gripped the wheel hard and concentrated on his driving for the next long minute.

Then, when he was in control of himself, he asked, "I only hope it's within my power. What do you need of me?"

"Your circuit to Hamburg," he said. "I have to let the

Führer know that every one of his agents in this country is in the hands of the English. He has to know—before the English trick him again! We'll use your control in Hamburg."

Johnny said nothing, but concentrated on driving.

V

There was a ranger's cottage on a lonely sheep track off the road up Snowdon where the North Wales members of the party were wont to gather at weekends. The ranger was a sympathizer, the road was easily observed, and the place was so isolated that they could even sing "Land of My Fathers" at the tops of their voices and only the sheep could hear them.

There was good burning wood in the hearth and Johnny had brought baked beans, sausages, and a loaf of bread, and he soon had a frying pan sizzling and a pot of tea stewing on the Butogaz range. As darkness fell, he lit the lantern over the primitive wooden table, pushed the dirty tin plates aside, and stared at the written sheets of paper which the Druid had handed him. He read them through twice, and then sat there, staring at them.

"Well?"

The Druid had his radio set assembled, the battery connected, and an aerial running out on to the crag facing toward the east.

Johnny coughed, twisted awkwardly in his seat, and finally blurted out, "Laddie, I don't think you ought to send this."

"What! Why not? Don't you realize what it will mean when the Führer sees that message?"

"I know what it will mean *if* the Führer sees it," Johnny said, still squirming. "But I don't think it's going to get through to him."

The Druid was staring at him as if he could not believe

what his ears were telling him. He stabbed a finger at the sheets of paper.

"Read it! Read it! This message reveals that all the Abwehr's agents in England have been caught and turned by the enemy! Here is the explanation for why the German armies were tricked on D-Day—and why they are still being tricked! And you say it will never reach the Führer? What sort of damn foolery is that?"

The Welshman sighed.

"I'm trying to tell you," he said softly, "that they already know! Or suspect, anyway. My control suspects me. All the other controls suspect their cases."

"Suspect what, you fool?"

"That their agents in England have been turned, and have been doubling with the English for months, that's what. And do you know the reason why they haven't done anything about it? Because they don't dare! They're afraid! There's a purge going on in the Abwehr at the moment, and blood is flowing—real blood, laddie. It isn't nice at all what the SS is doing to the old boys. Can you imagine what would happen to my control or the controls who run Arabel and Brutus and Tate and Ivan if they were to let their new masters know that their charges are being manipulated by the English— and have been manipulated for months. Why, it would be more than their lives are worth!"

"I don't believe it," the Druid said.

"You don't have to because you're not back in Hamburg and Berlin under the new regime! But they have to face what's going on there. Why, laddie, do you know what happened three days ago? The Abwehr persuaded the Führer to award an Iron Cross Second Class to that miserable little twerp in London who masquerades under the name of Arabel! Do you think his control can now go to the Führer and confess that Arabel's a traitor—and has been a traitor for nearly three years! I tell you, laddie, my control will never send it through! And he'll make trouble for you with the new regime if you try to insist."

In the flicker of the firelight, the Druid's face looked like a gargoyle, pain and anger screwing up his features as the light and shade chased over them.

"Oh, God," he said, at last, "what am I going to do?"

The Welshman got up and went to the nail where his leather overcoat was hanging, and pulled out a liquor flask. He poured some whisky into the mugs and pushed one toward the younger man.

"I know one way we can get through," he said. "I still have the contact at the Spanish embassy, and we can get a letter by bag to Madrid. All you have to do is put the message in a spook letter—I've still got a supply of secret ink—and we'll have it taken through to Lisbon and cabled straight on to Berlin."

The Druid asked, with weary skepticism, "And who have you got who is to be trusted in Lisbon?"

"Why, Trudy, of course," said Johnny. "Who else but old Trudy?"

The Druid stood up in a sudden blazing anger.

"Why, you stupid idiot!" he shouted. "I've already told you that von Fidrmuc has gone over to the enemy—and that means Trudy's betrayed us, too!" When he saw Johnny staring up at him in stupefaction, he leaned forward in exasperated fury, taking the little Welshman by the shoulders and shaking him. "Don't you understand? She's in this with him! Trudy's von Fidrmuc's mistress, has been for months and months!"

Johnny had slumped in his chair, almost slipping to the floor under the Druid's hands, his whisky slopping wildly.

"Poor old Trudy, poor old Trudy!" he kept whispering.

"Not poor old Trudy!" shouted the Druid, shaking harder. "She's his willing mistress! She likes him. The way she likes lots of men. The way she's always liked men—except for dupes like you! Did you really believe it when Trudy said she loved you? Why, it's Trudy's favorite story, the way she seduced

230

you! Did you never guess that she works for the SS? Did you really think she was just sitting around and waiting for you?"

"Yes," said Johnny, in a whisper, "I honestly did."

"Then you deserve all you've got from that treacherous bitch!" said the Druid savagely. "But I don't! I don't deserve any of this!"

Tears were suddenly running down the Druid's face, glinting and flashing in the firelight. He turned away into the darkness, and his shoulders heaved.

"After all I've done! After all I've risked!" he muttered between sobs. And then, in a panicky whisper: *"What am I going to do?"*

It was the first time Johnny had seen the young man show any emotion, but he took no notice. One hand held his flask of whisky, the other his mug. But he did not drink. His face had gone so gray it looked almost translucent in the light of the lamp above him, and his eyes were so blank that he might have been dead. He sat there, as still as a corpse, while the Druid shook with barely controlled sobs behind him.

VI

It was just after eight o'clock the next morning when the telephone rang in Philby's bedroom in Carlyle Square, Chelsea.

He listened for a few moments and then nodded and whispered, "I'll come at once."

Sliding out of bed carefully, so as not to disturb Aileen, he carried his clothes into the bathroom, shaved, and dressed quickly. He was just in time to catch the morning train for Liverpool. He figured that if he could pick up some sort of military transport in Chester, he could be in Wales by the early afternoon. Luckily, in his job, there was no need to reveal the nature of his mission.

CHAPTER 13

Change of Party

I

THERE WAS A SMALL hostelry in Llanberis called, ironically enough, the Druid's Nest, with a splendid view up the small-gauge railway track to the Snowdonia peaks. Johnny was at the bar nursing the remains of a pint of stout when Philby came in. The Englishman ordered a whisky for himself and one for Johnny, watched him pour it into the remains of his stout, and then suggested they move to the rear of the taproom.

"What's happened to you?" Philby asked, his eyes taking in the Welshman's unshaven face, the bloodshot eyes, the shaking hand gripping hard on the glass.

"I don't feel well, and I hope it's fatal," Johnny said bleakly, taking a swallow.

He had just passed the worst night and day of his life, and he despised himself. Time and again, as he tossed on the floor of the cold, dark cottage, he had told himself not to be an old fool, and had clamped his jaw tight to prevent himself from moaning aloud: "Oh, Trudy, Trudy, Trudy!" A couple of yards away from him, the Druid, with the resilience of youth, had eventually staunched his tears and gone to sleep like a baby. Johnny hated him. He felt like taking his booted foot and stamping it into that bright, youthful face until it was a bloody pulp. He hated him not because he had been the bearer of bad news but because he had deceived him, because he had known the truth about Trudy for all this time, and had lied about her, flattered him about her, and all the time despised him for being such a naïvely foolish old man.

Finally, just about dawn, he had crept out of the cottage and cruised down the mountain to a telephone box and called London. "I have the Druid," he had said.

It was not the first time he had shopped one of his fellow-agents to the English, but this time he felt good about it. This one was not the amenable type, and this one they would surely hang. The thought of that handsome face contorted by a rope around the neck made him feel better.

Later that morning, after they had breakfasted on Spam and tea and the Druid had looked through the paper—to get it was Johnny's excuse for his trip down the mountain—Johnny went out to the old car and dug out a remnant from his last Eisteddfod, at Bangor in 1939. It was a druid's costume complete with cowl and he threw it across to the Druid and suggested he wear it when the Nats arrived.

"They'll get a kick out of it," he said. "You know us Welsh—anything for a bit of drama. And in any case," he added, "it will keep you hidden. You don't want them identifying you when they go back to their villages and start talking to their girls."

The costume was far too small and any other man of his size wearing it would have looked like a clown, but it draped the Druid's shoulders with a kind of awesome dignity that made the Nats hiss in their breath when they eventually arrived. They came on bikes, across the hills on foot, some squashed in the backs of butchers' vans and one of them on a mountain pony, and Johnny was right when he said they were a bunch of yokels. But by the time the Druid had finished with them, they were Welsh warriors. He told them he had come from across the seas to help the fight to bring freedom to his country. He spoke to them of their ancestors who had been driven out of Wales a century before because they had dared to speak the language of their fathers and tried to teach its poetry to their children. He spoke of Welsh heroes like Henry Tudor, who became King of the English, and the Ordovices and Owen Glendower. He spoke of the rigors of the voyage of the brig *Mimosa* on its journey from Cardiff to Patagonia, and of the struggles of his great-grandfather and his kin to fashion a new Wales out of the Chubut Valley.

He put such fire in their bellies that when he finally sent them on their way, they went off like soldiers setting off for war, and Johnny figured that quite a few English pipelines, post offices, telephone exchanges, and police boxes would be going up in flames in the next week or two.

Even Johnny had been impressed, and felt such remorse about his betrayal that he was tempted not to go down the mountain for his rendezvous with Philby. And then the Druid tossed off the robes and sneered that if that selection of idiots was the best the Nats could do, what Wales needed was a Hitler youth movement, and "maybe a Trudy or two to liven them up." And Johnny hated him again.

Now he faced Philby and contemplated the Druid's arrest without any particular compunction. His misery was not for him, but for himself. But why had the SIS man come alone?

"Let's talk about the Druid," Johnny said. "You're not thinking of taking him by yourself, are you? He can turn mean, that boy, and he's feeling desperate at the moment. Everybody's let him down. I think you should let me get out of here and then call up the police before you go up there. He could break you in two."

"Where is he?" Philby asked.

"Walking the mountains," Johnny said. "He's got things on

his mind. But he'll be back. He's left his kit behind. I'm supposed to be making a contact in Portmadoc, and then we're off to Holyhead. He thinks he'll get a passage out of there to Ireland. He'll wait in the cottage till I get back."

Philby finished his drink. "Then I mustn't keep him waiting," he said.

Johnny regarded him sourly.

"You chaps from SIS are so sure of yourselves you make me sick," he said. "You think you can turn the Druid just like you've turned all the others, and use him the same way you've used me. Well, I'll tell you, it's not going to be that easy. He wouldn't even share the same pisshouse with you. He hates the English more than you hate the Nazis, and you're not going to change him."

Philby said, "Why don't you just draw me a map of where the cottage is, and then you finish your drink and get out of here." He fumbled in his pocket as he saw Johnny hesitate, and pulled out a sheaf of pound notes, and then a piece of paper and a pen. "Here. You know, you don't look well at all," he added solicitously. "You ought to be home in bed."

"Home *where?*" Johnny asked sarcastically, pocketing the money.

He drew a simple plan and shoved it across to the Englishman, then rose to go.

"I ought to be dead," he said.

Philby went to the door with him and waited until the engine of the old car sprang to life and the car disappeared in a cloud of exhaust smoke down the road. Then he climbed into his sleek Humber and slid up the mountain in the opposite direction.

An hour later, when the Druid came back to the cottage, Philby was waiting for him.

He had the Druid's Argentine passport in his hand, and what he did was hold out his hand and say, "Hallo, Gwyn."

But what was said between the two men after that, neither has ever revealed. All we do know is that sometime in the early hours of the following morning, Philby and the Druid left together. They parted at Chester Station, and both of them took the same train back to London. But though they passed each other once in the corridor of the express, and made polite noises when they bumped in the swaying carriage, no one would have guessed that they had ever met each other before.

That night, however, Philby was able to make a telephone call.

"He's ours" was all he said.

Nicky Rostov, alias Ernst of the KGB, promptly sent a message to the Soviet embassy for ongoing transmission to Moscow.

"DRUID IS OURS," it said.

Epilogue

On September 25, 1944, Harold Adrian Russell (Kim) Philby was married at Chelsea Registry Office in London to the conjugal companion of his wartime years, Aileen Furst. Since Aileen was in an advanced state of pregnancy with their fourth child and not feeling well, it was a discreet ceremony. Descriptions of it in later years mention only two witnesses as being present. One was a female friend of Aileen's, the other Thomas Harris, described as an "art dealer." These two signed the marriage certificate.

But there was, in fact, a fifth person in the wedding party, though no one noted his name. The registrar remembered that he laughed and joked with the bride and groom in a lilting voice that proclaimed him a Welshman, and this was confirmed when he was heard to remark that he had to "get back to Cardiff this afternoon, because we've got a concert tonight." He went on to mention they had a Spanish guitarist on the program "who doesn't speak English, and I've promised to help out."

At which Thomas Harris had laughed and poked the young man in the chest, saying, "And to think I once believed you didn't understand Spanish! What a naughty boy you were to do that to me!"

They moved out of the office and went to the pub next door for a drink, and there they toasted the Philbys in gins-and-tonics. The young man, his blue eyes shining, made a little speech in Welsh, and then obligingly translated.

"There is only one way for a Welshman to learn to love the English, and that is when they are united in a common cause, with blood and class forgotten. That is how we are united. One day all the Welsh and all the English will be too!"

Aileen Philby looked completely astonished at this outburst, and Philby and Harris seemed embarrassed. But before anyone could make a remark, he had crushed them in a sort of communal embrace, said he had to run for the train, and hurried to the door.

"What on earth does that man *do?*" asked Aileen, adding sourly: "You know the oddest people, Kim."

Thomas Harris, who had been staring at the door, turned round to her.

"That young man," he said, "just happens to be one of the coming influences in music and the arts in Wales. *And* one of the most influential. Why, culture over there wouldn't be the same without him. Concerts, poetry readings, art shows, a revival of the national Eisteddfod—he's into them all. Wales would be a desert without him."

"And," interrupted Philby, with a grin, "Tommy would never have had an exhibition of Spanish art in Cardiff, Swansea, and Llandrindod Wells if it hadn't been for him!" He reached out and patted his old friend and comrade's arm. "But I agree with Tommy. He's doing marvels in Wales, that boy. I shouldn't be at all surprised if he doesn't get a K for it one of these days."

Tommy Harris looked skeptical. "Have to wait a bit for that, I think," he said. "But there is one thing he's got to get very soon. And he'll deserve it. When the next Eisteddfod comes around, I hear they're planning to name him a druid!"

"Let's drink to that," said Philby, lifting his glass. "To the Druid!"

"To the Druid!" said Harris, solemnly.

Aileen Philby couldn't understand why first her husband and then Tommy Harris burst into fits of uncontrollable laughter.

And where are they now, these spymasters, spies, and double spies whose activities caused such worry and woe among their adversaries during World War II?

Among the spymasters:

Walter Huppenkothen, released after serving ten years for war crimes, is living in obscurity in West Germany.

Hugo Hoffmann became a private inquiry agent after the war, mainly tracing missing persons in Berlin, and died there in 1978.

Paul von Fidrmuc changed his name at the end of the war, and in the next decade was heard of variously in Paris, Bonn, New York, and Vienna. He was last seen in Munich, running an employment bureau for Czech refugees.

Kreme von Auenrode was caught and killed by Russian troops in Austria in 1945.

Elizabeth von Auenrode, his wife, is living in Germany.

Gertrude von Körner was killed in a bombing raid in Berlin in 1945.

Nicholas Rostov (*"Ernst"*) of the MVD/KGB is retired and living quietly in a suburb of Moscow.

H. A. R. (*Kim*) *Philby* lives partly in an apartment in Moscow and partly in a dacha about eighty miles from the Russian capital. He still travels widely on behalf of the KGB, although retired, and advises the network on British and Middle Eastern affairs. He also keeps up a lively correspondence with ex-colleagues and acquaintances in the Western world (including the author). He was recently married for the fourth time, to a young and charming Russian.

Thomas Harris was killed in an automobile accident in Majorca in 1968.

Anthony Blunt was knighted by the Queen after the war for his services to art. He successfully concealed from the public his role as a Soviet spy until 1979, when he was unmasked in a statement made by Prime Minister Margaret Thatcher in the House of Commons. He made a public confession that he had worked for the KGB and was deprived of his knighthood. He is now living quietly in London and writing his reminiscences.

Denzil Roberts works in an official post in London.

Professor Sir John C. Masterman (who ran the Double Cross System) is retired and living in Oxford.

Among the spies and double spies:

Dusko Popov ("Ivan"/"Tricycle") is alive and well and living in the South of France.

Arthur Owens ("Johnny"/"Snow") disappeared after he was refused permission to publish his memoirs. He was last heard of in Eire.

Luis Calvo ("Arabel"/"Garbo") was last heard of in Spain.

Eddie Chapman ("Fritz"/"Zigzag") is living in Britain and wrote a cautious account of his wartime activities in *The Eddie Chapman Story* (with Frank Owen), 1954.

John Eppler, happily married, with a family, ran a successful book business in the Saarland and now spends much time in France.

The Druid? The KGB is the network probably best able to answer the question of what happened (or has happened) to him. Or does the secret intelligence service of the West German Republic know even more about him than Moscow?

Born in Manchester, England, and educated at the William Hulme School, the Sorbonne, and Berlin University, Leonard Mosley has been a foreign correspondent most of his working life. He joined Kemsley (now Thomson) newspapers and worked for their Berlin Bureau in 1939, and his experiences there—including interviews with Hitler and most of the Nazi leaders—provided the basic material for his book On Borrowed Time: How World War Two Began, *which was a Book-of-the-Month Club selection in 1969.*

When World War II began, he became chief war correspondent for the London Sunday Times *and associated newspapers, and reported the Battle of Britain, the Middle East campaign, and the Allied landings in Greece and Italy. He was part of the small expedition that went through the Italian lines and restored Emperor Haile Selassie to the throne of Ethiopia. While in the Middle East, he took a course in parachuting and on D-Day dropped into Normandy with the first wave of the Allied invasion of Europe.*

In the postwar years, he covered the Nuremberg trials and traveled widely in Africa, the Middle East and the Far East. From a long stay in Japan he produced Hirohito: Emperor of Japan, *which was a Book-of-the-Month Club selection in 1966 and the first biography of a Japanese ruler to be published in Japan, where it became an instant best-seller.* Power Play, *published in 1973, was the first book to warn the world of the strength of OPEC and of the oil crisis to come. Two other books,* Lindbergh *and* Dulles, *were full selections of the Literary Guild and the Book-of-the-Month Club, respectively, and* Blood Relations: The Rise and Fall of the du Ponts of Delaware *has been sold to TV for a miniseries.*

In addition to writing twenty books of history and biography and five novels, Mr. Mosley has worked as a theater and film critic in London and as a scriptwriter in Hollywood. For his literary works and war correspondence, he was made an Officer of the Order of the British Empire, and for his writings about the Middle East, a Commander of the Order of Saint John of Jerusalem. He now lives on Sanibel Island, in Florida.